1 Timothy

Reformed Expository Commentary

A Series

1 Timothy

Philip Graham Ryken

P&R
PUBLISHING
P.O. BOX 817 • PHILLIPSBURG • NEW JERSEY 08865-0817

Italics within Scripture quotations indicate emphasis added.

Page design by Lakeside Design Plus

Printed in the United States of America

Library of Congress Cataloging-in-Publication Data

Ryken, Philip Graham, 1966–
1 Timothy / Philip Graham Ryken.
p. cm. — (Reformed expository commentary)
Includes bibliographical references and indexes.
ISBN 978-1-59638-049-3 (cloth)
1. Bible. N.T. Timothy, 1st—Commentaries. I. Title. II. Title: First Timothy.
BS2745.53.R95 2007
227'.83077—dc22

2007015846

To Dick Lucas,

who is worthy of double honor
for his labor in preaching and teaching,

and

to the King of ages—
immortal, invisible, the only God,

who is worthy of honor and glory forever and ever, amen.

Contents

Series Introduction

In every generation there is a fresh need for the faithful exposition of God's Word in the church. At the same time, the church must constantly do the work of theology: reflecting on the teaching of Scripture, confessing its doctrines of the Christian faith, and applying them to contemporary culture. We believe that these two tasks—the expositional and the theological—are interdependent. Our doctrine must derive from the biblical text, and our understanding of any particular passage of Scripture must arise from the doctrine taught in Scripture as a whole.

We further believe that these interdependent tasks of biblical exposition and theological reflection are best undertaken in the church, and most specifically in the pulpits of the church. This is all the more true since the study of Scripture properly results in doxology and praxis—that is, in praise to God and practical application in the lives of believers. In pursuit of these ends, we are pleased to present the Reformed Expository Commentary as a fresh exposition of Scripture for our generation in the church. We hope and pray that pastors, teachers, Bible study leaders, and many others will find this series to be a faithful, inspiring, and useful resource for the study of God's infallible, inerrant Word.

The Reformed Expository Commentary has four fundamental commitments. First, these commentaries aim to be *biblical*, presenting a comprehensive exposition characterized by careful attention to the details of the text. They are not exegetical commentaries—commenting word by word or even verse by verse—but integrated expositions of whole passages of Scripture. Each commentary will thus present a sequential, systematic treatment of an entire book of the Bible, passage by passage. Second, these commentaries are unashamedly *doctrinal*. We are committed to the Westminster Confession of Faith and Catechisms as containing the system of doctrine taught in the Scriptures of the Old and New Testaments. Each volume will teach, promote, and defend the doctrines of the Reformed faith as they are found in the Bible. Third, these commentaries are *redemptive-historical* in their orientation. We believe in the unity of the Bible and its central message of salvation in Christ. We are thus committed to a Christ-centered view of the Old Testament, in which its characters, events, regulations, and institutions are properly understood as pointing us to Christ and his gospel, as well as giving us examples to follow in living by faith. Fourth, these commentaries are *practical*, applying the text of Scripture to contemporary challenges of life—both public and private—with appropriate illustrations.

The contributors to the Reformed Expository Commentary are all pastor-scholars. As pastor, each author will first present his expositions in the pulpit ministry of his church. This means that these commentaries are rooted in the teaching of Scripture to real people in the church. While aiming to be scholarly, these expositions are not academic. Our intent is to be faithful, clear, and helpful to Christians who possess various levels of biblical and theological training—as should be true in any effective pulpit ministry. Inevitably this means that some issues of academic interest will not be covered. Nevertheless, we aim to achieve a responsible level of scholarship, seeking to promote and model this for pastors and other teachers in the church. Significant exegetical and theological difficulties, along with such historical and cultural background as is relevant to the text, will be treated with care.

We strive for a high standard of enduring excellence. This begins with the selection of the authors, all of whom have proven to be outstanding communicators of God's Word. But this pursuit of excellence is also reflected in a disciplined editorial process. Each volume is edited by both a series editor and a testament editor. The testament editors, Iain Duguid for the Old Testament and Daniel Doriani for the New Testament, are accomplished pastors and respected scholars who have taught at the seminary level. Their job is to ensure that each volume is sufficiently conversant with up-to-date scholarship and is faithful and accurate in its exposition of the text. As series editors, we oversee each volume to ensure its overall quality—including excellence of writing, soundness of teaching, and usefulness in application. Working together as an editorial team, along with the publisher, we are devoted to ensuring that these are the best commentaries our gifted authors can provide, so that the church will be served with trustworthy and exemplary expositions of God's Word.

It is our goal and prayer that the Reformed Expository Commentary will serve the church by renewing confidence in the clarity and power of Scripture and by upholding the great doctrinal heritage of the Reformed faith. We hope that pastors who read these commentaries will be encouraged in their own expository preaching ministry, which we believe to be the best and most biblical pattern for teaching God's Word in the church. We hope that lay teachers will find these commentaries among the most useful resources they rely upon for understanding and presenting the text of the Bible. And we hope that the devotional quality of these studies of Scripture will instruct and inspire each Christian who reads them in joyful, obedient discipleship to Jesus Christ.

May the Lord bless all who read the Reformed Expository Commentary. We commit these volumes to the Lord Jesus Christ, praying that the Holy Spirit will use them for the instruction and edification of the church, with thanksgiving to God the Father for his unceasing faithfulness in building his church through the ministry of his Word.

Richard D. Phillips
Philip Graham Ryken
Series Editors

Preface

The Bible expositions that formed the basis for this book were first preached during Sunday evening services in the early years of my pastoral ministry at Philadelphia's Tenth Presbyterian Church. Preaching through 1 Timothy was as much for my own benefit as it was for anyone else's. Like Timothy, I was just beginning to learn how to pastor a church by reading and preaching the Scriptures, defending sound doctrine, developing godly leadership, and caring spiritually for every member of God's household. To study this epistle was like sitting shoulder to shoulder with Timothy during his pastoral internship with the best of teachers: the apostle Paul.

I am grateful to God for the opportunity to return to 1 Timothy and contribute this volume to the Reformed Expository Commentary. The original manuscript was greatly improved by suggestions from Rick Phillips, Iain Duguid, and Dan Doriani, who worked especially hard to make sure that my exegesis was informed by the best and latest scholarship. The following people also deserve special thanks: the session and congregation of Tenth Church, for their prayers, encouragement, and the gift of sabbatical time to complete a final revision of the manuscript; the staff at P&R Publishing, for their labors in bringing the book to press; and Lisa and the children, for their constant faith and abiding love. Together we are all members of the household of God, and confessors of "the mystery of godliness" (1 Tim. 3:16).

One special debt of gratitude remains. During the last year of my doctoral studies at Oxford University I traveled into London every Monday to listen to Dick Lucas lecture on preaching at the Cornhill Training Institute. For decades Reverend Lucas has had an influential preaching ministry at St. Helen's Bishopsgate, in the heart of London's financial district, and also more widely among evangelicals in England and America. By the grace of God, his ministry has been a model of excellence in Scripture exposition, and studying with him each week was an important part of my final preparation for gospel ministry. Reverend Lucas is also well known for his generous encouragement of younger ministers—a living example of what Paul said to Timothy: "Treat younger men like brothers" (1 Tim. 5:1). His willingness some years ago to read and comment on my exposition of 1 Timothy is typical of his kindness and commitment to expository preaching. To me and many others, he has been a true father in the faith.

1 Timothy

Defend the Faith

1

A True Son in the Faith

1 Timothy 1:1—11

Paul, an apostle of Christ Jesus by command of God our Savior and of Christ Jesus our hope, To Timothy, my true child in the faith: Grace, mercy, and peace from God the Father and Christ Jesus our Lord. (1 Tim. 1:1–2)

When I left for college my father gave me a copy of Louis Berkhof's *Manual of Christian Doctrine*, a small classic in the tradition of Reformation theology. The book was inscribed with these words: "For Philip upon entering college, in the hope that your theology will remain Reformed." My father wanted me to remain true to the biblical and evangelical doctrines defended during the Protestant Reformation, doctrines like the authority of Scripture and justification by faith alone. In other words, he wanted me to remain a true son in the faith.

A True Son

Paul had the same desire for Timothy. He considered himself to be the young minister's spiritual father, so he addressed his first Pastoral Epistle

"To Timothy, my true child in the faith" (1 Tim. 1:2). At the time he wrote this, Paul was coming to the close of his world-changing ministry. He was the great missionary of the New Testament, God's evangelist to the Gentiles (Acts 9:15). He was also an apostle, a messenger or ambassador for God. And as an eyewitness of the risen Christ (Acts 9:3–6), he was a man appointed to teach God's people with divine authority.

Paul was not a self-appointed apostle, or even an apostle commissioned by the church. On the contrary, he had been chosen, called, and commissioned directly by Jesus Christ. His apostleship thus came "by command of God our Savior and of Christ Jesus our hope" (1 Tim. 1:1). Not only is this a strong claim for Paul's authority, but it is also a strong claim for the deity of Jesus Christ. A command from the Father is also said to be a command from the Son, and vice versa. Therefore, the Son must be equal in power and authority to the Father. Jesus is God.

Already it is evident that this letter is full of profound teaching about the attributes and activities of God. "God our Savior"—this phrase looks back to the salvation God accomplished through Christ; "Christ Jesus our hope"—this looks forward to the day when Christ will return in power and glory. So, as John Stott explains, "Paul locates his apostleship in a historical context, whose beginning was the saving activity of *God our Savior* in the birth, death and resurrection of Jesus, and whose culmination will be *Christ Jesus our hope*, his personal and glorious coming, which is the object of our Christian hope, and which will bring down the curtain on the historical process."[1] Not bad for a return address! Paul's opening lines mention virtually everything God has done and will do to save his people.

Like his return address, Paul's greeting is full of profound theology. He offers Timothy "grace, mercy, and peace from God the Father and Christ Jesus our Lord" (1 Tim. 1:2). The apostle starts with the traditional Greek salutation of grace (*charis*), ends with the traditional Jewish greeting of peace (*shalom*), and inserts mercy (*eleos*) to make a distinctively Christian blessing.[2] From the very beginning, therefore, this epistle is full of Christ. It is full of the hope that Christ will return in glory, the grace Christ offers to

1. John Stott, *Guard the Truth: The Message of 1 Timothy and Titus* (Downers Grove, IL: InterVarsity, 1996), 39.

2. J. N. D. Kelly, *The Pastoral Epistles: Timothy I and II, Titus*, Harper's New Testament Commentaries (San Francisco: Harper and Row, 1960), 41.

sinners, the mercy Christ gives to the needy, and the peace Christ has made with God through his death on the cross. The letter brings grace, mercy, and peace from Christ to Timothy, Paul's spiritual son.

Timothy was a true son in the faith in several respects. Paul first met the young man when he passed through Lystra on his second missionary journey. Perhaps he introduced Timothy to Christ in the first place. In any case, Paul heard of his excellent reputation and invited him to join his missionary team (Acts 16:1–3). Timothy began his ministry under the apostle's tutelage. He seemed like a son because he was relatively young. This is why Timothy is such an excellent model for young ministers. He was probably in his thirties by the time this letter was written, yet Paul still tells him not to let anyone look down on him because he is young (1 Tim. 4:12; cf. 2 Tim. 2:22).

Paul also considered Timothy a son because of their close personal relationship. They traveled together to Thessalonica (1 Thess. 3:2), to Corinth (1 Cor. 4:17), and to Jerusalem (Acts 20:4). Timothy stayed at Paul's side when he was imprisoned in Rome (Phil. 2:19). They also collaborated to write six books of the New Testament. The letters of 2 Corinthians, Philippians, Colossians, 1 and 2 Thessalonians, and Philemon come from Paul *and* Timothy, with Paul of course serving as the primary writer. Timothy also served as Paul's pastoral representative, the church leader delegated to lead the church that Paul had planted in Ephesus.

After all they had been through, it is not surprising Paul considered Timothy his spiritual son. He uses a term of affection: *teknon*, meaning "dear child." He showed the same fatherly feeling when he wrote to the Corinthians and called him "Timothy, my beloved and faithful child in the Lord" (1 Cor. 4:17). Later, when he was in prison, he wrote, "I have no one like him. . . . But you know Timothy's proven worth, how as a son with a father he has served with me in the gospel" (Phil. 2:20, 22).

A True Faith

Paul's purpose in 1 Timothy is to help his spiritual son remain true. In the opening verses of the letter he exhorts him to hold on to the true faith (1 Tim. 1:2), to defend the true doctrine (1 Tim. 1:3–4), to uphold the true use of the law (1 Tim. 1:6–11), and to cherish a true love (1 Tim. 1:5).

First, then, Timothy had true faith. The important thing about him was not that he was Paul's child, but that he was God's child. He was a true child *in the faith.* So the relationship between these two men was spiritual as well as personal. Their family ties were bound by their common faith in Christ. Timothy was a true son of Paul because he was a true son of God.

Perhaps Paul called God "Father" at the beginning of his letter to remind Timothy that he was God's dear child. This is every believer's great privilege. As the apostle John exults, "See what kind of love the Father has given to us, that we should be called children of God; and so we are" (1 John 3:1). Everyone who is born again by God's Spirit is a son or a daughter of God, with a right to all of God's fatherly care and affection. The phrase Paul uses for "true child" (*gnēsio teknō*) refers to natural childbirth. Since Timothy's mother was Jewish, but his father was Greek (Acts 16:1), orthodox Jews would have considered his birth illegitimate. Yet Timothy was a genuine Christian, born of the Spirit, and thus he was Paul's legitimate spiritual heir.

Timothy learned this true faith at his mother's knee. In his subsequent letter to Timothy, Paul wrote, "I am reminded of your sincere faith, a faith that dwelt first in your grandmother Lois and your mother Eunice and now, I am sure, dwells in you as well" (2 Tim. 1:5). Timothy was a true son in the faith, not only to Paul, but also to his own believing mother.

True Christian sons and daughters often learn the faith from their mothers. Augustine wrote how his mother Monica travailed in prayer for his salvation. In the *Confessions* that he made to God, Augustine testified to her faithfulness:

> My mother, your faithful servant, was weeping for me to you, weeping more than mothers weep for the bodily deaths of their sons. For she, by that faith and spirit which she had from you, saw the death in which I lay, and you, Lord, heard her prayer. You heard her and you did not despise her tears which fell streaming and watered the ground beneath her eyes in every place where she prayed; indeed you heard her.[3]

Or consider J. Gresham Machen, the defender of Christian orthodoxy at Princeton and Westminster seminaries during the first decades of the twentieth

3. Augustine, *The Confessions of St. Augustine*, trans. Rex Warner (New York: Penguin, 1963), 3:11.

century. It was his mother, Mary Gresham Machen, who instructed him in the Bible, the Westminster Shorter Catechism, and the *Pilgrim's Progress.*[4]

The influence of mothers holds true for ordinary Christians as well as for great heroes of the faith. I think of my own mother, who was convinced that maternity was the better part of her life's work. She did not always find it easy to be at home with her children, but she prayed that God would bless her spiritual investment in their lives. To that end, she often took the prayer of Moses and made it her own: "May the favor of the Lord my God rest upon me; establish the work of my hands for me—yes, establish the work of my hands" (Ps. 90:17 NIV). Mothers who devote their maternity to the Lord are often blessed, in the end, with sons and daughters like Timothy: true children in the faith.

The True Doctrine

If a true son becomes a minister, he must teach true doctrine. This is the first thing Paul says in the body of his letter: "As I urged you when I was going to Macedonia, remain at Ephesus that you may charge certain persons not to teach any different doctrine, nor to devote themselves to myths and endless genealogies, which promote speculations rather than the stewardship from God that is by faith" (1 Tim. 1:3–4; cf. 2 Tim. 2:14, 16, 23).

This command helps put the entire epistle in context. Timothy was in Ephesus, a city Paul visited at least twice, once briefly (Acts 18:19–21) and once for more than two years of extended teaching (Acts 19:10). Perhaps 1 Timothy was written shortly after Paul's second visit, although it is more likely the letter was written sometime after Paul was released from his prison in Rome. In any case, Timothy was in Ephesus, the center of Paul's church-planting strategy for Asia Minor.

As it happens, Paul's first letter to Timothy was actually his second letter to the Ephesians. It was not private correspondence. The benediction at the end of chapter 6 is given in the plural (1 Tim. 6:21), indicating that like the rest of Paul's epistles, this letter was for the whole church. This means that 1 Timothy can and should be read on several different levels: as a personal

4. D. G. Hart, *Defending the Faith: J. Gresham Machen and the Crisis of Conservative Protestantism in Modern America* (Baltimore: Johns Hopkins, 1994), 13.

communication from an apostle to a minister delegated to lead a local church; as a pastoral letter from a church planter to the congregation he loves, with instructions for their ongoing work; and as a general statement of principles for life, ministry, and worship in the family of faith. Paul offers his purpose statement for the letter in chapter 3: "I am writing these things to you so that, if I delay, you may know how one ought to behave in the household of God, which is the church of the living God" (1 Tim. 3:14–15).

Timothy was to remain in Ephesus in order to "charge certain persons not to teach any different doctrine" (1 Tim. 1:3). The word Paul used to describe "different doctrine" is one he may have invented: *heterodidaskalein* (cf. 1 Tim. 6:3). In his letters Paul often condemned those who preached a different Jesus, a different Spirit, or a different gospel (2 Cor. 11:4; cf. Gal. 1:6). Any doctrine which is different from the true doctrine is a false doctrine. There is only one right theology; every other theology is wrong. There is only one orthodoxy; everything else is heterodoxy, although of course the church must give answers to the new questions and challenges that arise in every age. John Calvin put it well: "We therefore teach that faithful ministers are now not permitted to coin any new doctrine, but that they are simply to cleave to that doctrine to which God has subjected men without exception."[5]

Who were the heterodox teachers of the Ephesian church? Paul did not name any names. Instead, he ominously referred to them as "certain persons." No doubt Timothy knew exactly whom he was talking about! We might even imagine the sidelong glances that were cast at these men by other leaders in the church.

What were these men teaching? They were obsessed with myths and endless genealogies. "Myths" sounds like the stories or Gnostic philosophies of ancient Greece. Plato, for example, used this term to refer to the legends and fables of antiquity.[6] However, even though there was some Greek influence on the church (especially since Ephesus was the home of the goddess Diana), "myths and endless genealogies" more probably refers to the teaching of certain Jewish rabbis (cf. Titus 1:14: "Jewish myths"). In this connection, it is noteworthy that the false teachers in Ephesus desired to be "teachers of the law" (1 Tim. 1:7).

5. John Calvin, *Institutes of the Christian Religion*, trans. Ford Lewis Battles, 2 vols., Library of Christian Classics 20–21 (Philadelphia: Westminster, 1960), 4.8.9.

6. Plato, *The Republic of Plato*, trans. Francis MacDonald Cornford (New York: Oxford University Press, 1945), 330 D.

Two ancient Jewish texts shed further light on Paul's meaning. One is entitled *The Book of Jubilees*, written around 125 BC. Another was written after AD 70 and is called *The Biblical Antiquities of Philo*. These books retell the Old Testament story from a Pharisaic point of view and include extended genealogies. They go beyond the Scriptures to speculate about the biographies of the biblical saints. John Stott describes them as "tendentious rewrites of a section of Old Testament history. Both stress the indestructibility of Israel and of the law. And both embellish their story with fanciful additions."[7] The heterodox theologians in Ephesus seem to have been thinking along similar lines. They started with the Bible and made up the rest as they went along. Their teaching was little more than guesswork, the product of a lively imagination. Then, as now, such speculative theories were likely to excite the interest of weak or unsound hearers.

The presence of these false teachers was no surprise to Paul. When he made his tearful farewell speech to the Ephesian elders, he warned them about this eventuality: "I know that after my departure fierce wolves will come in among you, not sparing the flock; and from among your own selves will arise men speaking twisted things, to draw away the disciples after them" (Acts 20:29–30). Notice Paul's concern: that false teachers will draw the people of God away from the gospel truth.

The contemporary church faces the same danger. The myths and endless genealogies of the present day are extrabiblical texts which are treated as Scripture. Many cult writings, like the *Book of Mormon*, fall into this category. So does the *Apocrypha* (if it is regarded as sacred Scripture), for these ancient texts were rejected by the Jews as not belonging to the Word of God. Another example is the so-called *Gospel of Thomas* which the Jesus Seminar and other heretical groups have tried to make famous. The *Gospel of Thomas* was compiled in Egypt sometime between AD 150 and AD 350. It claims to contain 120 "secret words of the living Jesus," but although a few of its teachings echo the biblical Gospels, the rest are all myths.

Another myth is any attempt to find hidden knowledge in the Bible. A notorious example here is *The Bible Code*, which rearranges the letters of Genesis and claims to decipher them in order to predict world events. According to the author, events such as the Gulf War and the assassination

7. Stott, *Guard the Truth*, 44.

of Yitzhak Rabin were predicted by "the Bible code."[8] There are many serious problems with the specific details of *The Bible Code.*[9] But the whole approach is misguided: it neglects the plain meaning of Scripture in order to speculate on matters of merely contemporary concern. Similarly, Dan Brown's novel *The Da Vinci Code* purports to provide secret knowledge about Jesus, but this knowledge is based on an unreliable hodgepodge of discredited "gospels" and historical speculations.[10]

Many evangelical discussions about the end times also fall into this category. Even if they are not myths or genealogies, they are at least endless! Some people seem to run for their handbooks of Bible prophecy every time something happens in the Middle East, hoping to figure out where we are on the timeline to eternity. Usually, though, they are asking the wrong questions and getting the wrong answers. A good deal of Roman Catholic dogma is also mythical. Central Catholic doctrines such as purgatory, the veneration of saints, and the adoration of Mary come from tradition. They are speculations that go beyond biblical teaching—exactly the kind of "different teaching" the Bible condemns.

True sons and daughters in the faith are commanded not to teach such things for two reasons. The first is that they "promote speculations rather than the stewardship from God that is by faith" (1 Tim. 1:4; cf. 6:4 and 2 Tim. 2:14). Not every religious discussion is equally beneficial, as the Ephesians were starting to discover. Some topics lead to debates about ancient religious texts, the end times, heretical dogmas, or other matters not addressed in the Bible.

The other reason not to teach false doctrine is that it is a complete waste of time: "Certain persons, by swerving from these, have wandered away into vain discussion" (1 Tim. 1:6; cf. 2 Tim. 2:16). They have lost their theological bearings. They have drifted away, which is the way most people abandon Christian orthodoxy: one step at a time. The more they deviate, the more tedious and tendentious their doctrine becomes. Elsewhere in the New Testament—in Galatians, for example—Paul attacks false teaching because the gospel is at stake. Here the problem is not so much a gospel issue as a stewardship issue. Heterodoxy is a waste of time.

8. Michael Drosnin, *The Bible Code* (New York: Simon and Schuster, 1996).
9. See Benjamin Wittes, "Of Bible Codes and Idols," *First Things* 78 (Dec. 1997): 12–14.
10. Dan Brown, *The Da Vinci Code* (New York: Doubleday, 2003).

Today one place to find such meaningless talk is on the Internet, where people often engage in wearisome and unproductive theological dialogues. The same is also true at seminaries and divinity schools where scholars are on a perpetual quest for novelty. But some religious matters are not even worth a good argument. There is a trade-off here between talking and doing. Either we can promote controversy or we can exercise good stewardship in thinking about theology. Salvation in Christ is the most important thing God has ever planned or accomplished for his people. Therefore, it is the most important message for us to study, to teach, and to live. Nothing should distract us from that message, least of all some idle speculation which goes beyond Scripture. Why waste time when there is God's work to be done?

This is a warning not to major on minors. Those who want to be dogmatic must be sure they have the right dogma. Paul says the false teachers in Ephesus do not lack conviction. Their teaching is full of what he calls "confident assertions"; however, they speak "without understanding what they are saying" (1 Tim. 1:7). There is a dangerous combination here: arrogance and ignorance. Error can be taught with as much conviction as the truth. In fact, the more argumentative someone is about a theological issue, the more likely he or she is to be spiritually unbalanced. Philip Towner applies the obvious spiritual lesson: "These characteristics make a timeless portrait of the false teacher. Doctrinal subtleties, special interpretation, spurious claims to authority, controversy and dogmatism ought to make God's people suspicious. At the same time, evidence of these same tendencies in our own lives ought to cause alarms to go off."[11]

The True Use of the Law

The reason the false teachers in Ephesus were unbalanced had something to do with God's law. Their desire to be "teachers of the law" (1 Tim. 1:7) suggests that they claimed the right to interpret the law of Moses from the Old Testament. The false teachers wanted to be law-teachers, which brought to Paul's mind a third thing every true child in the faith must have: a true understanding of the law.

11. Philip H. Towner, *1–2 Timothy and Titus*, IVP New Testament Commentary Series (Downers Grove, IL: InterVarsity, 1994), 49.

Paul was opposed to the self-appointed teachers of the law in Ephesus, but not to the law itself. So he quickly went on to say, "Now we know that the law is good, if one uses it lawfully" (1 Tim. 1:8; cf. Rom. 7:12). There is an obvious wordplay here, which the New English Bible renders as follows: "We all know that the law is an excellent thing, provided we treat it as law."

What is the proper way to use the law? Reformation Christians have taught that there are three proper uses of biblical law. One is the spiritual use of the law to reveal sin. As Martin Luther wrote in his *Lectures on Galatians*, the law shows sinners their sin "so that by the recognition of sin they may be humbled, frightened, and worn down, and so may long for grace."[12] A second use of the law is its civil use to restrain wrongdoers. This is how the law is useful for society; it keeps criminals in their place. John Calvin added "a third and principal use" of the law, namely, to teach us God's will for our lives. This is how Christians use the law. As we meditate on the law, we are "aroused to obedience. . . and drawn back from the slippery path of transgression."[13] These three uses of the law might be termed the pedagogical use, the political use, and the pious use of the law.

Which use of the law does Paul have in mind when he writes, "the law is not laid down for the just but for the lawless and disobedient, for the ungodly and sinners" (1 Tim. 1:9)? Obviously, he is not describing the third use of the law in which the Christian obeys the law of Christ. Rather, he is referring to a use of the law which is not for law-abiding citizens who already know how to behave themselves. Thus he mainly has in view the second use of the law: its power in society to restrain those who are a law unto themselves. The law of the land is not for saints, but for sinners. Here some commentators point out that none of us is righteous; we are all commandment-breakers. This is true, of course, but it is not the point of this passage. Although Paul does not deny that the law has other uses, here he is mainly concerned about its civil use.

The second use of the law is implied by the apostle's list of vices: "the law is not laid down for the just but for the lawless and disobedient, for the ungodly and sinners, for the unholy and profane, for those who strike their fathers and mothers, for murderers, the sexually immoral, men who practice

12. Martin Luther, *Luther's Works*, ed. Jaroslav Pelikan (St. Louis: Concordia, 1963), 26:327.
13. Calvin, *Institutes*, 2.7.12.

homosexuality, enslavers, liars, perjurers, and whatever else is contrary to sound doctrine" (1 Tim. 1:9–10). Here Paul mentions the most extreme forms of defiance and insubordination. He condemns not shoplifting but kidnapping, not lust but perverse sexual acts, not white lies but perjury, and so forth. In fact, he chooses the kinds of gross sin that civil laws often prohibit. According to Roman law, most of these vices were punishable by death. The law has a serious purpose of restraining wicked behavior: "*This*, Paul says, is why God gave his Law, not for idle speculation and meaningless talk."[14]

The list in 1 Timothy also seems to echo many of the Ten Commandments.[15] One way to see this is to begin with "those who strike their fathers or mothers" and work backwards. Such domestic violence violates the fifth commandment to honor one's father and mother. The word "profane" aptly describes those who break the fourth commandment by profaning the Lord's Day. "Unholy" is just the term to use for those who fail to sanctify the Lord's name, and thereby break the third commandment. Perhaps this leaves the "ungodly" and "sinners" to break the first and second commandments, but whether Paul has in mind the first two commandments or not, he clearly refers to commandments six through nine. "Murderers" break the sixth commandment, while "the sexually immoral" and "men who practice homosexuality" break the seventh. Next come "enslavers." The New Testament is sometimes criticized for promoting slavery, but here Paul condemns slave traffic as the worst violation of the eighth commandment. Finally, he condemns "liars" and "perjurers," who break the ninth commandment by bearing false witness. Perhaps the tenth commandment—which prohibits coveting—is omitted because it governs a sinful attitude not punishable by civil law.

After this rehearsal of God's commandments, Paul's concluding comment about the law comes as something of a surprise: the law is for "whatever else is contrary to sound doctrine, in accordance with the glorious gospel of the blessed God with which I have been entrusted" (1 Tim. 1:10–11). The heinous sins just mentioned are the result of unsound doctrine. Not only are they against the law, but they also fail to conform to "the gospel which tells of the glory of God"

14. Gordon D. Fee, *1 and 2 Timothy, Titus*, New International Biblical Commentary (Peabody, MA: Hendrickson, 1988), 46.

15. See George Knight, *The Pastoral Epistles*, New International Greek Testament Commentary (Grand Rapids: Eerdmans, 1992), 83–85.

(NEB). The gospel thus requires the same conduct that the law requires—not as a way to merit grace, but as the appropriate response of gratitude.

It is sometimes argued that the gospel makes the law obsolete. It is true that the gospel does away with the law as a basis for justification. Thus the difference between law and gospel is that the law is powerless to save. As Paul says elsewhere, "by works of the law no one will be justified" (Gal. 2:16). Only the gospel—in which the righteousness of Christ is offered to us by faith—is able to justify. Yet the gospel does not lower God's legal standards. The law remains useful for driving sinners to Christ (pedagogical use), restraining sin (political use), and teaching believers how to live for Christ (pious use). Therefore, as George Knight explains, "when the law is rightly applied as an ethical restraint against sin, it is in full accordance with the ethical norm given in the gospel as the standard for the redeemed life."[16]

Not only does lawlessness fail to conform to the gospel, but it is also contrary to sound doctrine. The word for "sound" (*hygiainousē*) is a medical term meaning "healthy" or "wholesome." Life cannot be separated from doctrine. Unhealthy theology produces unhealthy conduct, and an unsound life always betrays unsound doctrine. Every sin comes ultimately from a failure to believe rightly about God.

It is significant that the Greek text of 1 Timothy describes correct teaching as "the sound doctrine" (1 Tim. 1:10). Not *a* sound doctrine, but *the* sound doctrine. This idea is repeated throughout the Pastoral Epistles: *the* faith, *the* truth, *the* teaching, and so forth. The Bible insists that there is one standard for Christian theology. This standard is the teaching of Christ and his apostles found in the pages of the New Testament, in full agreement with the prophetic witness of the Old Testament.

Paul's emphasis on the sound doctrine is a valuable corrective for these pluralistic times, in which people say, "Your theology is just your opinion. Christianity may be true for you, but not for me." A notable example of this way of thinking comes from *Man Friday*, a 1975 film based on *Robinson Crusoe*. The original novel by Daniel DeFoe was a deeply Christian work, but in the film Crusoe's friend Friday is a champion for religious pluralism. "Worship any way you like," he says, "as long as you mean it. God won't mind."[17]

16. Knight, *Pastoral Epistles*, 91.

17. Philip Zaleski, "The Strange Shipwreck of Robinson Crusoe," *First Things* 53 (May 1995): 41.

The truth is, however, that God *does* mind. There is only one true theology; every other doctrine is false. Here is how John Stott applies Paul's emphasis on the truth of sound doctrine to the contemporary Christian:

> The pertinence of this theme, at the end of the twentieth century, is evident. For contemporary culture is being overtaken and submerged by the spirit of postmodernism. . . . The postmodern mind . . . declares that there is no such thing as objective or universal truth; that all so-called "truth" is purely subjective, being culturally conditioned; and that therefore we all have our own truth, which has as much right to respect as anybody else's. Pluralism is an offspring of postmodernism; it affirms the independent validity of every faith and ideology, and demands in shrill tones that we abandon as impossibly arrogant any attempt to convert somebody (let alone everybody) to our opinion. In contrast to this relativization of truth, it is wonderfully refreshing to read Paul's unambiguous commitment to it.[18]

When John Calvin dedicated his commentary to the Duke of Somerset, he called 1 Timothy "highly relevant to our own times."[19] It is all the more relevant five centuries later. Now, as then, God wants his true sons and daughters in the faith to know and defend orthodoxy because it is *the* true doctrine.

TRUE LOVE

What connotations are brought to mind by the word "doctrine"? To many people the term sounds rigid, inflexible, impractical, probably boring. The last person most people want to meet is someone who will straighten out their theology. However, this is exactly what Paul tells Timothy to do: "charge certain persons not to teach any different doctrine" (1 Tim. 1:3). A charge is a military order. The Bible thus gives ministers the authority to oppose false doctrine. Yet notice that the purpose or goal of defending true doctrine is to create true love: "The aim of our charge is love that issues from a pure heart and a good conscience and a sincere faith" (1 Tim. 1:5). A true son in the faith must have true love, which, according to the Scriptures, flows naturally from a love for doctrine.

18. Stott, *Guard the Truth*, 10.

19. John Calvin, *The Epistles of Paul to Timothy and Titus* (1548–50; Edinburgh: Oliver and Boyd, 1964), 182.

False doctrine does just the opposite. The problem with heterodoxy is not just that it is unorthodox, but also that it leads to controversy. It disturbs the life and love of the church. In his book *The Cruelty of Heresy*, C. F. Allison argues that heresy is the ultimate cruelty.[20] This is because it does not love people enough to warn them about the judgment to come or to insist that Jesus is the only way to salvation. In the end, every false theology is murderous to the soul. Teaching heterodoxy is perhaps the most unloving thing a person can do. Is any sin greater than the murder of a soul?

Only true doctrine teaches people how to love God and others. True doctrine fosters the love that comes from "a pure heart" (1 Tim. 1:5). The heart is the center of the inner spiritual life. A pure or cleansed heart is a loving heart because it has no self-interest. It is untainted by mixed motives. Its only aspiration is to put others first. True love also comes from "a good conscience" (1 Tim. 1:5). The conscience is the center of the moral life. A guilty conscience leads to the hatred of one's neighbor. It creates distance or even animosity in a relationship. But a conscience made good by God's grace has nothing to hide. It brings people close to one another in intimate relationship. Then true love comes from "a sincere faith" (1 Tim. 1:5)—literally, an "unhypocritical faith." A hypocrite cannot love anyone as much as he loves himself. He is mainly concerned what others think of him, whereas true love is selfless.

This kind of love—true love from a pure heart, a good conscience, and a sincere faith—is the best advertisement for true doctrine. Love is also the best test of our theology, for true love and true doctrine go together. Liberal theology wants love without doctrine. It is willing to tolerate all kinds of doctrinal error, as long as people don't fight about it. On the other hand, some Reformation churches are willing to go without the love as long as they maintain sound doctrine. But that is neither true love nor true doctrine! Wherever doctrine is the purest, love must be the highest.

Do you practice the doctrine of love as much as you love your doctrine? The better you understand God's grace in Christ, the more your life will overflow with zeal for the lost, love for the church, and compassion for the needy. If we are not great lovers, there is something wrong with our love, or our doctrine, or both.

20. C. FitzSimons Allison, *The Cruelty of Heresy: An Affirmation of Christian Orthodoxy* (London: SPCK, 1994).

The Bible does not indicate if Timothy remained a true son in the faith. Presumably he did. But sadly the Bible does indicate that eventually his congregation wandered from the Lord. The New Testament contains yet another letter to the Ephesians. The short letter to the Ephesian church in Revelation 2 warmly commends the congregation for defending true doctrine: "you have tested those who call themselves apostles and are not, and found them to be false" (Rev. 2:2). Yet somewhere along the way the Ephesians lost their true love: "But I have this against you, that you have abandoned the love you had at first" (Rev. 2:4). These people loved their doctrine, but they were forgetting the doctrine of love.

This is a reminder that the true children of God must have true love as well as true faith and true doctrine. Who is sufficient for these things? Who is able to defend the truth of God's Word while at the same time living out the love of the gospel? We can only do this through the saving work of Jesus Christ and the transforming work of his Spirit. In our own strength we might be able to defend the truth without living in love, or to live in love without defending truth, but we could not have both together. Without the love of God we inevitably become harsh, judgmental, and legalistic in our defense of the truth; without the truth of God our love becomes an excuse for theological compromise. Sadly, this is what we usually see in the church: truth without love, or love without truth, rarely both together. But when we do find love and truth together, we know that this can only be a gracious work of the one true God,[21] who will use the union of love and truth to save dying sinners.

21. Francis Schaeffer makes a similar point about love and purity in *The Church at the End of the Twentieth Century* (Downers Grove, IL: InterVarsity, 1970), 98.

2

Mercy for the Worst of Sinners

1 Timothy 1:12–16

Formerly I was a blasphemer, persecutor, and insolent opponent. But I received mercy because I had acted ignorantly in unbelief, and the grace of our Lord overflowed for me with the faith and love that are in Christ Jesus. (1 Tim. 1:13–14)

Christians seem to sing fewer hymns these days, but when they do, sometimes they tinker with the lyrics. Consider the change made to a simple hymn by John Newton: "Amazing grace! How sweet the sound! That saved and strengthened me!"

There is a grace that strengthens, as we shall see, but Newton was talking about a grace that does more than strengthen; he was praising God for the grace that saves. In the original, therefore, Newton identified himself as the worst of sinners: "Amazing grace! How sweet the sound! That saved a wretch like me!" Brian Abel Ragen comments: "While Newton believed that human beings were wretches, in desperate need of a Savior, these 20th-century adapters clearly believe that they and the congregations who sing their words are perfectly nice people. . . . They are not bad—certainly not *wretches*; they have simply lost their way. They are not wicked; they merely have a handicap—a dysfunction—from which they hope to recover."[1]

Downplaying depravity like this inevitably has the result of minimizing the amazing grace of God. As Ragen concludes, "Grace is amazing because it saves *wretches*, not because it puts a final polish on nice people. . . . You cannot be saved if you are not lost. . . . You cannot be freed unless you are enslaved."[2]

Happy to Serve

The apostle Paul had experienced both God's saving grace and his strengthening grace, so he knew the difference. What a Christian needs for ministry is God's strengthening grace, a grace the apostle had received: "I thank Christ Jesus our Lord, who has given me strength, that he considered me faithful, appointing me to his service" (1 Tim. 1:12 NIV).

When it comes to serving the Lord, believers need divine enablement, and Paul had been thus enabled. His effectiveness as a missionary did not depend on natural talent, a first-rate education, or following the latest Christian fads. Rather, he was spiritually empowered. As he told the Philippians, he had learned to do everything through the God who gave him strength (see Phil. 4:13). First Christ appointed him to serve as an apostle; then Christ gave him the strength to serve. The God who gave Paul strength was the same God who put him into service in the first place.

What always amazed Paul is that God trusted him with this ministry at all. He had already mentioned to Timothy how God had entrusted the glorious gospel to him (1 Tim. 1:11). He proceeded to praise God for finding him trustworthy with this trust. In English we might render the wordplay here like this: Paul was considered "faithful" (*piston*) to be "enfaithed" (*episteuthēn*) with the gospel. This may refer to the period of preparation between Paul's conversion and his commission, between

1. Brian Abel Ragen, *America* (January 29, 1994), quoted in Michael S. Horton, "The Justification of the Guilty, Not the Righteous," *Modern Reformation* 6.6 (November/December 1997): 4.

2. Ibid.

becoming a Christian and becoming an apostle. God had confidence that Paul would be a reliable minister.

This does not mean, however, that Paul had proved himself worthy. Who could ever be worthy of an apostolate? The whole point of this passage is that he was *unworthy* to receive God's grace. Rather, in entrusting the gospel to Paul, God also made Paul trustworthy. Calvin paraphrased Paul's testimony like this: "I should have nothing that might be fit for this office, which is to bear the Gospel: but all my might, all my worthiness, cometh from the mere grace of our Lord Jesus Christ."[3]

What comes through strongly in this verse is Paul's thankfulness to God for the privilege of serving as an apostle. This is an example for every Christian. Do you praise God for the ministry he has given you in the family, the church, or the world? When you fold the laundry, stuff bulletins, drive a school bus, or do whatever it is that you do, thank God for the high privilege of serving in his name.

Sometimes we grow ungrateful because we are tired of ministry. We complain about *having* to serve the Lord rather than thanking him for *getting* to. On other occasions we are too proud to be grateful. We are tempted to think that God should thank *us* for our spiritual service. To help us avoid these temptations, Nancy DeMoss has drawn up a list of the difference between "Proud Spirits and Humble Hearts." Proud, unbroken people have a "desire for self-advancement." They are "driven to be recognized and appreciated." They say, "The ministry is privileged to have me!" Broken people, on the other hand, have a "sense of unworthiness." They are "thrilled to be used at all, eager for others to get the credit." When they think of their involvement in the church, they say, "I don't deserve to serve in this ministry!"[4]

Paul had a humble heart. He was not bashful about his credentials as an apostle, and on many occasions he insisted on his apostolic right to speak the Word of God. But he never lost his sense of personal unworthiness for ministry, or his profound gratitude for the privilege of serving God. He thanked God for giving him the strength to serve.

3. John Calvin, *Sermons on the Epistles to Timothy & Titus* (London, 1579; repr. Edinburgh: Banner of Truth, 1983), 67.

4. Nancy DeMoss, quoted in Dale Schlafer, *A Revival Primer* (Denver: Promise Keepers, 1997), 55–58.

Grace Abounding

Before Paul became an apostle, he had to become a Christian, and for this he did not need to be strengthened; he needed to be saved! Only God's amazing grace could save a wretch like him. In 1 Timothy 1 Paul gives a short personal testimony of his conversion to faith in Jesus Christ, the transformation that brought him from past sinfulness to present service.

The apostle began with his wretched past, describing himself as "a blasphemer, persecutor, and insolent opponent" (1 Tim. 1:13). The apostle was not exaggerating when he said this. Paul (who was then known as Saul) was present for the stoning of Stephen, giving approval to his death (Acts 7:58–8:1). He was also the ringleader of the terrible persecution that followed: "Saul was ravaging the church, and entering house after house, he dragged off men and women and committed them to prison" (Acts 8:3; cf. 22:19). Then, "still breathing threats and murder against the disciples of the Lord" (9:1), he traveled to Damascus to take more prisoners. In addition to his own blasphemy, he tried to force Christians to commit blasphemy (Acts 26:11).

In short, before he came to Christ Paul was a thoroughly disreputable individual. The fact that he committed his crimes in the name of God made them all the more outrageous. From Paul's perspective in those days, attempting to eradicate the church was one of the best ways for him to serve God. As he later explained in his testimony to King Agrippa:

> I myself was convinced that I ought to do many things in opposing the name of Jesus of Nazareth. And I did so in Jerusalem. I not only locked up many of the saints in prison after receiving authority from the chief priests, but when they were put to death I cast my vote against them. And I punished them often in all the synagogues and tried to make them blaspheme, and in raging fury against them I persecuted them even to foreign cities. (Acts 26:9–11; cf. 22:4–5, 19)

This was the violent, blasphemous, wretched life the man led in the days when he was persecuting the church.

Then Paul came to Christ. A Christian testimony is a story of God's grace overcoming a man's sin, so Paul tells the "after" as well as the "before." He explains, "I received mercy" (1 Tim. 1:13). Or, as Thomas Goodwin expressed it in good Puritan English, "I was bemercied."[5] Mercy refers especially to the forgiveness of sins, and Paul received this mercy when he met Jesus Christ on the road to Damascus. There God forgave Paul for all his violence, all his blasphemy, and all his persecutions. By the grace of God, the fiend became a friend.

Why did Paul receive this mercy? The apostle gives what seems to be at least a partial explanation: "I received mercy because I had acted ignorantly in unbelief" (1 Tim. 1:13). Before he became a Christian, Paul hardly knew what he was doing. In fact, when he met Jesus on the Damascus road, he was so surprised that he said, "Who are you, Lord?" (Acts 9:5). He was persecuting Christ almost unwittingly.

This does not mean that Paul's ignorance and unbelief somehow qualified him for salvation, or made his actions any less sinful. He was still guilty. God never excuses sin because of mitigating circumstances. Nevertheless, God had pity on Paul's desperate spiritual condition—his ignorance and unbelief. The man received mercy because God is merciful. As Paul explained on another occasion, God "saved us, not because of works done by us in righteousness, but according to his own mercy" (Titus. 3:5). It was only by the grace of God that Paul was found when he was lost, and enabled to see when he was blind.

God has great mercy on those who have yet to receive the message of salvation. They are still responsible for their sins, of course, but God pities their spiritual ignorance. When John Bunyan, the famous author of *The Pilgrim's Progress*, experienced this same mercy he wrote, "though I was such a great sinner before conversion, yet God never much charged the guilt of the sins of my ignorance upon me, only he showed me I was lost if I had not Christ because I had been a sinner."[6]

When Paul was converted, he not only received mercy, but he also received grace. Grace is the undeserved, unmerited favor of God, which Paul received in superabundance: "the grace of our Lord overflowed for me with the faith and love that are in Christ Jesus" (1 Tim. 1:14). This was the passage Bunyan had in mind when he entitled his spiritual autobiography *Grace Abounding to the Chief of Sinners*.

5. Thomas Goodwin, quoted in John Stott, *Guard the Truth: The Message of 1 Timothy and Titus* (Downers Grove, IL: InterVarsity, 1996), 51.

6. John Bunyan, *Grace Abounding to the Chief of Sinners* (New York: Penguin, 1987), 24.

Abounding grace is grace that overflows. It is a mighty torrent of divine favor that cannot be contained. It is the kind of grace described in a hymn by Julia Johnston:

Marvelous grace of our loving Lord,
Grace that exceeds our sin and our guilt,
Yonder on Calvary's mount outpoured,
There where the blood of the Lamb was spilt.

Grace, grace, God's grace,
Grace that will pardon and cleanse within;
Grace, grace, God's grace,
Grace that is greater than all our sin.

Johnston's hymn reminds us that God's abundant grace was poured out in the life blood of Jesus Christ. The grace which abounds flows from his cross.

Grace was not the only thing Paul received in abundance, however. His testimony is that "the faith and love that are in Christ Jesus" came along with that grace (1 Tim. 1:14). Here Paul is referring to faith in Christ and love for God. Earlier, he had condemned the false teachers for turning away from faith and love (1 Tim. 1:5–6); by contrast, he himself received faith and love when he came to Christ. This contrast clarifies the true gospel as over against the false gospel of the false teachers.

The various benefits of salvation in Christ cannot be separated, for with him it is all or nothing. Anyone who knows Christ has grace, and faith, and love, and everything else Christ has to offer. Whoever does not know him does not have his grace, or his faith, or his love. Every spiritual blessing comes in and with Jesus Christ. Even faith comes from God. God holds out the free gift of eternal life, but we are too sinful to take it. Our hands are curled up in defiance and rebellion. So God takes us firmly by the wrist, uncurls our fingers, presses his grace into our hands, and wraps our fingers back around it. We lay hold of eternal life with the hand of faith, but God opens the hand.

Paul is the perfect example. After he saw the glory of the risen Christ on the Damascus road, he was blind for three days. He fasted and prayed, waiting for God to save him. Then Ananias laid his hands on Paul in the name of Jesus, giving him sight and filling him with the Holy Spirit (Acts 9:17). It was all the gracious work of God from beginning to end, and Paul depended on that grace for the rest of his life.

The Chief of Sinners

In its spiritual dynamic of sin and grace, Paul's autobiography—his personal testimony of God's amazing, abounding grace for a wretched sinner—is basically the story of every Christian. Paul is not in some special category, but only one in a long line of unpromising sinners who became productive servants in the kingdom of God. True, his sins were worse than most, especially since he persecuted the church of Jesus Christ (cf. 1 Cor. 15:9). Nevertheless, every Christian has received what Paul received: mercy and abundant grace through faith.

The apostle thus takes his personal experience and applies it to every Christian: "The saying is trustworthy and deserving of full acceptance, that Christ Jesus came into the world to save sinners, of whom I am the foremost" (1 Tim. 1:15). This sounds like a slogan from the early church, possibly from a hymn or creed or catechism. We can almost imagine seeing it on posters and bumper stickers at the Christian bookstores in Asia Minor. Here Paul affirms that the popular saying is a true saying (cf. 1 Tim. 3:1; 4:9; 2 Tim. 2:11; Titus 3:8): Jesus Christ really did come into the world to save sinners.

This proposition deserves to be wholeheartedly accepted, and by everyone, because it contains the whole gospel, from the incarnation to the atonement. "Christ Jesus came into the world"—this speaks to the fact of the incarnation, of God becoming a man. The very Son of God left all the glories of heaven to become a human being. He did it for this reason: "to save sinners"—that is, to deliver them from sin and death. This statement speaks to the fact of the atonement, of Christ dying on the cross for sinners. A sinner is anyone who is alienated from God by disobedience. But the very reason Christ came into the world was to deliver his people from sin. He atoned for their sins by the blood he shed on the cross. "Christ Jesus came into the world to save sinners": that is the gospel, from the incarnation to the atonement.

Then Paul added a phrase to make that trusty gospel personal: "sinners, of whom I am the foremost." In this phrase the apostle literally identifies himself as the "first" (*prōtos*) of sinners, meaning that he was the "worst" or "foremost" or "chief" sinner of them all. But he also invites us to put ourselves in his sandals, as if to say, "Repeat after me: 'Christ Jesus came into the world to save sinners, of whom I am the foremost.' "

Jesus Christ did not just come to save sinners in general; he came to save me in particular! Becoming a Christian means making a personal commitment to Christ and a personal confession of sin. "Christ Jesus came into the world to save sinners"—this is a universal truth. "Of whom *I* am the worst"—this is the universal truth applied to my situation. As John Stott says, "The universal offer is one thing; its individual acceptance is another."[7]

Once there was a woman who wanted to be baptized into the church. So the elders asked her about her testimony of faith in Jesus Christ. She gave an accurate description of who Jesus was and what he had done, but something seemed to be missing. It was not so much a personal testimony as an impersonal testimony. So one of the elders asked her, "Do you believe that when Jesus was dying on the cross he was paying the price for *your* sins?" There was a long pause. Then she said, "I've never thought of it that way before." With further counsel, she proceeded to make a personal commitment to the Lord Jesus Christ, trusting that he died for her personal sins on the cross. This step was necessary for her to take. We are not able to receive God's grace until we admit we are sinners, because Jesus Christ came to save sinners. As Jesus said himself, "I came not to call the righteous, but sinners" (Matt. 9:13; cf. Luke 19:10). Do you believe that you are among the worst of sinners?

It is important to use the present tense because that is what Paul uses. His testimony is not that he *was* the worst of sinners, but that he *is* the worst of sinners, now redeemed. Our need for the gospel does not cease when we first receive it. Because we are still sinners, we need to go back to the good news of God's mercy every day. So I ask the question again: Do you believe yourself to be the worst of sinners?

Just as he had once said that he was the "least of the apostles" (1 Cor. 15:9), and the "least of all the saints" (Eph. 3:8), now Paul says that he is the least of all the sinners. The apostle was coming to a deeper awareness of his depravity, and at the same time he was growing in grace and service to God. Here is how Paul Tournier explained this dynamic of sin and grace in the

7. Stott, *Guard the Truth*, 52.

life of a growing Christian: "Believers who are the most desperate about themselves are the ones who express most forcefully their confidence in grace. . . . Those who are the most pessimistic about man are the most optimistic about God; those who are the most severe with themselves are the ones who have the most serene confidence in divine forgiveness. . . . By degrees the awareness of our guilt and of God's love increase side by side."[8]

Some people object to the apostolic teaching on sin because they think people should not get down on themselves. One immediately thinks of Dr. Robert Schuller, the sage of self-esteem, who wrote, "I don't think that anything has been done in the name of Christ and under the banner of Christianity that has proven more destructive to human personality, and hence counterproductive to the evangelistic enterprise than the unchristian, uncouth strategy of attempting to make people aware of their lost and sinful condition."[9] Paul, for one, would beg to differ, because one of the main goals of his ministry was to help people see their sinful condition, and therefore to see their need for a Savior.

Admittedly, some people thank God that they are *not* the worst of sinners. However, these people do not happen to be Christians. Consider the parable that Jesus taught "to some who trusted in themselves that they were righteous":

> Two men went up into the temple to pray, one a Pharisee and the other a tax collector. The Pharisee, standing by himself, prayed thus: "God, I thank you that I am not like other men, extortioners, unjust, adulterers, or even like this tax collector. I fast twice a week; I give tithes of all that I get." But the tax collector, standing far off, would not even lift up his eyes to heaven, but beat his breast, saying, "God, be merciful to me, a sinner!" I tell you, this man went down to his house justified, rather than the other. For everyone who exalts himself will be humbled, but the one who humbles himself will be exalted. (Luke 18:10–14)

Jesus could hardly have made it any clearer: those who are confident about their own righteousness are not justified. Unless you consider yourself the worst of sinners—knowing that the sinful attitudes in your heart are as dis-

8. Paul Tournier, *Guilt and Grace* (New York: Harper and Row, 1959), 159–60.
9. Robert Schuller, *Self-Esteem: The New Reformation* (Waco: Word, 1982), 98.

honoring to a perfectly holy God as any sins can be—you are still learning what it means to be a Christian, because genuine Christians are firmly convinced of the wretchedness of their sin.

What the tax collector said is significant. Literally, he said, "God, be merciful to me, *the* sinner." He was so painfully aware of his sin that it was as if he were the only sinner in the whole world. All he needed to do was to identify himself as *the* sinner and God would know exactly who was talking. The apostle Paul viewed himself the same way:

> For he had not investigated the sinful and criminal records of all the inhabitants of the world, carefully compared himself with them, and concluded that he was worse than them all. The truth is rather that when we are convicted of sin by the Holy Spirit, an immediate result is that we give up all such comparisons. Paul was so vividly aware of his own sins that he could not conceive that anybody could be worse. It is the language of every sinner whose conscience has been awakened and disturbed by the Holy Spirit.[10]

It is a hopeful thing to know that we are sinners, because "Christ Jesus came into the world to save sinners" (1 Tim. 1:15). This verse gives the only qualification needed to be saved by Christ. Take comfort in this qualification if you sometimes doubt your salvation. The only thing you can contribute to your salvation is the sin from which Christ came to save you.

Christianity is the only religion in the world that is for bad people. In one way or another, every other religion says people can become good enough for God. But what if we are not good enough? What then? What if we really are the worst of sinners? Then Christianity is the only religion that offers real hope. If we are wretched sinners, then Christianity is our only option. Jesus Christ is the only one who can or will save us, because he came into the world to save sinners.

There is a wonderful story about a sinner who came to faith in Christ through this very verse. It comes from the early days of the English Reformation, when the Cambridge scholar Thomas Bilney first read the New Testament in Greek:

> At last . . . I heard speak of Jesus, even then when the New Testament was first set forth by Erasmus . . . and at the first reading (as I well remember) I chanced

10. Stott, *Guard the Truth*, 53.

> upon this sentence of St. Paul (O most sweet and comfortable sentence to my soul!) in 1 Timothy 1. "It is a true saying, and worthy of all men to be embraced, that Christ Jesus came into the world to save sinners; of whom I am the chief and principal." This one sentence, through God's instruction and inward working, which I did not then perceive, did so exhilarate my heart, being before wounded with the guilt of my sins, and being almost in despair, that even immediately I seemed unto myself inwardly to feel a marvellous comfort and quietness.[11]

That comfort sustained Bilney to the end of his life, when he was burned at the stake for his faith in Jesus Christ.

The Prototypical Convert

The worst of sinners find mercy and abundant grace in Jesus Christ. In case any further encouragement to come to Christ is needed, Paul uses himself as an example: "But I received mercy for this reason, that in me, as the foremost, Jesus Christ might display his perfect patience as an example to those who were to believe in him for eternal life" (1 Tim. 1:16).

Again the apostle claims that he received mercy. Again he identifies himself as the worst of sinners. His point is that if God can transform the worst of sinners into an apostle, there must be no limit to the power of his grace. Even a bully, and a murderer, and a sworn enemy of Christ can become a servant of God. If God can save Paul, of all people, then he can save anyone.

The apostle thus serves as an illustration for others—figuratively, a "prototype." Every Christian can see himself or herself in Paul's conversion, even though many aspects of it were unique. Not every convert enters the kingdom of God with blinding light and the visible, audible presence of the risen Christ. Not every testimony is identical to Paul's, nor should it be. But his conversion experience on the Damascus road gives hope to everyone because it shows the full extent of God's patience. God is slow to judgment, giving sinners time to repent. In his grace God is willing to put up with a lot from people, as he did from Paul.

11. Thomas Bilney, quoted in *The Acts and Monuments of John Foxe*, 8 vols. (London, 1837), 4:635.

The first Christians took great encouragement from God's forbearance with Paul and the other apostles. In *The Epistle of Barnabas*, which was written in Alexandria around AD 100, we read that when Christ "chose his own apostles who were destined to preach his gospel," he chose men "who were sinful beyond all measure in order that he might demonstrate that 'he did not come to call the righteous, but sinners.'"[12]

With all of this encouragement, there is only thing left to do: believe in Jesus Christ. Paul is the prototype for those who "believe in him for eternal life." It is not enough to believe you are a sinner unless you also take Christ for a Savior. Everyone who does believe in him receives eternal life.

Earlier I quoted the words of John Newton's hymn "Amazing Grace." That hymn was written from personal experience, for Newton himself was among the worst of sinners. At the age of eleven he took to the sea, where he had many adventures: he was press-ganged into the navy; he was captured and flogged for desertion; he despaired almost to the point of suicide. Eventually Newton became a slave-trader, a hard and wretched man. But he was shown mercy. As he feared for his life in stormy seas, he threw himself on the grace of God, which he found in abundance. Later he testified, "How wonderful is the love of God in giving his Son to die for such wretches!"[13]

Even after he was saved, Newton continued to confess his need of God's amazing grace. He wrote in one of his letters, "In defiance of my best judgment and best wishes, I find something within me which cherishes and cleaves to those evils, from which I ought to start and flee, as I should if a toad or a serpent was put in my food or in my bed. Ah! how vile must the heart (at least my heart) be." Newton did not despair, however. Before closing the letter, he quoted Paul's words to Timothy: "I embrace it as a faithful saying, and worthy of all acceptation, that Jesus Christ came into the world to save sinners."[14]

Every Christian knows how to complete Newton's quotation in the quietness of a believing heart: "of whom *I* am the worst."

12. *The Epistle of Barnabas*, 5.9, in *The Apostolic Fathers*, 2d ed., trans. J. B. Lightfoot and J. R. Harmer, ed. Michael W. Holmes (Grand Rapids: Baker, 1989), 167.

13. John Newton, *Letters of John Newton* (Edinburgh: Banner of Truth, 1960), 11'1.

14. Newton, *Letters*, 129–30.

3

Immortal, Invisible, God Only Wise

1 Timothy 1:17

To the King of ages, immortal, invisible, the only God, be honor and glory forever and ever. Amen. (1 Tim. 1:17)

Demetrius was right to be worried. The Ephesian silversmith made shrines for the goddess Artemis, and what kept him up at night—worrying about his job security—was the rapid growth of Christianity in his city.

Up until a missionary named Paul arrived, the silver trade in Ephesus had been rather lucrative. The worship of Artemis "brought no little business to the craftsmen" (Acts 19:24). But Christianity meant the end of idolatry, and this posed a threat to their livelihood. So Demetrius called the silversmiths together and said:

> Men, you know that from this business we have our wealth. And you see and hear that not only in Ephesus but in almost all of Asia this Paul has persuaded and turned away a great many people, saying that gods made with hands are not gods. And there is danger not only that this trade of ours may come into

> disrepute but also that the temple of the great goddess Artemis may be counted as nothing, and that she may even be deposed from her magnificence, she whom all Asia and the world worship. (Acts 19:25–27)

The silversmiths wanted to defend the honor and majesty of their queen. More importantly, they wanted to keep their jobs. So "when they heard this they were enraged and were crying out, 'Great is Artemis of the Ephesians!' So the city was filled with the confusion" (Acts 19:28–29). A massive protest was held in the giant theater of Ephesus. For two straight hours, as many as twenty thousand people shouted, "Great is Artemis of the Ephesians!" (Acts 19:34).

Eventually the city clerk was able to quiet the crowd. He said: "Men of Ephesus, who is there who does not know that the city of the Ephesians is temple keeper of the great Artemis, and of the sacred stone that fell from the sky?" (Acts 19:35). Yes, the whole world did know this, for the temple of Artemis was one of the seven wonders of the ancient world. It was 425 feet long and 220 feet broad, with 127 columns of white marble, each 60 feet high. It took two centuries to build it. Edwin Yamauchi calls it "the largest structure in the Hellenistic world and the first of such monumental proportions to be built entirely of marble."[1] Inside stood the ancient and enormous statue of Artemis herself.

The goddess seemed immortal, but Demetrius was right to be worried. The coming of Christ meant the end of Artemis. She has now been tossed on the scrap heap of history. With the exception of a few scattered columns on a plain near ancient Ephesus, the last fragments of her temple—a handful of coins and a few broken columns—are now on display in the basement of the British Museum in London.

A Hymn of Triumph

The death of Artemis has turned Paul's doxology into a hymn of triumph: "To the King of ages, immortal, invisible, the only God, be honor and glory forever and ever. Amen" (1 Tim. 1:17). Paul addressed these words to Timothy in Ephesus, the guardian city of Artemis. The contrast

1. E. M. Yamauchi, *New Testament Cities in Western Asia Minor* (Grand Rapids: Baker, 1980), 103.

between God and the goddess could not be more absolute. God is a King; Artemis was a queen. He is immortal; she proved to be mortal. He is invisible; she was a statue. He is unique; she was mass-produced. While he will be honored and glorified forever, her praise and worship have ceased.

Christians have long sung this verse as a hymn of praise to God and triumph over every false god. It forms the basis for the opening stanza of the well-known hymn by Walter Chalmers Smith:

Immortal, invisible, God only wise,
In light inaccessible hid from our eyes,
Most blessed, most glorious, the Ancient of Days,
Almighty, victorious, thy great name we praise.

Paul may have sung nearly the same words to a different tune, for his doxology sounds like part of a Christian hymn. Since the language is Jewish, it may have been a song which was carried over from the synagogue into the early church.

But why does Paul sing the doxology here? The apostle has just given his Christian testimony. He has testified how God rescued him from a life of violence and blasphemy and gave him the grace, faith, and love which are in Jesus Christ (1 Tim. 1:13–14). He has confessed that Christ Jesus came to save sinners (1 Tim. 1:15). And he has explained how the mercy of God was shown to him, the chief of sinners (1 Tim. 1:16).

It is easy for a personal testimony to become self-centered, however, so Paul ends his spiritual autobiography by glorifying God. Having explained the one true gospel, he worships the one true God. According to Calvin, the apostle thereby "admonishes us all by his example, that we should never think of the grace shown in God's calling without being lost in wondering admiration. This sublime praise of God's grace swallows up all the memory of his former life. How great and deep is the glory of God!"[2] To put this another way, there comes a time to leave off praising God for what he has done in your life and simply to praise him for who he is in himself.

2. John Calvin, *The Second Epistle of Paul the Apostle to the Corinthians and the Epistles to Timothy, Titus and Philemon*, trans. T. A. Smail, Calvin's Commentaries (Edinburgh: Oliver & Boyd, 1964), 199.

Now unto the King Eternal

Who is this God we praise? Why should we praise him, and for how long?

The Scripture begins with God's kingship: "To the King of ages." God is praised first for his sovereign rule over the universe. Here the title of "King" is given to God the Father rather than to God the Son. Some scholars have found this puzzling because the New Testament usually identifies Jesus Christ as King. And so he is. Jesus entered Jerusalem in royal pomp before ushering in the kingdom of God. He is "Lord of lords and King of kings" (Rev. 17:14). But Paul also knew the Old Testament passages where God the Father is identified as King: "The Lord is king forever and ever" (Ps. 10:16); "The Lord is the true God; he is the living God and the everlasting King" (Jer. 10:10); and so forth.

It is appropriate to speak about both the kingdom of God and the kingdom of Christ. The Father and the Son exercise a co-regency: "The kingdom of the world has become the kingdom of our Lord and of his Christ, and he shall reign forever and ever" (Rev. 11:15). The Father and the Son reign together. There is no rivalry between them. The joint-kingship of the Father and the Son makes it natural for Paul to go from praising Christ to praising God as King. John Chrysostom preached that "the Father is most glorified, when the Son hath done great things. For the glory of the Son is referred again to Him."[3] The work of the Son is to glorify the Father. Glory to the Son is glory to the Father.

Here Paul especially emphasizes the duration of God's reign. God is the "King of the ages." This title is found nowhere else in Scripture, although it appears in ancient Jewish literature. It refers, not so much to God himself, but to his rule. God's kingship is everlasting. His reign will never come to an end.

God is the King of ages past. He ruled over the deeps when they were formless and void. He governed the galaxies when they were brought into being. He was King over the dinosaurs when they walked the earth. He was God and King to Abraham, Isaac, and Jacob, to Moses and all the prophets. He was the King of all the kings of Israel.

3. John Chrysostom, "Homilies on the Epistles of St. Paul the Apostle to Timothy, Titus, and Philemon," trans. and ed. Philip Schaff, *Nicene and Post-Nicene Fathers*, First Series, 14 vols. (Peabody, MA: Hendrickson, 1994), 13:421.

God is also the King of the present age, which commenced with the birth, life, death, and resurrection of Jesus Christ. God is sovereign over the church in this gospel age. He rules over the worldwide expansion of his kingdom, right up to the present moment.

God is King of both this age and the age to come. He will rule over every subsequent era of human history, however long it may last. In short, "God is the supreme king who governs all the ages from the creation of the world, including the age of the Messiah himself, until the end of time."[4] Then, at the second coming of Jesus Christ, he will be enthroned over the new heavens and the new earth. He will rule forever and forever. God was the King, he is the King, and he will be the King forever.

What other king can make the same claim? Every earthly monarchy is temporary. Kings are born, they ascend to the throne, they rule, and then they die. Even the greatest of royal dynasties must come to an end. It happened to the Pharaohs of Egypt, the Caesars of Rome, and the emperors of China. It will happen to every president, premier, and prime minister who is presently in power. But God is the King of the ages. There will never be an interregnum in the kingship of almighty God. He is the once and future King. He ruled in the past, he rules in the present, and he will rule forever.

This raises the most practical of all spiritual questions: Will you let God be King? Will you submit to his rule in your own life and heart?

One popular Christian bumper sticker reads: "GOD IS MY CO-PILOT." This is the kind of relationship many Christians want to maintain with God. They want to stay in the captain's chair. They are willing to turn over the controls only when there is an emergency. But anyone who relegates God to co-pilot is headed for turbulence! It is much safer to leave the cockpit altogether and go find a seat somewhere in coach class. God is the King, not a co-pilot.

So will you let God rule your life? Will you let him govern your moral behavior? Will you let him control your work situation? Your family? Your finances? Your conduct and your crises are best left in God's hands. This is what it means to be a servant of the King. A true king does not take orders; he gives them. If God is the King eternal, he needs to be trusted and obeyed.

4. J. N. D. Kelly, *The Pastoral Epistles: Timothy I and II, Titus*, Harper's New Testament Commentaries (San Francisco: Harper and Row, 1960), 56.

The King Immortal

God is also immortal. In Paul's doxology, eternity refers to God's kingship, whereas immortality refers to God himself, to his being and essence. The word "immortal" (*aphthartos*) is perhaps better translated as incorruptible. It means that God, unlike the milk in the refrigerator, does not have a use-by date. He is imperishable. He cannot decay.

This makes God different from everything else in his world. The natural world is changeable, corruptible. Pine trees enter the forest and drive out the aspens. Rivers alter their courses. Mountains erode. Entire galaxies collide and stars collapse into black holes. If the scientists are right, the cosmos itself is in gradual decline. This is explained by the scientific principle known as entropy. According to the Oxford English Dictionary, entropy is a "measure of the disorganization or degradation of the universe." Things are slowing down, cooling off, and returning to a formless void. Thermodynamic theory teaches entropy is always on the rise. In other words, the entire universe is running down.

Our bodies are also running down. Scientists are still trying to figure out a way to immortalize humanity, but the human body is corruptible. Human beings grow old and die. Only one thing can stop the aging process, and that is death itself. The older people get, the more wrinkles they get, the more aches and pains, and the less hair. The aging process goes on inside the body all the time. Cells replicate themselves again and again throughout a person's lifetime. But eventually, chromosomes shorten beyond the point of repair. It is a little bit like having a shoelace that keeps breaking. Eventually, the lace gets so short that the shoe cannot be tied. In the same way, the ends of a chromosome gradually deteriorate until finally the entire cell shuts down.

Corruption is a fact of daily human existence. Appliances stop working. Clothing gets torn and stained. Automobiles break down. Shops and factories close. The demographics change, the population shifts, and cities go into decline. Indeed, entire civilizations are corruptible, which is one of the main lessons of the twentieth century. In the aftermath of the First World War, William Butler Yeats wrote a famous poem about the corruptibility of humanity. It is entitled "The Second Coming":

Turning and turning in the widening gyre
The falcon cannot hear the falconer;
Things fall apart; the center cannot hold;
Mere anarchy is loosed upon the world,
The blood-dimmed tide is loosed, and everywhere
The ceremony of innocence is drowned;
The best lack all conviction, while the worst
Are full of passionate intensity.[5]

Things fall apart. Persons, families, towns, cities, nations, empires, civilizations—they all fall down. But not God. God is not eroding. He is not cooling off or winding down. He is not growing old and wrinkled. His chromosomes are not getting shorter. He is not falling apart. Unlike everything else he has made, God is immortal. Not only will he live forever, but every one of his divine attributes will remain undiminished throughout all eternity. God does not become less powerful, less loving, less just, or less holy with the passage of time. He is every bit as powerful, loving, just, and holy as he has ever been, and always will be.

God's incorruptibility is beautifully represented in the artwork of Mako Fujimura, a Christian artist who lives and works in New York City. Fujimura gives honor to his ethnic heritage by using traditional Japanese mineral pigments, each of which has symbolic significance. In Fujimura's paintings, God is represented by gold. Wherever gold appears, it is a symbol of things eternal. Humanity, by contrast, is represented by silver. Partly this shows the value of human beings. But it also shows the corruption of humanity because silver will tarnish and blacken with age. As the years pass, the paintings will become visual testimonies of the incorruptibility of God. Mortal silver will darken, while the gold of immortality continues to shine.

The best place to see God's immortality is in the resurrection of Jesus Christ. King David made this prediction about the Messiah: "You will not abandon my soul to Sheol, or let your holy one see corruption" (Ps. 16:10). This was a prophecy about Jesus of Nazareth. He died, and was buried, but he did not perish in the grave. He was raised on the third day in an incorruptible body.

5. William Butler Yeats, "The Second Coming," in *The Norton Anthology of English Literature*, 3d ed., ed. by M. H. Abrams, et al. (New York: Norton, 1962), 1925.

By raising Jesus from the dead, God gave immortality to mortals. Jesus Christ was the first to be raised with an everlasting body, but only the first. Part of his work is to give his people immortal, incorruptible bodies. As the Scripture says, "What is sown is perishable; what is raised is imperishable. . . . For this perishable body must put on the imperishable, and this mortal body must put on immortality" (1 Cor. 15:42, 53). Because God himself is immortal, he can guarantee eternal life to mortal flesh (see 1 Tim. 1:16).

The King Invisible

The eternal, immortal God cannot be seen. God is invisible. This fact comes up again in chapter 6, where we read that God is the immortal King "who dwells in unapproachable light, whom no one has ever seen or can see" (1 Tim. 6:16).

What about Moses? Didn't he see God? No, not in his divine essence:

> Moses said, "Please show me your glory." And he said, "I will make all my goodness pass before you and will proclaim before you my name 'The Lord.' And I will be gracious to whom I will be gracious, and will show mercy on whom I will show mercy. But," he said, "you cannot see my face, for man shall not see me and live." And the Lord said, "Behold, there is a place by me where you shall stand on the rock, and while my glory passes by I will put you in a cleft of the rock, and I will cover you with my hand until I have passed by. Then I will take away my hand, and you shall see my back, but my face shall not be seen." (Ex. 33:18–23)

Elisha saw the chariots and horsemen of Israel (2 Kings 2:11–12), but not the God of Israel. Isaiah "saw the Lord sitting upon a throne, high and lifted up" (Isa. 6:1), but he must have seen a theophany of the pre-incarnate Christ, as the apostle John confirms (see John 1:2–4), because the Scripture is emphatic: no one has ever seen God—meaning God the Father—nor can anyone see God. The most that anyone has ever seen is the glorious light within which God himself remains hidden—the outward refulgence of his inner majesty.

The invisibility of God is sometimes considered a disadvantage. The skeptic says, "If God is so real, why can't I see him? If only he would come down from heaven and reveal himself to me, then I would believe in him. So where is he?" The answer is that God is invisible. This is one of the first things little people learn in the *Children's Catechism* (Q & A 11): "Can you see God?" "No, I cannot see God, but he always sees me." By his very nature, God is invisible. We can no more see God than we can see gravity.

That God is invisible does not mean that he is unknowable, however. Also like gravity, there is abundant evidence for his existence. He has revealed something of himself in everything he has made: "For his invisible attributes, namely, his eternal power and divine nature, have been clearly perceived, ever since the creation of the world, in the things that have been made" (Rom. 1:20). We can see the things that God has created, and when we see them, our thoughts and desires are lifted from the seen to the unseen. The visible creation draws us to praise the invisible God.

For some, the invisibility of God may come as something of a disappointment. Human beings have a natural curiosity. We want to uncover what is hidden and gaze upon what is unseen. But we cannot lift the curtain on God. Invisibility is of the essence of his deity.

Therefore, God is to be praised for his invisibility. This may be one of God's most underrated attributes. Which is more worthy of worship, a visible God or an invisible God? The fact that God cannot be seen shows that there are aspects of his divine being which are not subject to our scrutiny. God is without limits and without boundaries. He cannot be probed and dissected. We must accept that there are some divine mysteries which the human mind cannot penetrate. There are some things about God—like his invisibility—which are so great and so far beyond our comprehension that they are known only to God. Otherwise, God would not be God.

There is one thing we can see, however, and that is God's incarnate Son. God has made himself visible in Jesus Christ, who is both human and divine. Jesus Christ is God in the form of a human being; therefore, in Christ the unseen God can be seen by human eyes. This is what Scripture means when it says that Jesus "is the image of the invisible God" (Col. 1:15).

God knows that his invisibility makes him inaccessible, so he made himself visible in and through Jesus Christ. The apostle John knew that when he saw God the Son he was looking at God the Father: "And the Word became flesh and dwelt among us, and we have seen his glory, glory as of the only Son from the Father, full of grace and truth. . . . No one has ever seen God;

the only God, who is at the Father's side, he has made him known" (John 1:14, 18). To see Jesus in all his majesty is to see the glory of God. As Calvin preached, "God can be known by no other means, but by beholding him in our Lord Jesus Christ."[6]

The hope of every Christian is to see Jesus face to face, and in seeing Jesus, to see the image of the invisible God. King David desperately longed to gaze upon the beautiful face of the Messiah. He wrote, "One thing have I asked of the LORD, that will I seek after: that I may dwell in the house of the LORD all the days of my life, to gaze upon the beauty of the LORD and to inquire in his temple" (Ps. 27:4). The beauty of the Lord—this is what Moses was asking to see when God showed him his goodness (Ex. 33:18).

Job wanted to see the same thing. Even after he had lost everything else, he never let go of the hope that he would meet his Savior face to face: "For I know that my Redeemer lives, and at the last he will stand upon the earth. And after my skin has been thus destroyed, yet in my flesh I shall see God, whom I shall see for myself, and my eyes shall behold, and not another. My heart faints within me!" (Job 19:25–27). Job could hardly contain himself. By faith, the resurrection was as certain to him as death, and the prospect of seeing the invisible God filled him with inexpressible joy.

The Puritans often wrote about studying divinity in the face of Jesus Christ. Many old New England gravestones depict a simple human face with lidless eyes staring wide open. The artwork was to show that the Christian was ready to behold the risen Christ on the day of resurrection. As the Puritan poet Edward Taylor once prayed, "Oh! Glorious Body! Pull my eye lids open: Make my quick Eye, Lord, thy brisk Glory greet."[7]

The desire of all these saints will be satisfied: "We know that when he appears we shall be like him, because we shall see him as he is" (1 John 3:2). In the beautiful face of Jesus Christ, the invisible God will be made visible. If you know God through faith in Jesus Christ, then one day you will get to see this for yourself. "Blessed are the pure in heart," Jesus promised, "for they shall see God" (Matt. 5:8).

6. John Calvin, *Sermons on the Epistles to Timothy & Titus* (London, 1579; repr. Edinburgh: Banner of Truth, 1983), 93.

7. Edward Taylor, *Meditations*, 2:74.

The Only King

God is not only immortal and invisible, but he is also incomparable. The last divine attribute Paul mentions is God's uniqueness. He is "the only God" (the King James Version famously calls him "the only wise God," but the word for wisdom is not found in the best and oldest manuscripts). God has no rivals. There is no other being in the universe who shares his attributes. He alone is King of the ages. Although God has given us eternal life, he alone is immortal in his very nature. And he alone is invisible.

The fact that the eternal, immortal, invisible God is also "the only God" (1 Tim. 1:17) opens up the mystery of the Trinity. It is sometimes pointed out, especially by Mormons and Jehovah's Witnesses, that the word "Trinity" does not appear in the Bible. On this basis, they proceed to argue that there is only one person in the Godhead, not three.

The truth is that the doctrine of the Trinity finds abundant support throughout the New Testament. Paul's first letter to Timothy is one among many places where the doctrine must be true for a Bible passage to make sense. Here we have two members of the Trinity clearly presented: God the Son, who came to save sinners (1 Tim. 1:15), and God the Father, who is immortal and invisible (1 Tim. 1:17). Yet we also have a strong statement of monotheism: there is only one God. What other explanation is there for this, except that the one and only God exists in more than one person?

Since the early days of the church, Christians have made this confession. As Augustine wrote in his famous treatise *On the Trinity*:

> The Father, and the Son, and the Holy Spirit intimate a divine unity of one and the same substance in an indivisible equality; and therefore they are not three Gods, but one God: although the Father hath begotten the Son, and so He who is the Father is not the Son; and the Son is begotten by the Father, and so He who is the Son is not the Father; and the Holy Spirit is neither the Father nor the Son, but only the Spirit of the Father and of the Son, Himself also co-equal with the Father and the Son, and pertaining to the unity of the Trinity.[8]

8. Augustine, *On the Trinity*, 1.4.7, quoted in Philip Schaff, *Nicene and Post-Nicene Fathers*, First Series, 14 vols. (1886; repr. Peabody, MA: Hendrickson, 1994), 3:20.

The Athanasian Creed stated the same doctrine rather more simply: "The Father is God, the Son is God, and the Holy Spirit is God; And yet they are not three Gods, but one God." This definition of the Trinity represents what all Christians, everywhere, have always believed about the triune being of God.

Admittedly, the doctrine of the Trinity is easier to state than it is to explain, as every Christian parent has learned. Immanuel Kant, the philosopher of the German Enlightenment, complained that "the doctrine of the Trinity, taken literally, has *no practical relevance at all*, even if we think we understand it; and it is even more clearly irrelevant if we realize that it transcends all our concepts."[9] Yet the truth is that the doctrine of the Trinity has a great deal of relevance. It is relevant for our salvation, where each person of the Trinity plays a part in redemption: the Father administrates redemption, the Son accomplished redemption, and the Spirit applies redemption. It is in the name of this Triune God that Christians are baptized. But even apart from the plan of salvation, knowing that the one and only God exists in three persons is relevant to our worship, which makes it relevant enough! This is how God has told us to address him: as Father, Son, and Holy Spirit. Even if we never unravel all the mysteries of the Trinity, we can praise God for the mystery.

Many of the most profound Christian hymns simply praise God for his triune being. There is an echo of the Trinity in the hymn "Holy, Holy, Holy." The thrice-holy God is the thrice-personal God: "God in three Persons, blessed Trinity." God's triune name also comes at the beginning of the Gloria Patri: "Glory be to the Father, and to the Son, and to the Holy Ghost." It comes at the end of the doxology: "Praise Father, Son, and Holy Ghost." It comes, too, in the glorious final stanza of a Latin hymn from the seventh century: "Laud and honor to the Father, laud and honor to the Son, laud and honor to the Spirit, ever Three and ever One, One in might, and One in glory, while unending ages run." God can receive no higher praise than to be addressed and adored as one God in three Persons, both in our private and in our public worship.

True Christian worship is always trinitarian worship. To worship God as Trinity is to enter into the joy expressed by the great fourth-century theologian Gregory of Nazianzus:

9. Immanuel Kant, *The Conflict of the Faculties*, trans. Mary J. Gregor (New York: Abaris, 1979), 65.

> I cannot think of the One without immediately being surrounded by the radiance of the Three; nor can I discern the Three without at once being carried back to the One. . . . When I think of any One of the Three I think of him as a whole, and my vision is filled, and the greater part of what I conceive escapes me. I cannot grasp the greatness of that One so as to attribute a greater greatness to the others. When I contemplate the Three together, I see but one luminary, and cannot divide or measure out the undivided light.[10]

Honor and Glory, Forever and Ever, Amen

All that is left to do is to praise God, giving him "honor and glory forever and ever" (1 Tim. 1:17). The apostle Paul is not simply listing God's attributes; he is praising God for them. He is giving honor and glory to God for his kingship, his eternity, his immortality, his invisibility, and his uniqueness.

To give "honor" is to give God his due. It is to show him the respect and reverence his kingship deserves (to give him his worth, which is what worship truly means: "worth-ship"). "Glory" refers to the radiant and luminous manifestation of God's majestic being. To give God the glory is simply to testify that he *is* glorious. The English word "doxology" is derived from the Greek word for "glory" (*doxa*). Our praise cannot add anything to God's glory because he is completely glorious in himself. But we can at least acknowledge God's splendor and majesty for what it is.

We do this with our songs and praises. We also do it with our lives. Chrysostom suggested that "honor and glory are not mere words; and since He has honored us not by words only, but by what He has done for us, so let us honor Him by works and deeds."[11] And let us do so forever. If God is the King of the ages, then he deserves to be praised for all eternity. The destiny of every child of God is to be wrapped up in the adoration of God throughout the endless ages.

To this we can only say, "Amen," as Paul does. "Amen" is not an afterthought; it is a word of agreement and affirmation. It means "truly," "so let it be," or "may this be the case." When Christians say "Amen" at the end of a hymn or a prayer, they are making that hymn or prayer their own. In effect, they are saying, "Yes, Lord, I give you from my heart all the praise I have just uttered with my lips."

10. Quoted by Christopher Hall, "Adding Up the Trinity," *Christianity Today* (April 28, 1997), 28.
11. Chrysostom, "Homilies," 13:421.

The "Amen" at the end of Paul's doxology invites a personal response. When Timothy first read this letter aloud to the church at Ephesus, he undoubtedly paused when he came to the end of this verse, so that all the people could say "Amen."

Down through the centuries many other Christians have added their own "Amen" to Paul's doxology. In his "Personal Narrative," Jonathan Edwards records his life-changing experience of reading 1 Timothy 1:17 as a young man: "The first instance that I remember of that sort of inward, sweet delight in God and divine things that I have lived much in since, was on reading the words 'Now unto the King eternal, immortal, invisible, the only wise God, be honor and glory for ever and ever' (1 Tim. 1:17)." America's greatest theologian went on to describe the impression these words made on his soul:

> As I read the words, there came into my soul, and was as it were diffused through it, a sense of the glory of the Divine Being; a new sense, quite different from any thing I ever experienced before. Never any words of Scripture seemed to me as these words did. I thought with myself, how excellent a Being that was, and how happy I should be, if I might enjoy that God, and be rapt up to him in heaven, and be as it were swallowed up in him for ever! I kept saying, and as it were singing over these words of Scripture to myself; and went to pray to God that I might enjoy him, and prayed in a manner quite different from what I used to do; with a new sort of affection. . . . An inward, sweet sense of these things, at times, came into my heart; and my soul was led away in pleasant views and contemplations of them. And my mind was greatly engaged to spend my time in reading and meditating on Christ, on the beauty and excellency of his person, and the lovely way of salvation by free grace in him.[12]

Paul's words will make a similar impression on all those who believe in the God they praise: "To the King of ages, immortal, invisible, the only God, be honor and glory forever and ever." Everyone who believes this doxology will want to add his or her own personal expression of affirmation, and in doing so to make a personal confession of faith in the one true God of the Bible: "Amen!"

12. Jonathan Edwards, *A Personal Narrative*, quoted in Sam Storms, "Jonathan Edwards' Personal Narrative," *Enjoying God Ministries* (June 25, 2005).

4

Fight the Good Fight

1 Timothy 1:18–20

This charge I entrust to you, Timothy, my child, in accordance with the prophecies previously made about you, that by them you may wage the good warfare. (1 Tim. 1:18)

If there is going to be a war, men must be ready to fight. This is the lesson of the first battle of Manassas (or Bull Run), the first major engagement of the American Civil War.

There had been talk of war for months, ever since South Carolina fired on Fort Sumter in early April of 1861. Both the North and the South hurriedly prepared for the conflict. By early July, each side was ready for war and certain of an easy victory. When Union general Irvin McDowell addressed his troops on the eve of battle, his only fear was that the enemy would be unable to put up a good fight.

The first shots were fired in northern Virginia late on the 8th of July. News of the skirmish reached Washington by nightfall. Since a Union victory seemed inevitable, the battle was treated as the social event of the summer. The next morning, the ladies and gentlemen of high society gaily packed their hampers, piled into carriages, and rode to Bull Run for a picnic.

But the day turned out to be anything but festive. The scene of battle was one of unimagined chaos and horror. The commanders were unaccustomed to warfare on such a grand scale. The armies did not so much engage as collide. The fighting was fierce until Stonewall Jackson led the Confederate soldiers on a bayonet charge. The Union was routed, with three thousand soldiers left dead or bleeding on the battlefield. The Washington socialites ran for their lives, their army defeated because it was not ready to fight.[1]

In the Lord's Army

The apostle Paul did not want Timothy to go so unprepared into battle. He knew the invisible war between God and Satan is no picnic, but a struggle to the death. So he ordered his young assistant to prepare for spiritual combat: "wage the good warfare" (1 Tim. 1:18), or as other translations have it, "fight the good fight."

Paul speaks to Timothy partly as a father in the faith, but especially as a general: "This charge I entrust to you, Timothy" (1 Tim. 1:18). These are Timothy's marching orders, for Paul's charge is Timothy's command. The orders come through God's field general (the apostle Paul) from the Commander-in-Chief of Christ's army, who is God himself.

Spiritually speaking, Timothy was no longer a civilian, but a soldier in God's army. He could sing the old children's song from Sunday school: "I may never march in the infantry, ride in the cavalry, shoot the artillery; I may never fly over the enemy, but I'm in the Lord's army, yes, sir!" Here at the end of chapter 1, Timothy is told to report for duty. And since he is a minister of the gospel, he is not simply a foot-soldier, but a standard-bearer.

His military orders are "in accordance with the prophecies previously made" about him (1 Tim. 1:18). This personal comment piques our curiosity. What was prophesied concerning Timothy? This may refer to the reports Paul heard about him in Lystra, reports that led to his joining the apostle's missionary team (Acts 16:1–3). More likely, Paul was referring to something that happened at Timothy's ordination, an event he mentions more than once. Later we will learn that Timothy was given a spiritual gift

1. For a full account of the first battle of Manassas, see Shelby Foote, *The Civil War: A Narrative*, 3 vols. (New York: Random House, 1958), 1:56–72.

"by prophecy" at his ordination (1 Tim. 4:14; cf. Acts 13:1–4; 2 Tim. 1:6). It is not necessary for us to know the content of this prophetic message; otherwise, the Bible would mention it. All we know is that Timothy's call to the ministry was affirmed by a prophetic word. He had the confidence of Paul, the endorsement of the church, and the confirmation of the Holy Spirit.

Don't Fight the Bad Fight

In answering his call to the ministry, Timothy was ordered to "wage the good warfare" (1 Tim. 1:18), which raises an obvious question: "What is this good fight?"

The expression itself implies that some fights are not good. Throughout this epistle, Timothy is repeatedly warned against the dangers of needless warfare. He should stay away from issues that promote controversy (1 Tim. 1:4). As an elder in the church, he must not be quarrelsome (1 Tim. 3:3; cf. 2 Tim. 2:23–24). Indeed, anyone who has "an unhealthy craving for controversy and for quarrels about words" is a false teacher (1 Tim. 6:4).

The Scriptures warn against such disputes because most Christian fights are bad fights. Quarrels and controversies are perennial dangers for the church. Most of the wars the church wages turn out to be civil wars; most of the casualties come from friendly fire. One is reminded of the 1991 Gulf War, when almost all of the U.S. casualties came as the result of friendly fire.

A fight over a doctrine not essential to the Christian faith is usually a bad fight. Every biblical truth needs to be taught, discussed, believed, and practiced. But not every biblical truth needs to be argued for in every situation, and no biblical truth should ever be defended with a contentious spirit.

Church traditions often make for bad fights, too, as do practical matters with little spiritual consequence. Craig Barnes, who pastored the National Presbyterian Church in Washington, D.C., once found himself embroiled in a bitter dispute over a coffee table:

> Last spring the hospitality committee put a little coffee stand in the narthex. The next day the head usher of twenty-five years quit in protest, saying this was a sacrilege to the church sanctuary. All the ushers quickly became upset.

> Since a committee had put the coffee there, the session had to decide on the issue, so they set up a task force that met for eight weeks to listen to the ushers and the hospitality committee.
>
> One Sunday a bunch of ushers decided not to show up to usher because we hadn't brought back the head usher yet. So then the elders were ticked off at the ushers.
>
> In the middle of that, I'm not talking about Jesus to anybody, I'm not making hospital calls, or shepherding people through grief. I'm trying to figure out whether we should serve coffee in the narthex.[2]

Some fights are not worth fighting. Some wars are not worth waging. Some battles are not worth contesting. Too often, God's sheep end up battered and bloodied because they have been attacked by other members of the fold!

How does one tell the difference between a good fight and a bad fight? Ask questions like these: *Will this matter a year from now?* If it won't matter then, it probably doesn't matter much now, either. *Am I enjoying this dispute, in a perverse sort of way?* If so, you may be fighting for the wrong reasons. *Am I fighting for myself, or for others?* It is one thing to defend someone else's spiritual interests, or the glory of God himself; it is very different to look out for your own interests. *Do I find myself trying to justify my actions, either to myself or to others?* Something really worth fighting about is too obvious to require much explanation.

Fight the Good Fight

There are plenty of bad fights, but there is only one good fight, which is why Paul calls it *the* good warfare (1 Tim. 1:18). The warfare he has in mind is the defense of the central doctrines of the Christian faith.

Sometimes, when the Bible speaks about spiritual warfare, it means the Great War between heaven and hell. When Paul told the Ephesians to "put on the whole armor of God," for example, it was so they could "stand against the schemes of the devil" (Eph. 6:11). Yet within that Great War between the lovers of God and the minions of Satan—what Donald Grey Barnhouse aptly called *The Invisible War*[3]—there is a battle for the truth.

2. M. Craig Barnes, "Finding the Eye of the Storm," *Leadership* (Winter 1998), 20–21.
3. Donald Grey Barnhouse, *The Invisible War* (Grand Rapids: Zondervan, 1965).

This letter began with Paul urging Timothy to oppose false doctrines. He has digressed to praise God for his salvation (although even this was pertinent, because it clarified the true doctrine of God and the gospel). Now the apostle returns to the matter at hand, which is the problem of heresy in the church. In fact, the letter could flow smoothly from verse 7 to verse 18 with little interruption in thought. When Paul refers to his "charge" in verse 18, he means the charge he had already given in verse 3 for Timothy to oppose false teaching. Thus he has returned to "Timothy's responsibility for extirpating heresy and establishing sound teaching."[4]

The good fight is the fight for sound theology. So when Paul proceeds to talk about "holding faith and a good conscience" (1 Tim. 1:19), he draws an explicit contrast with the false teachers he described back in verse 5 as letting go of "a good conscience and a sincere faith." When he mentions Timothy's opponents, he says they have made a shipwreck, not of "their faith," as the English Standard Version interprets the Greek, but of "*the* faith" (1 Tim. 1:19). He will return to this theme at the end of the letter when he repeats Timothy's marching orders: "Fight the good fight of the faith" (6:12).

The good warfare is the struggle to defend those doctrines which are essential to the Christian faith. This includes doctrines like the reality of the Trinity, the deity of Jesus Christ, the necessity of atonement for sin, the sufficiency of Christ's death on the cross, the efficacy of faith alone for justification, and the infallibility of Holy Scripture. Such deep theological truths are well worth fighting for.

Paul's command is a reminder never to take sound doctrine for granted. The people of God have never been able simply to rest in the faith; they have always had to fight for it. This good fight began in the Old Testament. By the time Moses came down from the mountain, the children of Israel were already worshiping the golden calf (Ex. 32). Joshua had to confront them with the choice between serving God and serving the gods (Josh. 24). Elijah was outnumbered by the prophets of Baal, 450 to 1 (1 Kings 18). Although not all God's prophets faced the same odds, they all faced the same enemy. Like Ezekiel, they had to oppose "the prophets who see false visions and who give lying divinations" (Ezek. 13:9).

4. J. N. D. Kelly, *The Pastoral Epistles: Timothy I and II, Titus*, Harper's New Testament Commentaries (San Francisco: Harper and Row, 1960), 56–57.

The warfare was resumed in the New Testament. The preponderance of Jesus' teaching contradicts the false theology of the Pharisees. Every New Testament epistle is concerned with sound doctrine. Apparently, there were as many enemies inside the early church as there were outside. Even the little epistle of Jude urges the church "to contend for the faith that was once for all delivered to the saints" (Jude 3).

The subsequent history of the church is largely a story of doctrinal confrontation. First the church had to defend the doctrine of the Trinity, settled by the Council of Nicea (AD 325). Then the church had to defend the sovereignty of God's grace against the man-centered doctrines of Pelagius (the Council of Ephesus, 431). All the while there were arguments over the deity of Jesus Christ, which were gradually settled by the Councils of Constantinople (381), Ephesus (431), and Chalcedon (451).

In the Middle Ages, the way of salvation came under attack. Eventually, because of doctrinal error, it was necessary for the Holy Spirit to reform the church. Scripture had to be defended as the alone standard for faith and practice (*sola scriptura*). Christ had to be defended as the alone mediator between God and man (*solus Christus*). Faith had to be defended as the alone instrument of justification (*sola fide*). Grace had to be defended as the alone power of God for salvation (*sola gratia*). And all these doctrines had to be defended in order to promote the greater glory of God, who alone is worthy of praise (*soli Deo Gloria*).

The good fight continued up through the twentieth century. There was the good fight between fundamentalism and modernism, fought by J. Gresham Machen and others. It was a fight between Christianity as a supernatural religion and Christianity explained away as human experience. This later became the fight between evangelicalism and liberalism, which Billy Graham, Carl F. H. Henry, and others waged during the middle part of the century, and which continued afterward.

The point of this sketch of church history is that there has never been a time when God's people were not in danger of falling into error. The history of the church confirms the necessity of Paul's charge to Timothy. Until Christ returns, the people of God will be engaged in a perpetual war against unsound doctrine. The Christian faith always needs to be defended, not only from paganism, but especially from heresy.

Whereas persecution often ends up helping the church by advancing the gospel, heresy always harms the church and hurts its ministry.

Christians long for peace in the church, and rightly so. Our Lord Jesus prayed that his people would be united with him, with the Father, and with one another (see John 17). However, anyone who believes that doctrinal unity can be achieved without a struggle understands neither the history of the church nor the teaching of Scripture. It is not enough to say, "Why don't we just all believe in Jesus?" As soon as one says that, one needs to explain who Jesus is, what he has done, what difference it makes, and how he is received.

Biblical realism warns Christians against naive ecumenism. There is an inevitable and perpetual warfare between truth and error. Since a minister is a warrior, Timothy needed to brace himself for the fight, and so do we. So what is our good fight?

First, it is the fight for biblical inerrancy. The evangelical church won the battle for the Bible which James Boice, Francis Schaeffer, and others fought during the 1970s and 80s, but it may be losing the war. Inerrancy is still regarded as a cardinal affirmation. Members of the Evangelical Theological Society affirm every year that "the Bible alone, and the Bible in its entirety, is the Word of God written and is therefore inerrant in the autographs." However, students and teachers in some evangelical churches and seminaries hold more loosely to the orthodox doctrine of Scripture, in some cases drawing a spurious distinction between infallibility and inerrancy, or else advocating interpretations that call biblical authority into question. Thus there is still a need to teach and defend the truth that the Bible is the Word of God written.

Second, there is the fight for salvation through Christ alone. So-called post-conservative evangelicals are increasingly open to the idea that Jesus Christ is not the only way to salvation. He is *a* way but not *the* way. Meanwhile, some leaders in the so-called emerging church are de-emphasizing the blood atonement of Jesus Christ. Therefore, confessing evangelicals must continue to defend the truth Paul teaches in the very next chapter: "there is one God, and there is one mediator between God and men, the man Christ Jesus" (1 Tim. 2:5).

Third, the good fight is for justification by grace through faith alone. The Bible teaches that sinners are declared righteous in the sight of God solely on the basis of the righteousness of Jesus Christ, imputed to them by faith. The 1990s witnessed several attempts to bring "Evangelicals and Catholics Together" over the doctrine of justification. These discussions put the evangelical church in danger of denying the biblical doctrine of justification. Where the evangelical-Catholic documents failed was in their understanding of the gospel itself. D. A. Carson, who participated in the dialogues, concludes that the Roman Catholic Church has not moved a single step closer to the biblical doctrine of justification. He writes: "the official teaching of the [Roman] church is that we are as far apart on this doctrine as Protestants and Catholics were at the time of Trent—notwithstanding the formal agreements that can be forged by handfuls of scholars from the two sides meeting in New York."[5]

In short, the battles the church must wage in the twenty-first century are the battles it has always waged. They center on questions like "What is the Word of God?" "Who is Jesus Christ?" and "What is the way of salvation?" The enemies of sound doctrine will not simply run away. They must be driven away. The good warfare for the Christian faith must always be waged.

The reason Christians must fight is that we have an enemy. That enemy has received his death blow, but he will not be vanquished until the second coming. Thus Calvin warned that when it comes to sound theology,

> the devil makes as great resistance as he can, because the doctrine of salvation which is preached unto us by the Gospel, is as it were the soul of the church, the kingdom of our Lord Jesus Christ, the bliss of men. And therefore . . . the Gospel can never be preached, but the devil is in such a rage, that he goes about to break off the course of the Gospel. . . . They that have to preach the Gospel, deceive themselves, if they think to execute their office quietly. . . and do nothing but expound the scripture. And why so? For the devil can not abide that they should preach the word of God purely, but he will resist it. . . . Therefore we must be ready to fight.[6]

A Good Conscience

The good fight is not simply a matter of faith; it is also a matter of practice. Paul charges Timothy to hold on to "faith and a good conscience" (1 Tim. 1:19). Given the military context, he must "arm himself" with faith

5. D. A. Carson, "Reflections on Salvation and Justification in the New Testament," *Journal of the Evangelical Theological Society* 40.4 (Dec. 1997): 581–608 (p. 606).

6. John Calvin, *Sermons on the Epistles to Timothy & Titus* (London, 1579; repr. Edinburgh: Banner of Truth, 1983), 100–101.

and a good conscience. Since a good conscience comes from a good life, Timothy must practice what he preaches. Christian life is as important as Christian faith, and the defense of sound doctrine is a matter of practice as well as belief.

These two virtues—faith and a good conscience—are joined together three times in 1 Timothy (1:5; 1:19; 3:9). They belong together. If a water molecule loses its oxygen atom, or a hydrogen atom, it is no longer water. In the same way, if a Christian loses faith or conscience, he or she is no longer living as a Christian.

Faith and conscience go together in several ways. Obviously, false doctrine leads to moral failure; wrong views about God's Word lead inevitably to wrong practices. But the reverse is also true: a bad conscience often leads to bad doctrine. Calvin went so far as to say that "a bad conscience is the mother of all heresies."[7]

People often try to justify their sins, and when they do, their bad behavior leads to false doctrine. The British historian Paul Johnson has shown how this happens in the world of ideas. His book *The Intellectuals* shows that many leading modern thinkers led private lives that were grossly immoral. In part, the philosophies of Karl Marx, Bertrand Russell, Jean-Paul Sartre, and others were attempts to justify their own sinful behavior.[8]

Faith and conscience always belong together, but especially in the life of a pastor. Nothing destroys a ministry more completely than immorality. Thus, the Scottish divine John Willison gave this counsel to ministers: "If we would advance the church's credit, and avert her reproach, let us all be careful to preach to our people by our lives as well as by our lips, to conform our doctrine in the pulpit by our conversation out of it. Let us mind, that a loose way of living will soon demolish all that is built by the most lively way of preaching; for our people have eyes to see how we walk, as well as ears to hear what we say."[9] All this is to say that the Christian faith is not simply to be defended, but also to be lived.

7. John Calvin, *The Second Epistle of Paul the Apostle to the Corinthians and the Epistles to Timothy, Titus and Philemon*, trans. T. A. Smail, Calvin's Commentaries (Edinburgh: Oliver & Boyd, 1964), 202.

8. Paul Johnson, *The Intellectuals* (New York: Harper and Row, 1988).

9. John Willison, *The Practical Works of the Rev. John Willison*, ed. W. M. Hetherington (Glasgow, 1852), 837.

Shipwreck!

What happens when Christians let go of their faith or their practice? Paul ends his charge by getting specific and giving two tragic examples of men whose immorality was the shipwreck of their faith.

The men he has in mind were notorious in the Ephesian church: Hymenaeus and Alexander. Hymenaeus is mentioned again in Paul's second letter to Timothy, where he says that "Hymenaeus and Philetus have swerved from the truth, saying that the resurrection has already happened. They are upsetting the faith of some" (2 Tim. 2:17–18). Alexander may be mentioned elsewhere as well, for Paul complains that "Alexander the coppersmith did me great harm; the Lord will repay him according to his deeds. Beware of him yourself, for he strongly opposed our message" (2 Tim. 4:14–15; this may or may not be Alexander the Jew, who tried to speak during the Artemis riot in Ephesus; see Acts 19:33–34).

What Paul says about these two men is that by rejecting faith and a good conscience, they "have made shipwreck of their faith," and that for this reason he "handed [them] over to Satan that they may learn not to blaspheme" (1 Tim. 1:19–20). By calling their theological position a "rejection," the Bible makes it clear that these men made a deliberate and conscious choice to repudiate the Christian faith.

The result was a shipwreck. Hymenaeus and Alexander foundered on the shoals of false doctrine. Their testimony turned into the *Titanic.* Eventually, their own teaching became blasphemous (1 Tim. 1:20), and they were guilty of the defamation of God's character. The lesson is that Christian teachers must be good sailors as well as good soldiers.[10]

Handed Over to Satan

The shipwreck of these men is sometimes considered a difficulty for Calvinism. Hymenaeus and Alexander seem to have lost their faith. What does this say about the doctrine of the perseverance of the saints? If they have lost their faith, how can anyone be certain of salvation?

10. Walter Lock, *A Critical and Exegetical Commentary on the Pastoral Epistles (I & II Timothy and Titus)*, International Critical Commentary (Edinburgh: T & T Clark, 1924), 19.

One good way of handling this difficulty is to point out that Hymenaeus and Alexander did not shipwreck "their faith," but "*the* faith" (*tēn pistin*). Scripture never claims these men to have had saving faith in the first place. If they did not, it is no wonder they hit an iceberg somewhere along the way. Perhaps, then, their example shows how far people can seem to go in the Christian faith without ever trusting Christ in the first place (cf. 1 John 2:19).

A better way of handling the difficulty, though, is to recognize that there was still hope for Hymenaeus and Alexander. Paul (of all people!) knew that it is sometimes possible to survive a shipwreck. Although being lost at sea is always dangerous, sometimes it is possible to swim for it, as Paul had done at least three times himself (see 2 Cor. 11:25; cf. Acts 27). It is also worth noticing that the sin these men committed—namely, blasphemy—was one of the apostle's former sins (see 1 Tim. 1:13). Paul knew that it was possible to be forgiven for blasphemy as well as saved from a shipwreck.

All of this helps explain why Paul handed Hymenaeus and Alexander "over to Satan" (1 Tim. 1:20). This phrase, which refers to church discipline, also appears in 1 Corinthians 5:5. It was carried over from the Jewish synagogues and refers to the correction of sin.

Church discipline includes everything Jesus described in Matthew 18:15–20. If a church member has fallen into scandalous sin, one of his Christian brothers or sisters should correct him privately: "If your brother sins against you, go and tell him his fault, between you and him alone" (Matt. 18:15). Hopefully, this will resolve the problem: "If he listens to you, you have gained your brother" (Matt. 18:15). The matter is settled and the church has been reconciled. However, if he refuses to listen, then two believers should go and plead with him to turn away from sin: "But if he does not listen, take one or two others along with you, that every charge may be established by the evidence of two or three witnesses" (Matt. 18:16). Only if all else fails should the matter be brought to the attention of the elders: "If he refuses to listen to them, tell it to the church" (Matt. 18:17).

In the end, a church member who refuses to repent must be put outside the church: "And if he refuses to listen even to the church, let him be to you as a Gentile and a tax collector" (Matt. 18:17). The decision to remove someone from the fellowship of the church is sometimes called "excommunication." It bars a former church member from receiving the sacrament of communion. It also removes him or her from God's care. To be handed over to Satan "did not simply mean that he left the Christian congregation and resumed a peaceful life in pagan society; such a man was thought to be really exposed to the malice of the Evil One, and physical disaster was fully anticipated."[11]

This is a warning about how dangerous it is to be caught outside the church of Jesus Christ. It is instructive to remember how much Job suffered when he was handed over to Satan, or to remember the Corinthians who fell sick because they were abusing the Lord's Supper (1 Cor. 11:30). Hymenaeus and Alexander were exposed to similar dangers when they were handed over to Satan. Although the details are not given, presumably Paul followed the biblical procedure. These men were denied Christian fellowship. They could no longer be considered part of the church of Jesus Christ. For them to return to fellowship with Christ and his church, they would need to be evangelized all over again.

All of this was done for the spiritual benefit of Hymenaeus and Alexander themselves. As Augustine observed, Paul was trying "to correct evil men by means of the evil one."[12] He excommunicated them so they would "learn not to blaspheme" (1 Tim. 1:20). Here "learn" (*paideuthōsin)* is a positive word meaning to instruct, train, and correct. Although he seems more pessimistic by the time he writes 2 Timothy, at this point Paul hopes that Hymenaeus and Alexander may yet make it back to port. As Towner points out, "For some it takes being cast off into the sea to realize the advantages on board ship."[13] It was Paul's fervent desire that God would bring Hymenaeus and Alexander back to himself.

Discipline is not intended simply to punish sin, but also to restore the sinner. Martin Luther pointed out that it has medicinal purposes.[14] It is not intended to harm, but to heal. When it is used properly, church discipline "maintains the glory of God, the purity of His Church and the keeping and reclaiming of disobedient sinners."[15] According to the *Book of Church Order*

11. Kelly, *Pastoral Epistles*, 58.

12. Augustine, *Letters*, 93.7, *The Confessions and Letters of Augustine*, trans. Philip Schaff, *Nicene and Post-Nicene Fathers*, First Series (1886; repr. Peabody, MA: Hendrickson, 1994), 1:384.

13. Philip H. Towner, *1–2 Timothy and Titus*, IVP New Testament Commentary Series (Downers Grove, IL: InterVarsity, 1994), 59–60.

14. Martin Luther, *Luther's Works*, ed. Jaroslav Pelikan (Saint Louis: Concordia, 1973), 28:255.

15. *The Book of Church Order of the Presbyterian Church in America*, 5th ed. (Atlanta: Committee for Christian Education and Publications, 1997), 27–3.

of the Presbyterian Church in America, its ultimate objectives are "the rebuke of offenses, the removal of scandal, the vindication of the honor of Christ, the promotion of the purity and general edification of the church, and the spiritual good of the offenders themselves."[16]

There is always the danger that spiritual authority may be abused. One thinks, for example, of the old Scottish elders who went into the villages during worship services to round up Sabbath-breakers for excommunication.[17] But the contemporary church errs in the opposite direction. Christians are so afraid of offending anyone that they rarely warn anyone away from sin. Church discipline needs to be restored to its rightful and helpful place in the church. It is not man's idea; it is God's idea. Calvin explained its proper function well: "Since it is in the Church that Christ holds the seat of His kingdom, outside the Church there is nothing but the dominion of Satan. Thus he who is cut off from the Church must necessarily fall for a time under Satan's tyranny, till he is reconciled to the Church and returns to Christ."[18]

A Warrior's Rest

It is sobering to realize that pastoral work sometimes includes putting sinners outside God's protection so that they might be saved. Ministry is not easy. But then, warfare never is. Christians must never forget that they are soldiers.

Paul stayed in the army until the end of his life. By the end of his second letter to Timothy, he was a veteran of many campaigns. He writes the dying words of a general to his second-in-command: "The time of my departure has come. I have fought the good fight, I have finished the race, I have kept the faith. Henceforth there is laid up for me the crown of righteousness, which the Lord, the righteous judge, will award to me on that Day, and not only to me but also to all who have loved his appearing" (2 Tim. 4:6–8).

These words would be wonderful to repeat at the end of a ministry, or at the end of life itself: *I have fought the good fight*. But it will be better still to receive the spoils of battle. For Christ must win the war, and all his soldiers

16. *Book of Church Order*, 27–3.

17. Gerald R. Cragg, *The Church and the Age of Reason, 1648–1789*, rev. ed., Penguin History of the Church 4 (Baltimore: Penguin, 1970), 85.

18. Calvin, *Second Epistle of Paul*, 203.

will wear the victor's crown. William Walsham How wrote a wonderful hymn for soldiers who have retired from the gospel campaign. Though it is often known by its first line—"For All the Saints"—its middle stanzas go like this:

> O may thy soldiers faithful, true, and bold,
> Fight as the saints who nobly fought of old,
> And win with them the victor's crown of gold.
> The golden evening brightens in the west;
> Soon, soon to faithful warriors comes their rest;
> Sweet is the calm of paradise the blest.

5

The Great Intercession

1 Timothy 2:1–7

First of all, then, I urge that supplications, prayers, intercessions, and thanksgivings be made for all people, for kings and all who are in high positions, that we may lead a peaceful and quiet life, godly and dignified in every way. (1 Tim. 2:1–2)

Joanne Shetler spent twenty years doing Bible translation among the Balangao tribesmen in the Philippine mountains. It was difficult work, and when Shetler returned to the United States for her first sabbatical, she was deeply discouraged: "I was frustrated. When I came home on my first furlough, after five solid years, only two people had believed—not a very good showing, is it? I didn't know what to do. I dumped the whole load on my home church. And I found something out. You can't do the job by yourself. You have got to have people praying for you."[1] Joanne Shetler was learning a valuable lesson about Christian ministry: spiritual work is not accomplished by might, ability, or technique, but by prayer.

1. Joanne Shetler, "Faithful in Obedience," in *Faithful Witness: The Urbana '84 Compendium*, ed. James McLeish (Downers Grove, IL: InterVarsity, 1985), 99–107 (p. 103).

Pray for Everyone

Praying is the most important thing God's people do. That is why, having charged Timothy to defend the faith, the apostle Paul gives intercession top priority in public worship: "First of all, then, I urge that supplications, prayers, intercessions, and thanksgivings be made for all people" (1 Tim. 2:1; cf. Phil. 4:6).

Scholars have long tried to distinguish among these different kinds of prayer. Writing sometime in the third century, Origen made them the basis for the classic analysis of prayer he wrote for Ambrose. More recently, George Knight has defined the Greek terms as follows: "*deēseis*, making requests for specific needs; *proseuchas*, bringing those in view before God; *enteuxeis*, appealing boldly on their behalf; and *eucharistias*, thankfulness for them."[2] This explanation is as good as any, but the real point is that all kinds of prayer should be offered for all kinds of people. Christians should offer every prayer for everyone.

The kind of prayer the apostle Paul especially has in mind is evangelistic prayer. It is intercession for the salvation of souls. This is clear from the rest of the passage, which is about God's plan for the salvation of the world. Christians pray for everyone (1 Tim. 2:1–2): first, because God wants everyone to be saved (1 Tim. 2:3–4); second, because Christ is a Savior for everyone (1 Tim. 2:5–6); and third, because the gospel is preached to everyone (1 Tim. 2:7).

The public prayers of the church should have a global perspective. Many evangelical churches have abbreviated the pastoral prayer or eliminated it altogether. The apostle Paul would have been shocked by this trend because he considered prayer of first importance in the public worship of God.

Even when it is offered today, however, congregational prayer is sometimes self-centered and fails to venture very far beyond today's offering or Aunt Edna's kidney. Pastoral prayers ought rather to be large, expansive, and wide-ranging. They should include the great issues of the day and the vast nations of the world. Intercession should be made for renewal, revival, and reformation in the church. Prayer should be offered for missionaries, evangelists, and

2. George Knight, *The Pastoral Epistles*, New International Greek Testament Commentary (Grand Rapids: Eerdmans, 1992), 115.

church planters. The sufferings of the persecuted church and the desperation of unsaved humanity should be brought weekly before the throne of grace.

The God who rules the world wants his people to pray for the world. Therefore, every church should locate itself at the center of something God is doing in the whole world. The Great Commission (Matt. 28:18–20) goes hand in hand with the Great Intercession. In his *Thoughts on Public Prayer*, the old Princeton theologian Samuel Miller wrote:

> A good public prayer ought always to include a strongly marked reference to *the spread of the gospel*, and earnest petitions for the success of the means employed by the Church for that purpose. As it forms a large part of the duty of the Church to spread the knowledge of the way of salvation to all around her, and to send it, to the utmost of her power, to all within her reach who are destitute of it; so she ought never to assemble without recognizing this obligation, and fervently praying for grace and strength to fulfill it.[3]

Some of the most remarkable prayer meetings I ever attended were held at the Gilcomston South Church in Aberdeen, Scotland, when William Still was the minister. Every Saturday (!) night the congregation gathered for two solid hours of intercession for the worldwide progress of the gospel. At the front of the prayer hall was a large board listing the names and locations of ministers and missionaries who had been sent out by the church. The members began praying their way around the city of Aberdeen. Then they prayed for Scotland and the British Isles. Soon, someone would mention one of the other continents and prayer would continue, country by country, until nearly the whole world was surrounded in prayer. It was part prayer meeting, part geography lesson. Gilcomston was committed to praying for everyone, the way a gospel-preaching church should.

Royalty Included

When Paul urges the church to pray for everyone, he means everyone. Praying for the world includes praying "for kings and all who are in high positions" (1 Tim. 2:2). There may well have been a murmur of surprise

3. Samuel Miller, *Thoughts on Public Prayer* (1849; repr. Harrisonburg, VA: Sprinkle, 1985), 239–40.

when Timothy read this to the Ephesians. The traditional prayers of the Jewish synagogue did not include petitions for people in authority, especially Gentiles. Furthermore, there were no Christian kings in those days, only pagans—men like the Roman Emperor Nero, who threw Christians to the lions and used them as torches to light his garden. When John Calvin surveyed the rulers of those times he concluded that they were all "enemies of the Gospel, persecutors of the poor Christians, murderers, and wicked men."[4] Nevertheless, the Bible commands intercession (with thanksgiving!) "for kings and all who are in high positions."

The early church took this responsibility seriously. Consider how Clement of Rome prayed for the rulers and governors of the earth in the early second century: "Grant to them, Lord, health, peace, harmony and stability, that they may blamelessly administer the government which you have given them. . . . Lord, direct their plans according to what is good and pleasing in your sight, so that by devoutly administering in peace and gentleness the authority which you have given them they may experience your mercy."[5]

Clement's mention of peace and stability is fully in keeping with Paul's instructions. We pray for our leaders "that we may lead a peaceful and quiet life, godly and dignified in every way" (1 Tim. 2:2; cf. 1 Thess. 4:11–12). Like the captives in Babylon (see Jer. 29:7), Christians are to pray for the peace and prosperity of their rulers, even when they are living among pagans.

Christians are not always known as peacemakers. This was true already during Paul's lifetime, when Christians were blamed for the burning of Rome. It was also true during the Reformation. Calvin first wrote his *Institutes* (1536) to show that the Reformers were not trying to undermine the social order.[6] The church's reputation is in need of almost continual defense, for Christian involvement in public life is often greeted with skepticism, even hostility. This is partly because the gospel is so radical that Christians are always potential revolutionaries. Yet in the face of opposition, God wants his people to keep it quiet. He wants them to

4. John Calvin, *Sermons on the Epistles to Timothy & Titus* (London, 1579; repr. Edinburgh: Banner of Truth, 1983), 129.

5. *1 Clement*, 61, trans. J. B. Lightfoot and J. R. Harmer, ed. Michael W. Holmes (Grand Rapids: Baker, 1989), 63.

6. See John Calvin, "Prefatory Address to King Francis I of France," in *Institutes of the Christian Religion*, trans. Ford Lewis Battles, 2 vols., Library of Christian Classics 20–21 (Philadelphia: Westminster, 1960), 1:9–31.

lead orderly, dignified, reverent lives in all tranquility and serenity. In the words of the New English Bible, Christians are to maintain "full observance of religion and high standards of morality." They are to be respectful and respectable.

The reason Paul insisted on good deportment is that it is essential to the witness of the church. Christians who do not pray for their political leaders tend to disturb the peace. They are cynical about their political opponents and rejoice when they fall into disgrace. Since cynicism about the government is so prevalent in the evangelical church today, we may well conclude that Christians are not always diligent in prayer for people in authority. For as John Chrysostom rightly claimed, "no one can feel hatred towards those for whom he prays."[7] Prayer replaces hostility with compassion.

One good reason to pray for the government is that a peaceful society is a good society. These verses show the proper relationship between church and state: not separation, but partnership. John Stott offers a balanced perspective:

> It is the duty of the state to keep the peace, to protect its citizens from whatever would disturb it, to preserve law and order, and to punish evil and promote good, so that within such a stable society the church may be free to worship God, obey his laws and spread his gospel. Conversely, it is the duty of the church to pray for the state, so that its leaders may administer justice and pursue peace, and to add to its intercession thanksgiving, especially for the blessings of good government as a gift of God's common grace.[8]

When the state protects the church and the church prays for the state, everyone lives in peace. Although Christianity no longer enjoys the favor it once did, Americans can still praise God for religious liberty and pray for its preservation. Peace, in turn, aids the worldwide spread of the gospel. This was true during the Roman Empire of the *pax Romana*, when safe roads sped the first missionaries on their journeys. It was true during the British Empire, when British missionaries spanned the globe. It was true in the American Century, during which missionaries went out from the United

7. John Chrysostom, "Homilies on the Epistles of St. Paul the Apostle to Timothy, Titus, and Philemon," trans. and ed. Philip Schaff, *Nicene and Post-Nicene Fathers*, First Series, 14 vols. (Peabody, MA: Hendrickson, 1994), 13:426.

8. John Stott, *Guard the Truth: The Message of 1 Timothy and Titus* (Downers Grove, IL: InterVarsity, 1996), 63.

States to translate the Bible, evangelize unreached people groups, and plant churches in every nation. Peacetime missions is part of God's plan for the salvation of the world, so pray for peace.

Everyone Is Invited

As a general rule, the best prayers come from the soundest theology. Whenever God is approached on the basis of his plan, his work, or his character, he will hear and answer. As Paul laid his theological foundation for the Great Intercession, his key word was "all" (*pantōn*): there is prayer for all (1 Tim. 2:1–2) because there is an invitation for all (1 Tim. 2:4) and a ransom for all (1 Tim. 2:6).

Christians are to pray for everyone, first, because God wants everyone to be saved. "This is good"—in other words, it is good for Christians to have a global prayer concern—"and it is pleasing in the sight of God our Savior, who desires all people to be saved and to come to the knowledge of the truth" (1 Tim. 2:3–4). Here is the strongest incentive to pray for the worldwide work of the gospel: such prayers are pleasing to God. Here also is the strongest incentive to take an active role in missions: God's concerns are not parochial, but universal.

"To come to the knowledge of the truth" is another way to describe becoming a Christian. Christianity is based upon what is true. To be saved is to know the truth about Jesus Christ—that he came to deliver his people from sin and death. God wants you to know that. He wants everyone to know it. So he invites everyone to come to him through Jesus Christ.

The God who wants everyone to be saved is also the God who saves. He is "God our Savior." This is a somewhat unusual title in the New Testament, where God the Son is usually identified as Savior. But salvation is the work of the Father and the Spirit as well as the Son. Paul uses the phrase here to call to mind an important passage from the Old Testament: "There is no other god besides me, a righteous God and a Savior; there is none besides me. Turn to me and be saved, all the ends of the earth! For I am God, and there is no other" (Isa. 45:21–22). Here Scripture teaches the universal offer of the gospel. The only God, the God who saves, invites everyone to receive him.

In Timothy's day, there were several attempts to limit salvation to one elite group. Some Jewish Christians believed that Gentiles had to become cultural Jews before they became professing Christians. The pagan Gnostics were equally exclusive. They taught that salvation is not for everyone, but only for those who have special knowledge.

Churches today fall into the same trap whenever they treat the gospel as exclusive property, as if it belongs only to a certain race or class. One of the principal errors of liberation theology is its belief that God has a "preferential option for the poor." On the other hand, one of the major failings of American evangelicalism has been its middle-class mindset. But the gospel is for everyone. It is for peasants as well as tycoons, geniuses as well as people with average or below average I.Q., the Third World as well as the West.

God's universal offer of the gospel has global implications for evangelism. John Calvin taught that since God "intends the benefit of His death to be common to all, those who . . . exclude any from the hope of salvation do Him an injury."[9] On the contrary, every non-Christian should be invited to come to Christ. Jesus Christ is available to all. Christians offer this hope to the world: "God wants you to be saved and to come to a knowledge of the truth."

The universal gospel offer also has implications for prayer. The reason the church prays for everyone is that God invites everyone. Christians do not to have to guess whom God plans to save. Evangelistic prayer should be indiscriminate. Paul even told Timothy to pray for Caesar. However useless it may seem to pray for the Neros of the world, God wants them prayed for: "The truth is that God loves the whole world, desires all people to be saved, and so commands us to preach the gospel to all the nations and to pray for their conversion."[10]

This seems to create a theological problem. What does it mean that God wants all men to be saved when Scripture plainly teaches that not all will be saved (see, for example, Matt. 25:31–46)? Doesn't God get what he wants? How does this fit in with the doctrines of election and the sovereignty of God? These problems would seem to be especially acute for Calvinists. A. T. Hanson asserts: "This noble statement of the universality of God's love runs directly counter to the strict predestinarian tradition in Christianity which Augustine so emphatically championed, and Calvin, eleven hundred years

9. John Calvin, *The Second Epistle of Paul the Apostle to the Corinthians and the Epistles to Timothy, Titus and Philemon*, trans. T. A. Smail, Calvin's Commentaries (Edinburgh: Oliver & Boyd, 1964), 210.

10. Stott, *Guard the Truth*, 64.

later, reaffirmed. Consequently both Augustine and Calvin had to evade the obvious meaning of these words by saying that it means God chooses his elect from all classes of men."[11]

Although such objections draw us into mysteries of God's will that are known only to God, they also beg for answers. One way to handle the difficulty is to draw a distinction between God's general and specific wills. God's desire—what God *wants*—is somehow less strong than what he *wills*. The apostle Peter used the same terminology as the apostle Paul when he wrote: "The Lord . . . is patient toward you, not wishing that any should perish, but that all should reach repentance" (2 Peter 3:9). So perhaps there is a difference between God's desire and God's decree, which "works all things according to the counsel of his will" (Eph. 1:11). Or perhaps we can make a theological distinction between God's revealed will (that all should be saved) and his secret will (that only certain persons should be saved). These solutions are possible theologically, but there is a much better solution exegetically, as we shall see momentarily.

THE ONLY ONE

Paul has begun to build the theological foundation for the Great Intercession. The church is to pray for everyone because God wants everyone to be saved. Now the apostle adds two further reasons to pray: "For there is one God, and there is one mediator between God and men, the man Christ Jesus" (1 Tim. 2:5). We are to pray for everyone because there is a God for everyone and a mediator for everyone.

This verse speaks first to the unity of God. There is only one God. This is the bedrock of Old Testament theology: "Hear, O Israel: The LORD our God, the LORD is one" (Deut. 6:4; cf. Isa. 45:5). The unity of God is also central to New Testament theology (see 1 Cor. 8:6; Eph. 4:6), especially since the pagans in cities like Ephesus worshiped so many gods. By itself, however, the statement that there is one God only proves monotheism, not Christianity. Perhaps there is one God, but more than one way to be saved, as some are arguing today. John Stott states the objection like this: "Why should not the one

11. A. T. Hanson, *The Pastoral Epistles*, New Century Bible Commentary (Grand Rapids: Eerdmans, 1982), 68.

God, who wants all people to be saved, save them in different ways, some through Hinduism or Buddhism, others through Judaism or Islam, and yet others through New Age and other contemporary cults?"[12]

Jane Fonda once took a similar position in a conversation with the archbishop of Canterbury. When the archbishop said, "Jesus is the Son of God, you know," Fonda answered by saying, "Maybe he is for you, but he's not for me." To which the archbishop rightly replied, "Well, either he is or he isn't."[13] Jane Fonda was speaking as a religious pluralist (or perhaps a "Fondamentalist"?). She was saying that there are many roads to one God, whereas the archbishop rightly maintained that there is only one road to God. Just as there is only one God, there is only one way to God, through the only mediator between God and man.

Now a mediator is a go-between. The reason human beings need a mediator is our sin. We are alienated from God. We cannot go to him directly. He is too holy for us to bear, too transcendent. This is the problem Job was struggling with when he said:

> For he is not a man, as I am, that I might answer him,
>   that we should come to trial together.
> There is no arbiter between us,
>   who might lay his hand on us both.
> Let him take his rod away from me,
>   and let not dread of him terrify me.
> Then I would speak up without fear of him,
>   for I am not so in myself. (Job 9:32–35)

Jesus Christ is the arbitrator Job was looking for. Because he is the God-man, Jesus bridges the gap between the Creator and the creature. He is fully God. Therefore, he is able to meet God's standards. But as "the man Christ Jesus," to quote what Paul said to Timothy, he is also fully human. Therefore, Jesus is able to meet our obligations.

The reason Jesus is the only mediator is that he is the only one who has both a divine nature and a human nature—not the angels, or Mary, or the

12. Stott, *Guard the Truth*, 68.

13. From the Dick Cavett show, as cited in C. Stephen Evans, *The Quest for Faith: Pointers to God* (Leicester, UK: InterVarsity, 1986), 125.

saints, or even your favorite local minister, for none of them is divine. If we want to get to God, we have to go through this one divine person. Jesus is *the* mediator.

Jesus is able to represent and to reconcile both man and God because he has the most intimate sympathy with both parties. As a member of the Trinity, he has communion with the Father and the Spirit. As a member of the human race, he has union with us. Therefore, in the words of John Wesley, he is able to "to reconcile man to God, and to transact the whole affair of our salvation."[14] As the Puritans loved to say, Jesus Christ is able to strike hands on both sides of the covenant of grace.

Here is Christianity at its narrowest, and also its widest. Christianity is a thoroughly exclusive religion: it teaches that there is only one God, one Savior, and one salvation. Yet it is also broadly inclusive. It is just because there is only one God that the unique way of salvation is open to everyone: "Our *exclusive* faith (*there is one God*, and no other) leads necessarily to our *inclusive* mission (the one God *wants all men to be saved*)."[15]

A Ransom for Everyone

Paul moves from defining the mediator's person to describing his work. This brings us, as any discussion about salvation must bring us, to the cross of Calvary. There Jesus Christ "gave himself as a ransom for all, which is the testimony given at the proper time" (1 Tim. 2:6). This is where Paul's argument has been leading all along. The church prays for everyone because there is one God for everyone—a God who wants everyone to be saved—and because there is one mediator for everyone—a mediator who gave himself as a ransom.

The fact that Jesus "gave himself" speaks to the sacrificial nature of his death on the cross. His crucifixion was a voluntary offering, a willing sacrifice. No one took his life from him; he laid it down of his own accord (John 10:18).

The fact that Christ did this for others speaks to the substitutionary nature of his death. Jesus died in our place. His blood was the atonement for our sins. This doctrine of the substitutionary atonement has largely

14. John Wesley, *Explanatory Notes upon the New Testament* (London: Epworth, 1954), 775.
15. Stott, *Guard the Truth*, 67.

been forgotten in the contemporary church. George Lindbeck, a Lutheran theologian who teaches at Yale, complains that "even those who regard themselves as faithful conservers of the trinitarian and Christological orthodoxy of the ancient creeds have largely abandoned traditional Western atonement language, and with it, talk of salvation through Christ's death on the cross has weakened."[16] Yet the substitutionary nature of Christ's death is clearly taught here and everywhere else in the Scriptures.

The work of Christ on the cross is further described as a "ransom." This rich biblical term refers to the release of a captive by the payment of a price. When Jesus died on the cross, he was making an exchange for sin. It was not a price paid to the devil (as some of the early church fathers taught), but a payment made to satisfy the justice of God. The reason Christ could pay the price for our sins is the reason already mentioned: he is the mediator. He had to be God as well as man in order to pay the ransom. This was perhaps best explained by Anselm of Canterbury, who said that salvation "could not have been done unless man paid what was owing to God for sin. But the debt was so great that, while man alone owed it, only God could pay it, so that the same person must be both man and God. Thus it was necessary for God to take manhood into the unity of his person, so that he who in his own nature ought to pay and could not should be in a person who could."[17] This is what Jesus did when he died on the cross: he paid the price that only man could owe and only God could pay.

Jesus made this payment in a timely fashion. This seems to be the point of Paul's next phrase: "the testimony given at the proper time" (1 Tim. 2:6). The Revised English Bible puts it like this: "revealing God's purpose at God's good time." At just the right time (see Rom. 5:6–8; Gal. 4:4), Jesus died on the cross to demonstrate the love of God for the sinful world.

The various aspects of ransom are helpfully summarized in a sermon by Charles Spurgeon:

> When a prisoner has been taken captive, and has been made a slave . . . it has been usual, before he could be set free, that a ransom price should be paid

16. George Lindbeck, "Justification and Atonement: An Ecumenical Trajectory," unpublished paper.

17. Anselm of Canterbury, "Why God Became Man," in *A Scholastic Miscellany: Anselm to Ockham*, ed. and trans. Eugene R. Fairweather, Library of Christian Classics 10 (Philadelphia: Westminster, 1956), 176.

> down. Now . . . by the fall of Adam . . . we were by the irreproachable judgment of God given up to the vengeance of the law; we were given into the hands of justice; justice claimed us to be his bond slaves forever, unless we could pay a ransom, whereby our souls could be redeemed. . . . We were . . . "bankrupt debtors"; . . . all we had was sold . . . and we could by no means find a ransom; it was just then that Christ stepped in . . . and, . . . in the stead of all believers, paid the ransom price, that we might in that hour be delivered from the curse of the law and the vengeance of God, and go our way clean, free, justified by his blood.[18]

When Paul speaks of Christ as a ransom for all men, yet another theological difficulty is raised. This verse seems to teach a universal atonement, which is the Arminian position: Christ died for each and every soul who ever lived. The difficulty is that other Scripture passages teach a more definite atonement. This is one of the "Five Points of Calvinism," the "L" in "TULIP." The "L" stands for "limited atonement," which is perhaps better expressed as "definite atonement." It means that when Jesus paid for our sins he knew what he was paying for, and for whom, and he actually paid for it. He did not die simply to make salvation possible, but to make salvation actual for those whom the Father had given him (see Matt. 1:21; John 10:11, 14–15; 17:9; Eph. 5:25).

The question is this: when the Bible says Christ died for "all men," does it mean that he atoned for the sins of each and every human being who ever lived? The answer is "no." To understand this, it helps to know that "all" does not always mean "each and every single one." Sometimes "all" means "all kinds." For example, in his account of the last week of Jesus' earthly ministry, Luke tells us that "in the morning all the people came to him in the temple to hear him" (Luke 21:38). Does this mean that each and every inhabitant of Jerusalem heard Jesus every morning at the temple, including the tens of thousands of pilgrims who were there for Passover? Rather obviously, the word "all" is being used in a looser sense to refer to people in general.

That seems to be the way "all" is used in 1 Timothy 2. The phrase appears not only in verse 4 ("who desires all people to be saved") and verse 6 ("a ran-

18. Charles Haddon Spurgeon, "Justification by Grace," *The New Park Street Pulpit* (Pasadena, TX: Pilgrim, 1975), 3:153–54.

som for all"), but also in verse 1 ("prayers for all people"). In the case of verse 1, the Scripture does not command every Christian to pray, name by name, for every individual in the entire world. This would be a practical impossibility. Rather, Christians are to pray for all kinds of people.

This also helps explain what Paul meant when he said that God wants "all men" to be saved. According to Calvin, "the apostle's meaning here is simply that no nation of the earth and no rank of society is excluded from salvation, since God wills to offer the gospel to all without exception."[19] (This is the "better solution" promised earlier; see p. 65.)

In the same way, Jesus paid a ransom for all kinds of people. He does not discriminate on the basis of race, color, gender, ethnicity, or economic status. As Hendriksen helpfully explains, he did not die "one by one for every member of the entire human race, past, present and future, including Judas and the antichrist." Rather, Christ died for "all men regardless of social, national and racial distinctions."[20] Whatever neighborhood you come from, Christ is the Savior for you.

Calling Jesus a ransom for all men is something like calling your local physician the town doctor. In a small town, he is the only doctor there is. When you see him on the street, you say, "There goes our doctor." This does not necessarily mean that we are presently going to him for treatment. Whether or not he turns out to be our doctor depends on whether or not we get sick, and whether we are willing to go to him when we do. But he is still the town doctor.

Jesus is like the town doctor. He is the Savior of the world. He is accessible to everyone. He has promised to save anyone who comes to him in faith and repentance. But the fact that his death is a ransom does not mean that our own sins have been paid for. Whether we go to him for salvation or not depends on whether or not we realize that we need to be saved, and whether we are willing to go to him when we do. But whether we go to him or not, he is still the Savior of the world, "who gave himself as a ransom for all."

Once it is understood that "all" means "all kinds" rather than "each and every," we can reconcile what Paul said to Timothy with what Jesus said to

19. Calvin, *Second Epistle of Paul*, 208–9.

20. William Hendriksen, *New Testament Commentary: Pastoral Epistles* (Grand Rapids: Baker, 1957), 100.

his disciples: "The Son of Man came not to be served but to serve, and to give his life as a ransom for many" (Mark 10:45). Paul is not saying anything more than Jesus said. A ransom for many is a ransom for all when "all" means "all kinds."

One Gospel for Everyone

Any lingering doubts about Paul's meaning are put to rest in the next verse: "For this I was appointed a preacher and an apostle (I am telling the truth, I am not lying), a teacher of the Gentiles in faith and truth" (1 Tim. 2:7; cf. 2 Tim. 1:11). Christ's ransom for all men leads naturally to the church's mission to all nations, Gentiles as well as Jews.

This is the commission God gave to Paul when he was converted. He appointed him to be "his witness to all men" (Acts 22:15 NIV; the ESV reads "a witness to everyone"). Note the phrase well: "all men." Obviously God did not intend Paul to evangelize each and every human being who ever lived. Rather, when God called Paul to witness to all men, he made him a missionary to the Gentiles (see Acts 22:21), so that all people everywhere could hear the gospel. The salvation first given to the Jews is now extended throughout the whole world. There is one God, one Savior, and one ransom for everyone; therefore, there is one gospel for everyone.

This commission was not just for Paul; it is for every Christian. Here is how John Stott summarizes the first half of 1 Timothy 2: "It is the unity of God and the uniqueness of Christ which demand the universality of the gospel. God's desire and Christ's death concern all people; therefore the church's duty concerns all people too, reaching out to them both in earnest prayer and in urgent witness."[21] The one true gospel is to be proclaimed the way Paul proclaimed it: as a preacher who announced the coming of Christ the King and as a teacher who explained the way of salvation from the Scriptures. Paul did this truly and faithfully, as every Christian should.

The apostle also preached the gospel with prayer. He understood that the worldwide success of the gospel depends on prayer. A small group at Tenth Presbyterian Church in Philadelphia has been learning this lesson. More than a decade ago we made a commitment to do nothing except pray for

21. Stott, *Guard the Truth*, 73.

unsaved humanity, by name, every Friday during lunch time. Several months after we began to meet, our prayers began to be answered. Men, women, and children were coming to faith in Christ: parents, siblings, children, international students, coworkers, Muslims, and Jews. Scarcely a week passes without us celebrating news of another conversion, or hearing about some obvious work of the Holy Spirit in someone's life, or learning about someone else who needs our prayers. God is willing and able to save. He waits only to be asked. Since he invites everyone, we pray for everyone we can.

The church must pray for its missionaries the same way. This study began with the story of Joanne Shetler, who learned to depend on the prayers of her congregation back home. Shetler went on to describe what happened when her supporters accepted the responsibility to pray for her ministry: "My church no longer prayed 'Dear God, please bless Jo wherever she's at and whatever she's doing.' They took up the burden. And when I went back after furlough, things started to happen."[22] The Balangao began to respond to the gospel. This started with the biblical genealogies, which impressed them because they wanted to know more about their ancestors. They began to ask how they could become God's children. When a few of them received Christ, they asked if it would be all right to tell everyone else about him. Eventually, the Balangao came by the hundreds to put their faith in Jesus Christ.

God's plan is to build his church by the prayers of his people. Missionaries all over the world stand and wait for the Holy Spirit to bless their labor in the gospel. The Spirit waits only for the church to pray. Even now he is urging "that supplications, prayers, intercessions, and thanksgivings be made for all people."

22. Shetler, "Faithful in Obedience," 104.

6

Men and Women at Prayer

1 Timothy 2:8–10

I desire then that in every place the men should pray, lifting holy hands without anger or quarreling; likewise also that women should adorn themselves in respectable apparel, with modesty and self-control, not with braided hair and gold or pearls or costly attire, but with what is proper for women who profess godliness—with good works. (1 Tim. 2:8–10)

Are the differences between men and women facts or fictions? My two-year-old daughter offers me a barrette to put in my hair. I politely decline. "Barrettes are for girls," I say. "Boys and daddies don't wear barrettes." Am I simply making this up, or am I reflecting some essential distinction between males and females?

Lorna Smedman believes that gender is a fiction. Each year she teaches a course called "Reimagining Gender" at Hunter College in New York City and begins her first class session with the following words: "My working assumption in this course is that gender is already imaginary in the first place, meaning that it's a construction—a fiction that we all live and work with in our daily lives."[1]

1. Lorna Smedman, as quoted in a ministry newsletter.

If Smedman is right, then the line between the masculine and the feminine can be erased. There is no inherent reason why women should not behave like men, and vice versa. This view seems to be becoming more dominant in Western culture, with the result that some women no longer want to be women, and many men no longer know what it means to be men.

House Rules

The Bible stands against the androgyny of these postmodern times. It insists that gender is a God-given fact. It recognizes that the identity of every human being is gender-specific. There are essential differences between men and women.

The differences between the masculine and the feminine go back to the sixth day of creation, when "God created man in his own image, in the image of God he created him; male and female he created them" (Gen. 1:27). Creation thus establishes the true equality of men and women. Both the male and the female are created in the image of God. At the same time, the distinction between man and woman is divinely ordained.

It comes as no surprise, therefore, that God sometimes has special instructions for men and for women, especially in the church. The church is God's household, as the apostle will emphasize in his purpose statement for this epistle (1 Tim. 3:15), and every household has its own rules. The Bible addresses men and women separately, as well as jointly, so there will be order in the house.

When it comes to public worship, the Holy Spirit does not hesitate to say there are differences between men and women. Some instructions, while not inapplicable to women, are most necessary for men. Other instructions, although they have practical implications for men, are especially appropriate for women.

The Place for Prayer

To the men of the church the apostle Paul writes, "I desire then that in every place the men should pray, lifting holy hands without anger or quarreling" (1 Tim. 2:8). Bear in mind that this is not simply Paul's private wish or personal opinion; he is speaking as an apostle of Jesus Christ (see 1 Tim.

2:7). The word "desire" (*boulomai*) is a word for an authoritative command. This command is addressed to the men of the church, since the word "men" (*andras*) refers to males in distinction from females. God wants his sons to be men of prayer.

Paul has already outlined the content of prayer (1 Tim. 2:1–7); now he addresses the conduct of prayer. First, its location: prayer is to be offered everywhere. This may refer to every house of worship. God has a universal rule for worship, wherever his people happen to meet. However, the word "everywhere" also promises the worldwide success of the gospel. In the Old Testament, God was worshiped in his temple; soon he will be worshiped everywhere. The God who wants all men to be prayed for (1 Tim. 2:1), who desires all men to be saved (1 Tim. 2:4), and whose Son offered his life as a ransom for all men (1 Tim. 2:6), will be praised in all places. His kingdom will continue to grow until he is praised from every square inch of this planet.

Here the apostle seems to be alluding to the prophet Malachi: "From the rising of the sun to its setting my name will be great among the nations, and in every place incense will be offered to my name, and a pure offering. For my name will be great among the nations" (Mal. 1:11). The God who rules the world deserves worldwide praise. Paul's command to pray answers to Malachi's promise of a day when God's name will be great among all nations, from East to West. In the words of the great hymn by Isaac Watts:

> Jesus shall reign where'er the sun
> Does his successive journeys run;
> His kingdom stretch from shore to shore,
> Till moons shall wax and wane no more.

In the second stanza, Watts explains how God extends his kingdom to expand his praise:

> To him shall endless prayer be made,
> And praises throng to crown his head;
> His name, like sweet perfume, shall rise
> With every morning sacrifice.

There is no place where God's people cannot pray, and in the end, there is no place where they will not pray.

The Posture of Prayer

When God's people pray in every place, they are to lift "holy hands" (1 Tim. 2:8). While this mainly refers to the purity of prayer, it also has implications for its posture. The Bible does not demand any single position for prayer. Sometimes it speaks of bowing the head to pray, which is a good way of giving honor and worship to a king: "But I, through the abundance of your steadfast love, will enter your house. I will bow down toward your holy temple" (Ps. 5:7); "Oh come, let us worship and bow down; let us kneel before the Lord, our Maker!" (Ps. 95:6).

The mention of kneeling suggests another suitable position for prayer. Getting on one's knees is a sign of humility and absolute dependence upon God. It is the position Daniel assumed when he retired to his prayer closet: "He got down on his knees three times a day and prayed and gave thanks before his God" (Dan. 6:10). It is how Stephen prayed in the hour of his martyrdom (Acts 7:60). The Lord Jesus knelt in the garden to pray (Luke 22:41). These and other examples led the Old Princeton theologian Samuel Miller to describe kneeling as "a significant and becoming posture in prayer, strongly expressive of humility, reverence and earnestness."[2]

Other prayers are best offered flat on the ground. Moses often fell facedown in the presence of the Lord (e.g. Num. 16:22; 20:6), as did Joshua after him (Josh. 5:14). When Job entered into the depths of woe, he "fell on the ground and worshiped" (Job 1:20). Ezekiel assumed a prone position when he saw "the appearance of the likeness of the glory of the Lord" (Ezek. 1:28). This is how the angels and the elders pray at God's heavenly throne; they fall down on their faces and worship (Rev. 7:11). When a person is overwhelmed by either the troubles of life or the glories of almighty God, the appropriate thing to do is fall prostrate on the ground.

For public worship, standing for prayer is often to be preferred. At the dedication of the temple, Solomon knelt to pray, but the people all stood

2. Samuel Miller, *Thoughts on Public Prayer* (Philadelphia, 1849; repr. Harrisonburg, VA: Sprinkle, 1985), 119.

up (2 Chron. 6:3, 13). Similarly, "Jehoshaphat stood in the assembly of Judah and Jerusalem, in the house of the Lord" (2 Chron. 20:5; cf. Neh. 9:5). It thus became customary to stand for prayer in the Jewish synagogues. Standing was also the nearly universal practice of the early church. The writings of Justin Martyr, Origen, Jerome, and Augustine all indicate that Christians stood for public prayer.[3] This is how the Puritans prayed too, as well as nearly every Presbyterian prior to the twentieth century. Standing is a sign of respect; when a judge enters his courtroom, all rise. In the same way, Christians have often stood to pray before the great Judge over all the world.

Whether they kneel or stand, Christians may also raise their hands in prayer. This is the way the priests customarily worshiped in the temple: "Come, bless the Lord, all you servants of the Lord, who stand by night in the house of the Lord! Lift up your hands to the holy place and bless the Lord!" (Ps. 134:1–2; cf. 28:2; 141:2). Lifting hands was common in the early church, even though 1 Timothy 2 is the only place it is mentioned in the New Testament. Tertullian alluded to this passage when he said, "We Christians pray for all the emperors, &c., looking up to heaven, with our hands stretched out, because guiltless; with our heads uncovered, because we are not ashamed."[4]

The practice of lifting hands is confirmed by early Christian artwork. The murals in the Roman catacombs depict believers raising their hands in praise. C. K. Barrett also shows a Christian sarcophagus from the third century. Carved into the stone is a human figure with hands gently uplifted in prayer.[5] This posture is especially appropriate for the minister who leads in public prayer. When he stands in God's presence to offer prayer on behalf of God's people, he may raise his hands to show that the church's prayers are offered to God as a sacrifice of praise.

To summarize, Scripture allows several postures for prayer. As a general rule, Episcopalians kneel, Presbyterians bow, and charismatics lift. But a variety of postures is a help to private devotion and is suitable for the public worship of God.

3. Ibid., 122–25.
4. Tertullian, *Apology*, 30, quoted in Miller, *Public Prayer*, 63.
5. C. K. Barrett, *The Pastoral Epistles* (Oxford: Clarendon, 1963), 53.

The Purity of Prayer

God is not nearly as interested in the posture of prayer as he is in the purity of prayer. He wants men, especially, to be "lifting holy hands without anger or quarreling" (1 Tim. 2:8). The reference to holy hands refers to temple worship in the Old Testament. God's people consecrated themselves by washing their hands before prayer. Cleanliness really was "next to godliness"! Pools of water were scattered all around the temple mount. As God's people went up to worship they said, "I wash my hands in innocence and go around your altar, O Lord" (Ps. 26:6; cf. James 4:8). Clean hands symbolize a pure heart.

When Paul mentions the outward sign of holy hands, he is talking about the inward reality of a holy life. One kind of unholiness, especially, was causing problems in the Ephesian church: the sin of dissension. Paul warned the church, therefore, to pray "without anger or quarreling." Quarreling was exactly the problem at Ephesus. Angry words were being exchanged. They must have been, because this subject keeps coming up. The false teachers were creating controversies rather than doing God's work (1 Tim. 1:4). The result was "constant friction among people who are depraved in mind" (1 Tim. 6:5).

The sins of anger and argument have particular relevance for men. It is true that, on occasion, women disturb the peace of the church. One thinks of the infamous conflict between Euodia and Syntyche (see Phil. 4:2). But as a general rule, men are more likely to agitate the church, especially when it comes to doctrine. Men are typically like that. They are critical and competitive. They tend to argue first and listen later. They would rather be right than be reconciled. They get angry when they don't get their way. So the Bible reminds Christian men not to fight.

Arguments are harmful to the body of Christ in many ways, but especially because they hinder the church's prayers. Bitterness and resentment make for sour prayers. In fact, Jesus taught that if we are having a dispute, we should not come to worship at all until the matter is settled: "So if you are offering your gift at the altar and there remember that your brother has something against you, leave your gift there before the altar and go. First be reconciled to your brother, and then come and offer your gift" (Matt. 5:23–24). A man can lift up holy hands in prayer only if he has a right relationship with his brothers, not only in the local church, but also in the wider Christian community (the same principle also holds true for sisters in Christ).

Reconciliation is especially important when it comes to leading public worship. When Paul refers to men, his "point is not that men only should pray but rather that everywhere the church of Jesus Christ exists there should be men who pray."[6] Although the first house churches may have had seasons of open prayer, congregational prayers were and are conducted by the elders of the church.

Any minister who represents God's people in prayer must be a holy man. The psalmist asks: "Who shall ascend the hill of the LORD? And who shall stand in his holy place?" (Ps. 24:3). In other words, "Who is qualified to pray on behalf of God's people?" The answer is: "He who has clean hands and a pure heart, who does not lift up his soul to what is false and does not swear deceitfully" (Ps. 24:4). There is a direct spiritual connection between personal piety and public prayer. It takes holy hands and a holy heart to lead God's people in their prayers. Samuel Miller wrote:

> None can hope to attain excellence in the grace and gift of prayer in the public assembly, unless they abound in closet devotion, and in holy communion with God in secret. . . . We may safely say, then, that no man ever attained any high degree of excellence in public prayer, who had not previously cultivated peculiar intimacy with his covenant God in secret devotion; who did not abound in closet prayer; who had not had his heart trained to more than common familiarity with, and affection for, new covenant blessings. . . He who neglects this, or who has little taste for this, might as well expect a miracle to be wrought for his help every time he enters the pulpit.[7]

The connection between the spiritual life and the prayer life holds true for everyone who prays, not just for elders. This mystery is encountered elsewhere in the New Testament: "Likewise, husbands, live with your wives in an understanding way, showing honor to the woman as the weaker vessel, since they are heirs with you of the grace of life, so that your prayers may

6. Thomas C. Oden, *First and Second Timothy and Titus*, Interpretation (Louisville: John Knox, 1989), 91–92.

7. Miller, *Public Prayer*, 260–68.

not be hindered" (1 Peter 3:7). An inconsiderate husband is an ineffective intercessor. The power of prayer is directly related to its purity. The prayers of an unholy man will go unanswered, while the petitions of a righteous man may move mountains. Of all the incentives we have to lead holy lives, this is among the most compelling: so that God will answer our prayers.

The thought that unholiness hinders prayer is a sobering one, not least for ministers. How can unholy men lift holy hands in prayer? We dare not come like the Pharisee who lifted his prayer to heaven with the hands of hypocrisy. The only sincere way to pray is as a confessing sinner. Therefore, we come like the publican to pray, "God, be merciful to me, a sinner" (Luke 18:13). The only pure prayer is a penitential prayer.

This explains why Christians always pray in the name of Jesus. He is the only mediator between God and man. He offers cleansing from sin through his blood shed on the cross. So the Christian prays like this: "Lord, I know you answer only the prayers of the righteous, but answer my prayer anyway, not because I am righteous, but because Jesus Christ is righteous, and because his blood is the atonement for my sin." Whenever we pray in the name of Jesus, God will hear us out, unrighteous though we are: "For we do not have a high priest who is unable to sympathize with our weaknesses, but one who in every respect has been tempted as we are, yet without sin. Let us then with confidence draw near to the throne of grace, that we may receive mercy and find grace to help in time of need" (Heb. 4:15–16).

Out of Style

The apostle Paul also gave instructions for the prayers of women. Since these instructions touch on the subject of fashion, it is hard not to approach them with some trepidation. Thomas Oden claims that "this paragraph of Paul's letter to Timothy cannot be read without raising hackles and blood pressure."[8] One assumes he means the hackles of women and the blood pressure of ministers!

The passage sometimes has drawn ministers into conflict. John Chrysostom, the golden-tongued bishop of Constantinople, was regarded as the greatest preacher of his times—until, that is, he started preaching against

8. Oden, *First and Second Timothy*, 92.

the lifestyles of the rich and famous. Then the Empress Eudoxia ran him out of town, and he later died in exile. What Chrysostom preached, in part, were the words of the apostle Paul: "I desire likewise also that women should adorn themselves in respectable apparel, with modesty and self-control, not with braided hair and gold or pearls or costly attire, but with what is proper for women who profess godliness—with good works" (1 Tim. 2:8–10). No wonder Eudoxia was upset! Nearly every word clashed with her worldly values. Modesty? Self-control? Propriety?

Needless to say, Paul never would have made it on Madison Avenue, or in Beverly Hills. No beauty salons? No fancy jewels? No fashion statements? If this verse seems out of touch with contemporary culture, that is all the more reason to listen to what it says. Which is more likely: that the Bible is out of date or that our culture is out of line? God's Word critiques every culture. Often the Scripture that most shocks and surprises us, or even angers and offends us, is the Scripture we most need to hear.

The word "likewise" is significant because it sets the context. Paul is still addressing the subject of public worship. He assumes that women will be present in the assembly to praise God, and perhaps even to pray aloud (see 1 Cor. 11:5). His point is that while men are to pray without argumentation, women are to pray without ostentation.

Here it helps to know something about Hellenistic society, in which elaborately braided hair was a sign of extravagant luxury. Paul's wording is significant: "not with braided hair *and* gold or pearls or costly attire" (1 Tim. 2:9). James Hurley helps us understand the social context:

> The sculpture and literature of the period make it clear that women often wore their hair in enormously elaborate arrangements with braids and curls interwoven or piled high like towers and decorated with gems and/or gold and/or pearls. The courtesans wore their hair in numerous small pendant braids with gold droplets or pearls or gems every inch or so, making a shimmering screen of their locks.[9]

The conjunction of a fancy hair style with fancy jewelry was a sign of vanity. Some women spent hours fixing their hair and spangling their

9. James B. Hurley, *Man and Woman in Biblical Perspective* (Grand Rapids: Zondervan, 1981), 199.

coiffures with gems. One ancient sculpture depicts a wealthy lady in her salon, pampered by four attendants.[10] The Jewish writer Philo used this image in describing Pleasure as a woman whose hair "is dressed in curious and elaborate plaits." She wears "costly raiment"; "bracelets and necklaces and every other feminine ornament wrought of gold and jewels hang round her."[11]

Such finery must have been a temptation to women in the Ephesian church. Some of them, at least, were wealthy (see 1 Tim. 6:17) and presumably frequented the famous Ephesian market. Later Paul will warn them not to be "self-indulgent" (1 Tim. 5:6). Luxurious living must have seemed particularly inappropriate in a community where other Christians were poor.

Excessive adornment was characteristic not only of the wealthy, but also of prostitutes. George Knight suggests that "the reason for Paul's prohibition of elaborate hair styles, ornate jewelry, and extremely expensive clothing becomes clear when one reads in the contemporary literature of the inordinate time, expense, and effort that elaborately braided hair and jewels demanded, not just as ostentatious display, but also as the mode of dress of courtesans and harlots."[12] Remember, too, that Ephesus was home to the goddess Artemis. Members of the Ephesian church could see the temple prostitutes loitering near the pillars of her temple. To dress in their style was tantamount to marital unfaithfulness.[13] But God wants Christian women to take their stand against everything associated with sexual immorality, as well as material luxury. In Ephesus, the way women dressed demonstrated the difference between chastity and adultery.

In part, Paul was telling women not to come to church dressed like prostitutes. Such attire was completely unsuitable for a prayer meeting. But the apostle was not simply telling women what *not* to wear. He was also telling them what to wear and how to wear it. Words like "modesty," "respectable," "self-control," and "proper" all signify positive virtues.

10. Barrett, *Pastoral Epistles*, 54.

11. Philo, *De Sacrificiis*, 21, trans. F. H. Colson and G. H. Whitaker, Loeb Classical Library (New York: Putnam, 1929), 2:107, 109.

12. George Knight, *The Pastoral Epistles*, New International Greek Testament Commentary (Grand Rapids, MI: Eerdmans, 1992), 135.

13. See Gordon D. Fee, *1 and 2 Timothy, Titus*, New International Biblical Commentary (Peabody, MA: Hendrickson, 1988), 71.

"Respectability" (*kosmios*) is a form of humility, which is the appropriate attitude for prayer. A prayer meeting is no place for a fashion plate. A Christian woman does not go to church to meet men; she goes to meet God. So "getting ready for church" is primarily a matter of preparing the heart for prayer. A woman who loves to be noticed must remember with whom she is competing. God is the one who ought to receive all our attentions and affections in prayer.

"Modesty" (*aidous*) has sexual overtones. J. N. D. Kelly says it "connotes feminine reserve in matters of sex."[14] It describes a woman who is chaste and honorable. It implies that women should not dress in a seductive or suggestive manner. This extends not only to dress, but also to demeanor, to the way a woman carries herself.

"Self-control" (*sōphrosynē*) is a broader concept. It was one of the four cardinal virtues of Platonic philosophy.[15] Jouette Bassler defines it as "prudence, temperance, discretion, soundness of judgment, and self-control."[16] It means to be sober and to exercise self-mastery.

By using these terms, the Scripture is not telling Christian women to make sure they are always out of style. What is forbidden here is not having a hair style, or owning jewelry, or wearing nice clothes, but using such things immodestly or indecently. God does not want his daughters to be overly concerned how they look. Calvin's comments here are especially helpful:

> The fault is excessive concern and eagerness about dress. Paul's wish is that their dressing should be regulated by modesty and moderation, for luxury and extravagance come from a desire to make a display, which can spring only from vanity or wantonness. . . . Paul attacks by name certain kinds of immoderation, such as curled hair, jewels and golden rings—not that jewels of gold are completely forbidden but, whenever there is a shining display of them, they tend to bring with them all the evils . . . which spring from self-concern or unchastity.[17]

14. J. N. D. Kelly, *The Pastoral Epistles: Timothy I and II, Titus*, Harper's New Testament Commentaries (San Francisco: Harper and Row, 1960), 66.

15. See Plato, *The Republic of Plato*, trans. Francis MacDonald Cornford (New York: Oxford University Press, 1945), 4:430.

16. Jouette M. Bassler, *1 Timothy, 2 Timothy, Titus* (Nashville: Abingdon, 1996), 58.

17. John Calvin, *The Second Epistle of Paul the Apostle to the Corinthians and the Epistles to Timothy, Titus and Philemon*, trans. T. A. Smail, Calvin's Commentaries (Edinburgh: Oliver & Boyd, 1964), 216.

What modesty means in practice may vary from culture to culture. But vanity and immorality come from the heart, and the Lord knows what lies in a woman's heart.

A Real Beauty

Why does the Bible address these comments to women? It is not because Christian men are permitted to be immodest or indecent. Nor is it because men never acquire a taste for fashion. One thinks of Achan, who stole fine clothes from Ai because he saw they had designer labels from Babylon (see Josh. 7:21).

No, the reason women are warned about ostentation is the same reason that men are warned about argumentation: in each case, the Bible addresses a besetting sin. Women, especially, are prone to lavish their attention on outward appearance. This is as true today as it was in Timothy's times. The fashion industry, the cosmetic industry, and the jewelry industry are supported largely by females. In fact, looking for clothes at the shopping mall is often identified as a leading form of recreation for American women. Yet God himself cares little or nothing for outward appearance. Remember what he said to Samuel when he went to anoint the next king of Israel: "the Lord sees not as man sees: man looks on the outward appearance, but the Lord looks on the heart" (1 Sam. 16:7).

God's standards for feminine beauty, therefore, stand diametrically opposed to the standards of modern culture. How often do ordinary-looking women appear in television advertisements? How many fashion magazines feature tips for inward beauty? The world says beauty is only skin deep, but God turns things inside out. He says that beauty comes from the spiritual life of the soul.

Men are usually part of the problem. By evaluating women primarily by their looks, men make women slaves to their appearance. Of course there must be a sexual attraction between a husband and wife. But a single man who looks primarily for outward beauty is not looking at women the way God looks at them. He has an ungodly aesthetic.

If a woman wants to become beautiful to God, here is the fashion statement she ought to make: adorn yourself "with what is proper for women who profess godliness—with good works" (1 Tim. 2:10). Some of the good deeds Paul has in mind are listed in chapter 5: bringing up children, showing hospitality, washing the feet of the saints, caring for the afflicted, and devoting oneself to every good work (1 Tim. 5:10). These are God's beauty tips for women. A woman who adorns herself with good works always has suitable attire. The Holy Spirit makes the same point in one of the Bible's other fashion sections: "Do not let your adorning be external—the braiding of hair, the wearing of gold, or the putting on of clothing—but let your adorning be the hidden person of the heart with the imperishable beauty of a gentle and quiet spirit, which in God's sight is very precious. For this is how the holy women who hoped in God used to adorn themselves, by submitting to their husbands" (1 Peter 3:3–5).

The way to become more attractive is through godliness, not gaudiness. A woman is made beautiful by what she does, not what she wears. This means that the older a woman gets, the more beautiful she can become! Outwardly, the aging process cannot be reversed (see Prov. 31:30); inwardly, a godly woman is becoming more and more beautiful all the time (see 2 Cor. 4:16).

True beauty comes from nurturing the inward woman. Ask questions like these: How much money do I spend on my appearance—on clothes, jewelry, cosmetics, beauty treatments, and the like? How does that compare with my giving to the Lord's work? How much time do I spend in front of the mirror, and how much time do I spend on my knees?

When a Christian woman does look in the mirror, she should look for good works, which are the proof of genuine faith in Jesus Christ. As John Stott rightly says: "The church should be a veritable beauty parlour, because it encourages its women members to adorn themselves with good deeds. Women need to remember that if nature has made them plain, grace can make them beautiful, and if nature has made them beautiful, good deeds can add to their beauty."[18]

Good works are what a man should look for in a woman. When a man notices a woman who is devoted to the Lord, who gives good counsel, who handles her professional work with integrity, who loves children, who cares for the sick, and who feeds the poor, he should not say, "She's not all that good-looking, but she really loves the Lord!" Instead, he should

18. John Stott, *Guard the Truth: The Message of 1 Timothy and Titus* (Downers Grove, IL: InterVarsity, 1996), 84.

say, "Now there is a beautiful woman!" A woman who is beautiful in the eyes of God ought to be beautiful in the eyes of godly men.

The author of an old book called *Sketches of the Women of Christendom* wanted to show "what Christianity has done and can do for women, by telling stories of the beautiful lives of Christian women from the days of when Christ our Lord was born of a woman, to our own." She began her book with these words:

> As I wonder how best to introduce the subject to you, a beautiful and blessed company seems to rise before me. . . . They shine on us for a time, in some deed of sacrifice and service, and then they are lost to sight again, hidden in the homes they bless. . . . Two beautiful companies of good women rise radiant before us: firstly, that of the daughter, the wife, the mother, the sister, treading the common path of duty. . . . And then the glorious army of succor: matrons and maidens, old and young, rich and poor, pouring out the treasures of woman's heart to relieve the sick, the suffering, the sinful, throughout the world . . . a great multitude whom no man can number, ceaselessly shedding benedictions on the world.[19]

Any woman who wants to stand with her sisters in this beautiful company must adorn herself with what is appropriate for women who profess godliness—with good works!

19. In Susan Hunt, *By Design: God's Distinctive Calling for Women* (Franklin, TN: Legacy, 1994), 2–3.

7

What Paul Really Said about Women in the Church

1 Timothy 2:11–15

Let a woman learn quietly with all submissiveness. I do not permit a woman to teach or to exercise authority over a man; rather, she is to remain quiet. (1 Tim. 2:11–12)

When it comes to understanding biblical teaching about the role of women in the church, there seems to be danger on every side. First, there is the danger of controversy. Few issues have brought more division in recent years than the role of women in the church. Entire denominations have either split or formed over the question of women's ordination.

Second, there is the danger of letting culture overrule Scripture. No matter how they are understood, God's instructions for women stand against the prevailing attitudes of contemporary society. To the postmodern ear 1 Timothy 2:11–12 sounds like gender discrimination. The very idea that women would be forbidden to teach men would cause a scandal in the classroom or the marketplace. Why should things be any different in the church? On this issue, perhaps more than any other, there is tremendous pressure to let the tail of culture wag the dog of biblical truth.

Third, there is the danger of allowing church history to dictate how Scripture should be applied. When questions arise about the role of women in ministry, many churches say, "We've never done it that way before." As a result, the spiritual gifts of women often have been marginalized, to the impoverishment of the church.

Fourth, there is the danger of allowing personal opinion to distort our understanding of Scripture. One pastor experienced this firsthand when his church entered a prolonged conflict over the role of women: "The struggle began as one day an elder said to me, 'I expect to moderate the Elders' Board this year when we change our Constitution to allow women to be elders.' In response, I asked what his understanding was of 1 Timothy 2:13, where Paul, addressing the matter of a woman teaching or exercising authority over a man, writes, 'For it was Adam who was first created, then Eve.' He responded, 'I don't like that verse.'"[1] Admittedly, some Bible verses are hard to like; nevertheless, they reveal the mind of God the Holy Spirit, so like them or not, they are to be believed and applied to daily life.

Finally, there are difficulties with the text itself. What do these words mean: "quietly," "submissiveness," "teach," "exercise authority" (1 Tim. 2:11–12)? Each term calls for careful definition. Then there are further questions: What is the precise relevance of Eve's deception (1 Tim. 2:14)? Or what can it possibly mean to say that "she will be saved through childbearing" (1 Tim. 2:15)?

The passage defies simple answers. In the face of these dangers and difficulties, the only way to proceed is to recognize that we bring prior assumptions to this passage, asking the Holy Spirit to correct those assumptions as necessary and working through the passage as carefully as possible.

To Learn . . .

The previous section of Paul's letter to Timothy (1 Tim. 2:9–10) ended with warnings about being immodest. This section contains warnings about

1. Timothy B. Bayly, Executive Director, Council of Biblical Manhood and Womanhood, circular letter, December 5, 1997.

being insubordinate (1 Tim. 2:11–15), beginning with a positive command: "Let a woman learn quietly with all submissiveness" (1 Tim. 2:11).

With this statement Paul shatters conventional stereotypes—not modern stereotypes, but ancient ones. In the Roman world, women were considered to be intellectually second-class. It was widely accepted that females were academically inferior. Thus, the educational system was designed primarily for men, not for women. If possible, the Jewish rabbis were even more chauvinistic. According to the Jerusalem Talmud, "It would be better for the words of Torah to be burned, than that they should be entrusted to a woman."[2] In other words, educating women was a big waste of time. Not surprisingly, women played a very small role in the public life of the synagogue. The Babylonian Talmud explains the difference between men and women in worship: "The men came to learn, the women came to hear."[3]

The Word of God says nearly the opposite of what many Jews and Romans said. Before he makes any prohibition, the apostle writes words of liberation: "Let a woman learn" (1 Tim. 2:11). Because a woman is a human being made with a mind in his image, God requires her to learn. It is her responsibility before God to become a student of biblical doctrine.

This shows that the Bible is not afraid to confront culture. It is sometimes argued that Paul inherited negative attitudes about women from his rabbinic training, or that the New Testament is held prisoner by ancient, patriarchal attitudes about gender. Here we find exactly the opposite. The same is true throughout the New Testament, which is sprinkled with examples of women engaged in vital ministry, many of them close personal friends of the apostle Paul. It is not too much to say that one burden of his ministry was to ensure that the gifts of women were used to their fullest extent.

Christians ought to take great encouragement from what biblical truth has done to improve the status of women. The church has not always lived up to what the Bible says about gender, but whenever it has, women have been greatly blessed. A document signed by "Women of Renewal" states: "Because the Bible is the most effective force in history for lifting women to higher levels of respect, dignity, and freedom, we join an historic succession

2. In John Stott, *Guard the Truth: The Message of 1 Timothy and Titus* (Downers Grove, IL: InterVarsity, 1996), 85.

3. George Knight, *The Pastoral Epistles*, New International Greek Testament Commentary (Grand Rapids: Eerdmans, 1992), 139.

of women whose Christian faith is forged from biblical truth and whose lives are shaped into Christ's image on the anvil of obedience."[4] The church has some reason to be ashamed of the way it has treated women, but no reason to be ashamed of what God has said about women in his Word.

If a woman must learn, how should she do it? "Let a woman learn quietly with all submissiveness" (1 Tim. 2:11). The word "quietly" (*hēsychia*) is repeated at the end of verse 12. "Quiet" is a much better translation than the one provided in the New International Version: "silent." The word does not mean that women have to keep their mouths shut. Rather, it refers to a gentle demeanor, as it does earlier in the chapter, where Paul says that Christians should lead "a peaceful and quiet life" (1 Tim. 2:2; cf. 1 Peter 3:4).

A notable episode from the life of Paul helps to show what the apostle means by "quietly." On his last trip to Jerusalem, Paul was confronted by an angry mob outside the barracks where he was to be imprisoned: "And when he had given him permission, Paul, standing on the steps, motioned with his hand to the people. And when there was a great hush, he addressed them in the Hebrew language, saying: 'Brothers and fathers, hear the defense that I now make before you.' And when they heard that he was addressing them in the Hebrew language, they became even more quiet" (Acts 21:40–22:2). Two different Greek words are used to describe this crowd: first the people became "hushed" (*sigēs*); then they became "quiet" (*hēsychia*). It is the latter word which Paul uses in 1 Timothy 2:11–12—not the word for keeping silent, but the word for being respectful. Paul is telling women to give their ministers the same undivided attention that he himself received when he spoke in Jerusalem.

Women are also to learn with all "submissiveness" (*hypotagē*). To submit is to be obedient, to yield to authority. Here it means to respect the leadership and authority that God has given to the elders of the church. It means to receive their teaching in a spirit of cheerful agreement.

When these two words are put together—"quietly" and "submissiveness"—they do not describe an unusual style of learning that is unique to women. Rather, they describe the only way a person can learn at all. Any teacher knows it is impossible to teach someone who is talking all the time. Good teachers

4. "Women of Renewal: A Statement," Ecumenical Coalition of Women and Society, Institute on Religion and Democracy, 1997.

maintain order in their classrooms because good learning requires good listening. Learning also requires a teachable spirit. It is impossible to teach someone who thinks he or she knows all the answers already. To learn is to submit to the knowledge and authority of a teacher. Every good student is quiet and receptive.

A wonderful example of this kind of submissive learning is Mary, the sister of Martha and Lazarus. Jesus had stopped in their home to rest. While he was there, Martha "was distracted with much serving" (Luke 10:40). Meanwhile, Mary sat at the Lord's feet listening to everything he said (Luke 10:39). It made Martha mad to see Mary loafing around when there was work to be done. In her exasperation, she finally complained to Jesus, "Lord, do you not care that my sister has left me to serve alone? Tell her then to help me" (Luke 10:40). Notice what Jesus did not do in response. He did not tell Mary to go back to the kitchen where she belonged. He did not relegate her to so-called women's work. Instead, he said, "Mary has chosen the good portion, which will not be taken away from her" (Luke 10:42).

The words of Christ confirm the dignity and necessity of women becoming students of the Bible. They also serve as a rebuke to any man or woman who thinks theology is mainly for men. What Mary was learning from Jesus was the Word of God. She was learning true doctrine and how to apply it in daily life. God wants women to be knowledgeable in the Scriptures and sound in their theology.

Notice the way Mary learned: she "sat at the Lord's feet and listened to his teaching" (Luke 10:39). Mary learned in the rabbinic style. She kept her place; she was listening rather than talking; and she was sitting at Jesus' feet, which was the place of submission to teaching authority. In other words, as Mary sat in the seminary of Christ, she "learned quietly and with all submissiveness."

This is the way all God's people learn. They sit at the feet of their Master, even when he is speaking through the voice of a minister. I often have occasion to hear other men preach. When I do, my aim is to learn in quietness and full submission. I strive to resist the urge to say, "Well, that's not quite how I would handle that text." Rather, I must submit, not so much to another minister, but to the Lord himself, who wants me to sit at his feet the way Mary did.

. . . To Submit . . .

Submission is carefully defined here as "all submissiveness." Elsewhere, the Bible says much the same thing to women about marriage: "Wives, submit to your own husbands, as to the Lord. . . . Now as the church submits to Christ, so also wives should submit in everything to their husbands" (Eph. 5:22, 24). The Bible does not say partial submission. It does not say grudging submission. It says "full submission" or "entire submissiveness" (1 Tim. 2:11 NIV, NASB).

The Bible says "all" submissiveness because full submission is the only kind of submission there is. Anything less than full submission is no submission at all. Partial submission reserves the right to rebel; it leaves room to manipulate and to control. Grudging submission reserves the right to grumble; it leaves room for resentment and bitterness. But true submission is total submission. It is a heart surrendered to God.

Submission is a dirty word in contemporary culture, especially to feminists. It goes against everything Americans hold most dear: freedom, power, independence. Submission can also be a threatening word because sometimes it has been taken as an excuse for abuse. One woman writes, "Every single one of my feminist friends was abused by a man who was supposed to be her protector: a father, an uncle, a husband. . . . Is it any wonder these women don't trust men or that they equate 'submission' with co-dependence, downright mindlessness, or worse, masochism?"[5]

The real and present danger of these sinful patterns of relationship means that Christians have a responsibility never to allow the idea of submission to become a justification for abuse. We also have a responsibility to understand submission in its true biblical sense, which includes resisting the urge to think of submission as something negative. Keep in mind that the men to whom women are called to submit in the church are men who meet the qualifications for elders that Paul will provide in the following chapter—not domineering tyrants, but gentle servant leaders (see 1 Tim. 3:1–4). Furthermore, wherever the idea of submission appears in the New Testament (e.g. Heb. 12:9; James 4:7; Eph. 1:22; 5:21–24), it is always stated in the most

5. Anonymous, quoted in Susan Hunt, *By Design: God's Distinctive Calling for Women* (Franklin, TN: Legacy, 1994), 68.

positive terms. The Bible insists that it is a wonderful thing to submit to God-given authority. Not an easy thing, mind you, but a wonderful thing nonetheless. I know this because I myself submit to the authority of the elders of the church. On those rare occasions when I disagree with one of my fathers in the ministry about the direction of the church, I am called to defer to his judgment. It is not an affront to my dignity when I do so. Instead, it brings the peace and joy of knowing that I have honored the Lord and allowed his work to continue unhindered by my disobedience.

But of course the best place to understand the beauty of submission is in the example of Jesus Christ. Between God the Father and God the Son there is the most perfect equality. The Son has every attribute the Father has; they are equal in power and glory. Nevertheless, the Son submitted to the will of the Father, even unto his death on the cross (see Matt. 26:42; 1 Cor. 15:28). In the cross of Christ we see that submission does not entail coercion. Rather, it is willing, voluntary obedience to God's will for God's glory.

The relationship of the Son to the Father is a helpful analogy for understanding the relationship of women to men in God's house. Like the Son in his relationship to the Father, men and women are equal in their essence. Both the male and the female are created in the image of God (Gen. 1:27). Both men and women are redeemed by the blood of Christ (Gal. 3:28). They are equal in creation and equal in redemption.

At the same time, and without denying their fundamental equality, God commands wives to submit to their husbands and women to submit to their elders in the church. To submit in this way is to be like Jesus Christ. This is why the women of the church must never let go of God's command to learn in all submissiveness. Whenever they put this command into practice, they display the character of Jesus Christ.

. . . But Not to Preach

At the same time the Bible rules learning in, it rules teaching out—or at least a particular kind of teaching. The command is followed by a prohibition: "I do not permit a woman to teach or to exercise authority over a man; rather, she is to remain quiet" (1 Tim. 2:12). Verse 11 and verse 12 are joined together by the conjunction "but" (*de*): women are to learn but not to teach.

Some Christians have taken this verse to mean that no woman should ever teach any man anything (which is sometimes hard to do anyway!). In some churches women are forbidden not only to preach, but also to teach Sunday school, participate in home Bible studies, or give any other kind of instruction. The problem with this view is that it flies in the face of what the Bible teaches about the prophethood of all believers. When Peter preached at Pentecost, he quoted the prophet Joel: "And in the last days it shall be, God declares, that I will pour out my Spirit on all flesh, and your sons and your daughters shall prophesy, and your young men shall see visions, and your old men shall dream dreams; even on my male servants and female servants in those days I will pour out my Spirit, and they shall prophesy" (Acts 2:17–18).

According to the prophecy of Joel and the preaching of Peter, all God's sons and daughters exercise a prophetic ministry. This does not mean that they are all called to serve the church in a teaching office, but they all bear witness to the gospel. In keeping with this principle, the apostle Paul gave the following instructions to women as well as to men: "Let the word of Christ dwell in you richly, teaching and admonishing one another in all wisdom" (Col. 3:16). It is clear that at least certain kinds of teaching are to be carried out universally within the church.

Prohibiting women from teaching men not only goes against biblical command, but it also goes against biblical example. One thinks especially of Priscilla, who, with her husband, invited Apollos into her home "and explained to him the way of God more accurately" (Acts 18:26). She did this despite the fact that Apollos "was an eloquent man, competent in the Scriptures" (Acts 18:24). There are times and places when it is necessary for Christian men to learn from Christian women.

There is at least one place where it is not appropriate for women to teach, however: in the authoritative proclamation of God's Word in the context of the public worship of the church. Here it is important to remember the context of Paul's command. Since the beginning of the chapter he has been giving Timothy instructions about corporate worship services. What he writes is not intended to govern men and women in every situation, but applies especially to those occasions when the church gathers for the preaching of the Word of God (cf. 1 Cor. 14:34–35).

The word "teach" (*didaskein*), which means to instruct, has a specific meaning in the Pastoral Letters, where it refers to the exposition of Scripture in the official teaching of sound doctrine—the fundamentals of the faith (e.g. 1 Tim. 4:11; 2 Tim. 2:2). Teaching is what Paul did in his official role as an apostle (1 Tim. 2:7). It is also what the elders of the church are ordained to do (1 Tim. 3:2; 5:17), which may explain why eldership is the next subject that Paul will address. What the Holy Spirit does not permit women to do is to transmit apostolic doctrine publicly and officially. To put it more simply, the main thing that God forbids women to do is to preach (or to exercise the doctrinal and disciplinary authority that is tied to the preaching ministry).

Incidentally, most men are forbidden to do the same thing. This verse does not mean that all men are to teach all women. Nor does the Scripture say that all women are to submit to all men. Rather, these verses teach that all women are to submit to the teaching and discipline of the pastors of the church. In this respect, they are no different from Christian laymen who are not ordained elders.

One sign that Paul and the Holy Spirit have preaching in mind in 1 Timothy 2:12 is the way that teaching is coordinated with having authority. "Teach" and "exercise authority" are closely related terms. The activity they most clearly suggest is preaching, or any other form of doctrinally authoritative teaching in the church. In short, "women should not teach the gospel fundamentals in the church assembly."[6]

The Greek word for "exercise authority" (*authentein*) causes some difficulty because this is the only place it appears in the New Testament. Some egalitarians argue that the word refers to violent behavior, but this argument is based on a confusion between *authentein* and *authentēs*, which comes from a different root altogether.[7] Others say that *authentein* means "to domineer" or to "usurp authority" (KJV).[8] On this reading, women are not forbidden to have authority, but only to abuse it. In addition, it is suggested

6. Dan Doriani, *Women and Ministry: What the Bible Teaches* (Wheaton, IL: Crossway, 2003), 91.

7. H. Scott Baldwin, "A Difficult Word: *authenteō* in 1 Timothy 2:12," in *Women in the Church: A Fresh Analysis of 1 Timothy 2:9–15*, ed. Andreas J. Köstenberger et al. (Grand Rapids: Baker, 1995), 65–80 (pp. 76–77).

8. See, for example, Linda L. Belleville, "Teaching and Usurping Authority," in *Discovering Biblical Equality: Complementarity without Hierarchy*, ed. Ronald W. Pierce, Rebecca Merrill Groothuis, and Gordon D. Fee, 2d ed. (Downers Grove, IL: InterVarsity, 2004), 209–17.

that the worship of Artemis had made Ephesus a hotbed for feminism, with many pagan women believing in the inherent superiority of their sex.[9]

There are several problems with this interpretation. One is that the abuse of power is as objectionable in men as it is in women, and thus it would be surprising for Paul to limit this instruction to women. Furthermore, there is little evidence for strident feminism in Ephesus, and no evidence at all that such attitudes gained any influence in the church.[10] More importantly, the grammatical link between verses 11 and 12 strongly suggests that the verb for authority (*authentein*) is being used in a positive sense ("exercise authority") rather than a negative sense ("usurp authority"). Just as "Let a woman learn quietly" in verse 11 is set over against "I do not permit a woman to teach" in verse 12, so also "with all submissiveness" in verse 11 stands in opposition to "I do not permit a woman to exercise authority over a man" in verse 12. Learning is contrasted with teaching; submitting to authority is contrasted with exercising authority. But if "exercise authority" (*authentein*) means "usurp authority," then the balance of the grammatical structure is upset and the meaning of the passage is lost.[11]

There is also an important link between "teaching" and "exercising authority" within verse 12. For the grammatical structure that is used in this verse, the Greek language insists on having either two words with positive connotations or two words with negative connotations, but not one of each.[12] Therefore, "exercise authority" must be as positive as "teach" is, and should be taken in its standard sense. George Knight summarizes by saying that "the use of the word shows no inherent negative sense of grasping or usurping authority or of exercising it in a harsh or authoritative way, but simply means 'to have or exercise authority.'"[13] Paul is not speaking about the abuse of authority here, but about its rightful use by the elders of the church.

9. See Richard Clark Kroeger and Catherine Clark Kroeger, *I Suffer Not a Woman: Rethinking 1 Timothy 2:11–15 in Light of Ancient Evidence* (Grand Rapids: Baker, 1992), 54.

10. See Stephen M. Baugh, "A Foreign World: Ephesus in the First Century," in *Women in the Church: A Fresh Analysis of 1 Timothy 2:9–15*, ed. Andreas J. Köstenberger et al. (Grand Rapids: Baker, 1995), 13–52.

11. Doriani, *Women and Ministry*, 177–78.

12. Andreas J. Kostenberger, "A Complex Sentence Structure in 1 Timothy 2:12," in *Women in the Church*, 81–103.

13. Knight, *Pastoral Epistles*, 141. See also Albert Wolters, "A Semantic Study of *authentēs* and Its Derivatives," *Journal of Biblical Manhood and Womanhood*, 11.1 (Spring 2006): 45–65.

Where is such authority exercised in the church? Certainly in the writing of creeds and confessions that summarize Christian doctrine, and also in the formulation of church policy on theological issues. The word *authentein* hints that church discipline also may be in view. These things are the exclusive work of the elders of the church. So is preaching, which is the authoritative proclamation of Scripture. Not that preaching is infallible. In fact, the Bereans were commended for searching the Scriptures to make sure Paul had his theology straight (Acts 17:11). Yet to preach is to exercise teaching authority.

Depending on the discretion of the elders in a church, some other teaching situations may fall under the category of teaching with authority. The training of elders, for example, or classes on fundamental doctrines of the Christian faith. But elders are by no means required to teach every Bible study and Sunday school class in the church. Women and men who are not ordained may teach on a wide variety of biblical, historical, and practical subjects (although they should not, in my view, teach confessional doctrine). The elders are responsible before God for what is taught in the classes and Bible studies of the church, but they can exercise spiritual oversight without doing all of the teaching themselves.

It is also good for church members to make sure their pastors know what they are teaching. For example, a student who leads a campus Bible study might ask his pastor to recommend a commentary or clarify a point of interpretation. Or a woman who is preparing to teach might let her elder see a copy of the study guide she is planning to use, and so forth. Pastors and elders should do the same thing among themselves. Sound theology is best preserved by the collective wisdom of the men God has ordained to exercise teaching authority within the church.

Perhaps this is the best place to emphasize that beyond this one biblical restriction, women are at liberty to use their spiritual gifts to their fullest extent in the church. Here is one example of how this principle might be applied to congregational life:

> The Session of this church reaffirms that all positions of leadership and service are open to women, except for the authoritative teaching and disciplinary role that the Bible, in 1 Timothy 2:12–14, reserves for men. In the Presbyterian form of church government that role is embodied solely in the

> Session, composed of ruling and teaching elders. Aside from that function, women are encouraged to seek out all avenues of leadership and service, including Bible teaching, leading small groups, serving on the various church boards and committees, assisting in deaconal work and by any other means fully exercising their gifts for the greater benefit of the body of Jesus Christ.[14]

Some Objections

The preceding explanation of 1 Timothy 2:11–12 (or something close to it) has been the nearly universal understanding of the Christian church.[15] Only in the late twentieth century did it come under relentless attack.

The liberal strategy has been to deny the authority of these verses. Some say that verse 12, in particular, is only Paul's private opinion. He is not speaking for God, but only for himself, as if to say, "I personally do not allow a woman to teach or claim inordinate authority."[16] Against this it must be stated that the biblical word for permission (*boulomai*) is a word for a command (cf. 1 Cor. 14:37). Furthermore, Paul is speaking with apostolic authority. Verse 12 should thus be understood as follows: "I"—that is to say, I Paul, who have been appointed by God to be a herald, apostle, and teacher of the true faith (1 Tim. 2:7)—"do not permit a woman to teach." This is not a private opinion but an apostolic command with ongoing authority in the church.

Others say that Paul was mistaken. He barred women from the pulpit because he was a chauvinist, or because he was limited by Jewish and Greek attitudes about the value of women. Given his background and training, his position was as unavoidable as it was unfortunate.

By way of response, it must be remembered that Paul wrote under the inspiration of the Holy Spirit. Paul did not allow women to preach because God does not allow it. Here it is good to heed the words of the apostle Peter, who said that Paul's letters contain some things "that are hard to understand, which the ignorant and unstable twist to their own destruction, as they do

14. Adapted from the statement on "Leadership and Service Opportunities for Women" adopted by the Session of the Tenth Presbyterian Church in Philadelphia on December 22, 1992.

15. See Daniel Doriani, "A History of the Interpretation of 1 Timothy 2," in *Women in the Church: A Fresh Analysis of 1 Timothy 2:9–15*, ed. Andreas J. Köstenberger et al. (Grand Rapids: Baker, 1995), 213–67.

16. Thomas C. Oden, *First and Second Timothy and Titus*, Interpretation (Louisville: John Knox, 1989), 97.

the other Scriptures" (2 Peter 3:16). Since they are Holy Scripture, Paul's letters are ignored at the church's peril. At the same time, it must also be denied that either the apostle or God himself is a chauvinist. The better these verses are understood, the clearer it becomes that they do not demean women in any way.

While the liberal approach is to deny the authority of these verses, the strategy of evangelical feminists is to limit their application by saying that Paul was addressing circumstances that were unique to Ephesus. Some point to the poor quality of education there for women.[17] Others argue that Hellenistic culture simply wasn't ready for women in ministry. Often, Galatians 3:28 is used as a manifesto for the ordination of women: "There is neither Jew nor Greek, there is neither slave nor free, there is neither male nor female, for you are all one in Christ Jesus." On the basis of such arguments, many churches have felt free to set the strictures of 1 Timothy aside and proceed with the ordination of women to pastoral ministry.

The evangelical feminist argument ought to arouse immediate suspicion, for it is good to be suspicious whenever anyone suddenly decides a particular Scripture no longer applies. Furthermore, these instructions were not just for Ephesus. The Holy Spirit gave them to all Christians everywhere, and for all women everywhere, regardless of their educational background (note that one of the women in Ephesus was Priscilla, who was probably as theologically well informed as anyone in the church; see 2 Tim. 4:19): "As in all the churches of the saints, the women should keep silent in the churches. For they are not permitted to speak, but should be in submission, as the Law also says" (1 Cor. 14:33–34). These explicit instructions about submission help to keep Galatians 3:28 in perspective. The oneness of men and women there refers to their unity in Jesus Christ. That principle of spiritual unity is in no way contradicted by recognizing that God has given men and women differing spiritual responsibilities in the home and in the church. It is thus a mistake to use the general principle of Galatians 3:28 to overrule specific commands about the role of women in 1 Timothy 2 and elsewhere.[18]

17. Aída Besançon Spencer, *Beyond the Curse: Women Called to Ministry* (Peabody, MA: Hendrickson, 1985), 84.

18. See Richard Hove, *Equality in Christ: Galatians 3:28 and the Gender Dispute* (Wheaton, IL: Crossway, 1999).

The Created Order

There is yet another problem with saying that Paul's instructions apply only to Ephesians. The Bible's rationale is not based on Hellenistic culture, or on the school system in Asia Minor, or on the particulars of the Ephesian church. Instead, it goes all the way back to the creation of the world: "For Adam was formed first, then Eve; and Adam was not deceived, but the woman was deceived and became a transgressor" (1 Tim. 2:13–14).

Here I wish to make an autobiographical comment. The summer before I began seminary, I interviewed for a pastoral position in a liberal Presbyterian congregation. Had I been offered the job, I would have been supervised by the woman who served as associate minister. The situation forced me to investigate more fully the biblical teaching about women in ministry. At the time, I found it difficult to accept that spiritual gifts were not equally distributed within the church. Why should it be the case, I wondered, that the gift of preaching would be limited to particular men? After carefully researching both sides of the issue, however, I became convinced that the historic position of the church was correct. What persuaded me more than anything else was that the Bible bases its instructions for men and women on the way God created them (cf. 1 Cor. 11:8–9). The roles of men and women are founded upon God-given distinctions between the male and the female.

We see this mode of argumentation here in 1 Timothy 2, where Paul's first reason for telling women to learn but not to preach comes from the order of creation: "Adam was formed first, then Eve" (1 Tim. 2:13). Some commentators take this to be a statement of superiority,[19] but nothing is said about the superiority of men, either in this verse, or anywhere else in Scripture. Instead, what Paul says is similar to the ancient and biblical law of primogeniture, in which the firstborn son held a place of spiritual responsibility within the family. He may or may not have been more talented or more beloved than his siblings. Yet the eldest son "inherited command of resources and the responsibility of leadership in the home and in worship. He became 'head' of the household."[20] So, too, Adam was God's first-formed

19. J. N. D. Kelly, *The Pastoral Epistles: Timothy I and II, Titus*, Harper's New Testament Commentaries (San Francisco: Harper and Row, 1960), 68.

20. James B. Hurley, *Man and Woman in Biblical Perspective* (Grand Rapids: Zondervan, 1981), 207.

son. The fact that he was made first was not an accident of chronology; it was part of God's best plan for humanity: "The proscription on women teaching men, then, does not stem from the fall and cannot be ascribed to the curse. Paul appeals to the created order, the good and perfect world God has made, to justify the ban on women teaching men."[21] The effect of this appeal is to look beyond culture to creation.

Paul's second line of reasoning is more complex: "Adam was not deceived, but the woman was deceived and became a transgressor" (1 Tim. 2:14; cf. 2 Cor. 11:3). This verse, too, is often misunderstood. On a first reading, it sounds as if Paul blames Eve for the fall. Thus some Christians have wrongly concluded that men should preach because women cannot be trusted. Guthrie speaks of "the greater aptitude of the weaker sex to be led astray."[22] Kelly says that "since Eve was so gullible a victim of the serpent's wiles, she clearly cannot be trusted to teach."[23] Even Martin Luther fell into this way of thinking: "It was not Adam who went astray. Therefore there was greater wisdom in Adam than in the woman."[24]

The problem with this interpretation is obvious: men cannot be trusted, either. In fact, most of the problems in the Ephesian church were caused by *men* who were teaching false doctrine. Indeed, the vast majority of heretical doctrines in church history have been disseminated by men. Paul can hardly mean that men should teach because they are less vulnerable to false theology!

The true meaning of this verse lies in its emphasis on the word "deceived" (*apataō*), which Paul is taking from Genesis 3:13: "The woman said, 'The serpent deceived me, and I ate.' " The point is that Adam was *not* deceived. Unlike Eve, he knew full well what he was doing when he ate the forbidden fruit. The woman fell partly because Satan blinded her to the true nature of sin, but the man sinned with his eyes wide open. James Hurley thus concludes

21. Thomas R. Schreiner, "An Interpretation of 1 Timothy 2:9–15: A Dialogue with Scholarship," in *Women in the Church: A Fresh Analysis of 1 Timothy 2:9–15*, ed. Andreas J. Köstenberger et al. (Grand Rapids: Baker, 1995), 105–54 (p. 134).

22. Donald Guthrie, *The Pastoral Epistles*, Tyndale New Testament Commentaries (Downers Grove, IL: InterVarsity, 1957), 77.

23. Kelly, *Pastoral Epistles*, 68.

24. Martin Luther, *Lectures on 1 Timothy*, trans. Richard Dinda, *Luther's Works*, ed. Jaroslav Pelikan and Walther T. Lehman (St. Louis: Concordia, 1955–72), 28:278.

that "Eve was *not* at fault; she was deceived. Adam, on the other hand, was not deceived but, deliberately and with understanding, chose to sin."[25]

Adam's willful disobedience hardly recommends him for pastoral ministry! But it does indicate something important about God's plan for humanity: God held Adam principally responsible for the fall into sin. This explains why he asked Adam, rather than Eve, to explain what had happened in the garden (see Gen. 3:9). Adam tried to pin the whole thing on Eve, of course, but God came looking for the man. The same principle of spiritual responsibility shows up in Romans, where Paul explains that "death reigned from Adam to Moses" and that "many died through one man's trespass" (Rom. 5:14–15). Eve seems to be entirely forgotten, even though she was the first to sin. This is because Adam was the one chosen as our representative in the covenant, the man responsible for the spiritual welfare of the whole household of humanity.

Now an analogous spiritual responsibility has been given to men ordained to have teaching authority in the church. The Bible does not teach that men should preach because they will do a better job. The argument is sometimes made that women need to enter pastoral ministry because men are failing in their pastoral duties, or it is pointed out that some women are as gifted at speaking as many ministers. These objections fail because the Bible does not base its prohibition against women preaching on merit. It is based rather on the order God established at creation.

The fall of Adam and Eve itself shows what can happen when that created order is reversed. Men and women who seek to overthrow God's order for the church are sons and daughters of Eve. Like their mother, they become transgressors.

Saved through the Childbirth

There is hope for sinners, however, and it comes in the most difficult verse in a difficult passage: "Yet she will be saved through childbearing—if they continue in faith and love and holiness, with self-control" (1 Tim. 2:15).

It is not hard to guess why Paul introduces childbirth into the discussion. It is one distinction between men and women that no one can deny

25. Hurley, *Man and Woman*, 215.

is fundamental. A culture may do everything it can to obliterate the differences between males and females, but there is one thing it can never do: make men give birth. Labor and delivery are unique to women, a divinely ordained fact which indicates that the differences between men and women are rooted in creation. This much is certain, yet the question remains: what does it mean to be "saved through childbearing"?

Obviously, the verse does not mean that a woman must give birth to be saved, for not all women give birth. One possibility, though, is that women who do give birth will make it safely through childbirth. Here it should be kept in mind that in most places in the world throughout most of human history childbirth has been regarded as a matter of life and death both for the mother and her child. This interpretation refers back to the curse of Genesis 3:16: "I will surely multiply your pain in childbearing; in pain you shall bring forth children." Salvation, then, is understood in a physical sense to mean the preservation of life. Childbirth is dangerous, but Christian women will survive.

The first problem with this interpretation is that it is not always true. Some godly women—Rachel, for example (see Gen. 35:16–20)—have died in labor. But a bigger problem is that Paul typically uses this word for salvation (*sōzō*) in its spiritual sense of deliverance from sin. In the Pastoral Epistles, "salvation" usually refers to redemption from sin through the crucifixion and resurrection of Jesus Christ (see 1 Tim. 2:4; 2 Tim. 1:9; 4:18; Titus 3:5). When Paul wishes to speak about physical safety he uses a different word entirely (*rhuomai*; e.g. 2 Tim. 3:11; 4:18).

Another way to interpret this verse is expressed by the New English Bible: "women will be saved through motherhood." Childbearing is thus taken to represent a woman's calling. It is "the feminine role *par excellence*,"[26] and therefore it serves as a kind of shorthand for a woman's home life. The place where a woman will find her true sanctification is not in the authoritative teaching office of the church, but in the domestic sphere. Her vocation, says Barrett, "is not to public life but to the task of bearing and bringing up children."[27] Not that all women are called to be mothers, of course, but all women should embrace their feminine identity as life-givers, which is biologically signified in the capacity to bear children. This capacity had special importance in the

26. Doriani, *Women and Ministry*, 97.
27. C. K. Barrett, *The Pastoral Epistles* (Oxford: Clarendon, 1963), 56.

Ephesian context, where some people were forbidding marriage altogether (see 1 Tim. 4:3), and presumably saw childbearing as a second-rate calling for women. While the Bible does not limit women to staying at home, it does seem to center a woman's calling in the life of the home, especially if she is married (see Prov. 31:10–31; 1 Tim. 5:14; Titus 2:4–5).

On this interpretation, the woman will be "saved" (in the sense of "kept safe" or "preserved," as the word *sōzō* was often used in everyday conversation) from seizing masculine roles by resting content in the quiet duties of her feminine calling. A woman is not saved by becoming a man, but by embracing her God-given calling as a woman. Indeed, this is one of the ways that she works out her salvation.

Although this interpretation seems to relate well to the rest of the passage, it does have some limitations. In addition to failing to take the verb for salvation (*sōzō*) in its typical Pauline sense, it requires us to make two inferences that are not altogether certain: that "childbearing" encapsulates every woman's calling (a form of speech that fails to explicitly include the circumstances of many women, and that women who are not mothers may find difficult to embrace) and that "saved" means preserved from usurping a calling that God has given to men only (since Paul does not specify what women are saved from, this meaning is not stated, but at most implied).

One more possible interpretation is worthy of mention. It emphasizes that in the Greek original, childbearing has a definite article: it is referred to as *the* childbirth, which is at least suggestive. So the verse reads, "Women will be saved through the bearing of a child." To be more specific, the Scripture may refer to the birth of Jesus Christ, even if this is a somewhat unconventional way of referring to that miraculous event. Walter Lock put the verse into a poetic couplet that draws out its meaning on this interpretation: "A child from woman's seed to spring; / Shall saving to all women bring."[28] This interpretation makes good sense in connection with Genesis 3:15, which first promises that the offspring of the woman will defeat the devil. Jesus accomplished this chiefly by dying on the cross, of course, but he had to be born before he could die, and in this sense, salvation comes through (not by) his birth.

28. Walter Lock, *A Critical and Exegetical Commentary on the Pastoral Epistles (I & II Timothy and Titus)*, International Critical Commentary (Edinburgh: T & T Clark, 1924), 29.

This interpretation also makes good sense out of the immediate context. Verse 14 ends with the reality of sin. What could be more natural than for verse 15 to begin with the hope of salvation, in its usual sense of deliverance from sin, and to connect that salvation with the submission of a woman to the plan of God? Such considerations lead John Stott to conclude that "even if certain roles are not open to women, and even if they are tempted to resent their position, they and we must never forget what we owe to a woman. If Mary had not given birth to the Christ-child, there would have been no salvation for anybody. No greater honor has ever been given to woman than in the calling of Mary to be the mother of the Savior of the world."[29] Thus 1 Timothy 2 ends with the best consolation of all. It is not meant simply to cheer women up because they do not get to preach. Rather, it is meant to give hope to us all because God offers salvation from sin in Jesus Christ.

The Faith to Submit

If the first part of verse 15 does refer to the coming of Christ, then the rest of the verse falls into place. How is salvation received? It is received by faith, of course. Then Paul mentions some of the virtues which always accompany saving faith: love, holiness, and self-control. These character traits are the proof of genuine faith, and women must continue in these graces to persevere in the faith.

"Self-control," or "propriety" as the New International Version has it, is the perfect word to end this chapter. It describes a woman of prudence and discretion. Back in verse 9 it referred to modesty in attire; here in verse 15 it suggests self-restraint in seeking authority within the church.

A wonderful example of this kind of self-control comes from the life of Joanne Shetler, a former missionary to the Philippines. The first part of her story was told in chapter 5 of this commentary. As a result of Shetler's ministry, many members of the Balangao tribe received Jesus Christ as their Lord and Savior. There was a difficulty, however. The Balangao were unwilling to teach the Bible for themselves, and Shetler tried in vain to convince them to preach in their own worship services. They wanted her to do all the teaching

29. Stott, *Guard the Truth*, 87–88.

because she knew so much more than they did. The problem was not resolved until Shetler began to translate Paul's letters to Timothy. She writes:

> I continued translating in Timothy with my daddy [adoptive Balangao father]. And we came to a verse where Paul says to Timothy, "I don't allow women to teach men." My daddy didn't bat an eyelash. But that afternoon, after we'd finished work, he said to me, "Now what is that we're going to study on Sunday?" I thought he was just curious. I didn't know what was on his mind since fathers don't report to their children. So I told him. Sunday morning came, and before I could stand up to start, *he* stood up and said, "My daughter here knows more about this than I do, but we found in the Bible that women aren't supposed to teach men. So I guess I have to be the one!" And that was the end of my career, and the beginning of their teaching.[30]

No doubt some people would be offended by what Shetler's daddy did, and perhaps by Shetler's own acquiescence. But God was not offended. He was glorified, as he always is when his sons and daughters trust what the Scripture says and submit to his will for the church—the men by stepping forward to assume spiritual leadership when they are called, and the women by encouraging such leadership through submission.

30. Joanne Shetler, "Faithful in Obedience," in *Faithful Witness: The Urbana '84 Compendium*, ed. James McLeish (Downers Grove, IL: InterVarsity, 1985), 99–107 (pp. 105–6).

8

Qualifications for Elders

1 Timothy 3:1–7

The saying is trustworthy: If anyone aspires to the office of overseer, he desires a noble task. . . . He must manage his own household well, with all dignity keeping his children submissive, for if someone does not know how to manage his own household, how will he care for God's church? (1 Tim. 3:1, 4–5)

A minister who once preached from this passage borrowed his title from one of its key phrases. The sermon was supposed to be called "Above Reproach: The Qualifications of Elders." When the bulletin came back from the printer, however, it stated that elders were "Above Approach" rather than "Above Reproach."

"Above Approach"—the phrase reflects the way Christians sometimes feel about their spiritual leaders. Few things seem to cause greater fear than meeting with the elders of the church. I remember how I felt, as a youngster, when I waited to give my testimony of faith in Jesus Christ to the session. There I sat in the church hallway, rubbing sweaty palms on my good church trousers and trying desperately to remember my salvation verse. The feeling returned with greater force when I appeared before my presbytery to be examined for ordination to pastoral ministry.

The officers of the church have not always made Christians so nervous. Back in the nineteenth century a churchman from Edinburgh named David Dickson wrote: "Our people know well the necessity and usefulness of the office of the eldership. All over Scotland there is a *happy prejudice* in favor of an elder's visit. No elder could ever say that they did not welcome his visits. The houses and hearts of the people are ever open to those whom they have called to the office."[1] This is how elders ought to be treated: with affection.

A Noble Task

Elders should also be treated with respect, for the Bible holds their office in high esteem: "The saying is trustworthy: If anyone aspires to the office of overseer, he desires a noble task" (1 Tim. 3:1). This is the second time the apostle has taken a popular saying and given it divine approval. Walter Lock offers a clever paraphrase to give it the flavor of a proverb: "He who would play a leader's part, / On noble task has set his heart."[2]

The Greek word for "overseer" is *episkopos*, which is sometimes translated as "bishop." *Episkopos* is the word that gives the Episcopal Church its name. It is synonymous with the biblical word *presbyteros*, which means "elder" and gives the Presbyterian Church its name. In the New Testament—in Acts 20:17–38, for example—the words for pastor (*poimēn*), elder (*presbyteros*), and bishop (*episkopos*) are used interchangeably (see also 1 Peter 5:1–2; Titus 1:5–7). This is true in 1 Timothy as well, since Paul later calls the overseers "elders" (1 Tim. 5:17).

We are bound to conclude from the biblical usage that there is no difference in rank among the elders of the church, and that therefore hierarchical forms of church government go beyond the teaching of Scripture. They did not develop, in fact, until after the close of the New Testament, especially in the ministry of Ignatius, the bishop of Antioch, who died several decades into the second century.

1. David Dickson, *The Elder and His Work*, ed. George Kennedy McFarland and Philip Graham Ryken (1883; repr. Phillipsburg, NJ: P&R, 2004), 27.

2. Walter Lock, *A Critical and Exegetical Commentary on the Pastoral Epistles (I & II Timothy and Titus)*, International Critical Commentary (Edinburgh: T & T Clark, 1924), 34.

The biblical pattern for the church is spiritual government by a plurality of elders. All the overseers are brothers in ministry. As we shall see, there is a difference between teaching elders (sometimes known as pastors or ministers) and ruling elders (see 1 Tim. 5:17). But the difference lies only in their function, not in their authority. A pastor is not superior in rank to a ruling elder.

The point of Paul's trustworthy saying is that the work of an overseer is honorable. It has a long and rich tradition among the people of God. The first elders were appointed by Moses to teach and to judge the children of Israel (see Ex. 18). Throughout the Old Testament, God's people were represented and governed by elders who sat in the city gates and taught in the synagogues. The same was true in the New Testament. When the first Christians sent a gift to the poor people of Jerusalem, Paul and Barnabas brought it to the elders of the church (Acts 11:30). On their missionary journeys they appointed elders in all the churches (14:23). So by the time Paul wrote to Timothy, the elder was a well-established officer in the church.

The work of an overseer is good work. As the word suggests, it involves the oversight (*epi-skopos* = "over-look") of God's people. By ruling and teaching, elders supervise the spiritual life of the church. They look after things on God's behalf. And if such oversight is good work, then it is also good for men to seek it. I say "men" because the Spirit has already stated that women are not to exercise teaching authority in the church (1 Tim. 2:12). The word "aspires" (*oregetai*) means to "reach out" for something, to stretch for it. The Scripture speaks further of "desire" (*epithymei*). So godly men should strive to become elders in the church.

This is true for ruling elders as well as teaching elders (pastors). Too many young men desire to become ministers; too few aspire to become elders. At the same time we pray for our children to become evangelists, missionaries, and Sunday school teachers, we should pray that some of our sons will undertake the noble task of oversight.

This does not mean that eldership should be an ambition. Elders do not campaign for the office. Far from it. No one ever decides to become an officer of the church on his own. That is for the church to decide, led by the Holy Spirit, following the guidelines set forth in this passage (see also 1 Peter 5:1–4; Titus 1:5–9). Yet the outward call of the church is always matched by the inward call of the man. The great Puritan preacher William Perkins asked,

"How can you know for yourself whether God wants you to go [into the ministry] or not?" His answer was, "You must ask both your own conscience and the church. . . . Your conscience must judge of your willingness and the church of your ability."[3] Serving as a pastor or elder can be a worthy aspiration without becoming a blind ambition.

Why does the Bible bother to say that an overseer does good work? Possibly because the task is so daunting. Calvin comments, "It is no light matter to represent God's Son, in such a great task as erecting and extending God's Kingdom, in caring for the salvation of souls whom the Lord Himself has deigned to purchase with His own blood, and in ruling the Church which is God's inheritance."[4] Or perhaps the value of elders is stressed because the job is so dangerous. Ministers often become martyrs. In the early church, and many times since, elders have been the first to give their lives for the sake of the gospel. Nevertheless, it is good work, because it has God's blessing in life and God's reward in death.

The Elder's Morals

Oversight is good work, not "if you can get it," but only if you are qualified for it. What are God's minimum requirements? What is the character of a gospel elder?

The first qualification encompasses all the others: "an overseer must be above reproach" (1 Tim. 3:2). Not that any mere man could ever be sinless, of course, but he must be blameless in his outward, observable conduct. He must be free from scandalous sin. As David Dickson wrote, "The office and work being spiritual, it is necessary that elders should be spiritual men. It is not necessary that they be men of great gifts or worldly position, of wealth or high education; but it is indispensably necessary that they be men of God, at peace with him, new creatures in Christ Jesus."[5]

The integrity of a gospel elder must be beyond question. Once there was an elder who was charged with a moral offense. It was the duty of his brothers to take the charges seriously and to look into the matter, which they did.

3. William Perkins, *The Art of Prophesying* (Edinburgh: Banner of Truth, 1996), 188–89.

4. John Calvin, *The Second Epistle of Paul the Apostle to the Corinthians and the Epistles to Timothy, Titus and Philemon*, trans. T. A. Smail, Calvin's Commentaries (Edinburgh: Oliver & Boyd, 1964), 222.

5. Dickson, *Elder*, 30.

But the elder who was accused was a man of such grace and godliness that the charge sounded preposterous from the very beginning. He was a man above reproach, as circumstances later confirmed.

To be above reproach, an elder must be "the husband of one wife" (1 Tim. 3:2). This does not prohibit bachelors from serving as elders. Commonly, elders will be married, and God will use the demands of their callings as husbands and fathers to do much of the sanctifying work that needs to be done in their lives before they are ready to serve as officers in the church. But remember that Paul himself was single and commended singleness to others as an opportunity for greater service in the kingdom of God (1 Cor. 7:17; 9:5). Some suggest that the phrase means "married only once." This would disqualify widowers who remarry, as well as men who have been through a divorce. If this is what Paul meant, however, one might expect him to be more explicit.

The point of the phrase is probably more general: elders must be morally accountable for their sexuality. The Greeks and the Romans of the day generally tolerated gross sexual sin. Polygamy was practiced by both Greeks and Jews.[6] Marriage was undermined by frequent divorce, widespread adultery, and rampant homosexuality.[7] The words of Demosthenes show the scope of the problem: "Mistresses we keep for the sake of pleasure, concubines for the daily care of our persons, but wives to bear us legitimate children."[8]

How should the church take its stand against such sexual immorality? Some of the false teachers in Ephesus went so far as to forbid people to marry (see 1 Tim. 4:3), as if that would help! God's plan is quite different. He wants the leaders of the church to be living examples of biblical marriage: one man and one woman in a love covenant for life. In the words of Theodore of Mopsuestia, a man who has but one wife is "a man who having contracted a monogamous marriage is faithful to his marriage vows."[9] Being faithful to marriage vows includes avoiding inapropriately intimate

6. George Knight, *The Pastoral Epistles*, New International Greek Testament Commentary (Grand Rapids: Eerdmans, 1992), 158.

7. Thomas C. Oden, *First and Second Timothy and Titus*, Interpretation (Louisville: John Knox, 1989), 141.

8. Demosthenes, "Against Neaera," *Private Orations*, trans. A. T. Murray, Loeb Classical Library (Cambridge, MA: Harvard University Press), vol. 6, oration 59:122 (pp. 445, 447).

9. Theodore of Mopsuestia, quoted in Knight, *Pastoral Epistles*, 158–59.

relationships with other women. Wise pastors and elders do not counsel women alone and in private, so as to avoid the kind of intimacy that would compromise their ministry.

The next several qualifications have to do with an elder's judgment. He must be "sober-minded, self-controlled, respectable" (1 Tim. 3:2). The King James Version translates "sober-minded" (*nēphalion*) as "vigilant." A sober-minded man is "free from every form of excess, passion, or rashness."[10] He is wary, circumspect, even cautious. The word "sober-minded" describes the way a person walks late at night in the city: not paranoid, necessarily, but alert. This is necessary for the protection of the church. A vigilant elder notices spiritual needs and warns of spiritual dangers.

Next comes "self-controlled." The Greek word *sōphrona* has to do with decision-making. It means to be sensible. Men who make vital decisions about the ministry of the church must be prudent. They must have balanced judgment. When elders (especially pastors) do not weigh their decisions carefully, the church is vulnerable to all the latest trends in ministry and theology—trends which may be far from salutary for the health of the church. "Self-control" also refers to the ability to control one's appetites. The French writer Rabelais posed a question every elder should ask himself: "How shall I be able to rule over others if I have not full power and command of myself?"[11]

Then elders are to be "respectable" (*kosmion*). They are to be orderly and well-mannered. Among other things, this applies to their drinking habits. Although he need not be a teetotaler, a respectable elder is "not a drunkard" (1 Tim. 3:3). An alcoholic cannot serve as an overseer because he is incapable of the kind of sober judgment that good spiritual leadership requires.

The Greek philosophers sometimes used the word for "drunkard" (*paroinon*) to refer to violence, like a drunken rage. What comes next, therefore, is not surprising, especially in the pagan environment of Ephesus: an elder is "not violent but gentle" (1 Tim. 3:3). Bullies are not eligible for ordination. An elder is not a browbeater. Men who are verbally or physically abusive cannot be trusted to tend God's sheep.

10. Gordon D. Fee, *1 and 2 Timothy, Titus*, New International Biblical Commentary (Peabody, MA: Hendrickson, 1988), 81.

11. François Rabelais, *Works*, trans. D. M. Frame (Berkeley: University of California Press, 1991), ch. 52.

Instead, elders must be "gentle" (*epieikē*). E. K. Simpson says this means "gracious, kindly, forbearing, considerate, magnanimous, genial."[12] Elders must be peaceable, which is the exact opposite of being violent. The true strength of a man lies in gentleness. Of course, an elder must be firm when he rebukes sin. When overseers lack the courage to confront, the church loses its conviction. But an elder must be gentle. He must live among God's people like a tender shepherd. He must be sympathetic with the weak and compassionate to the wounded.

Furthermore, an elder must not be "quarrelsome." Very likely, Paul had the false teachers in mind when he wrote this, for they were starting to become belligerent. Their disputes resulted in "envy, dissension, slander, evil suspicions, and constant friction among people who are depraved in mind" (1 Tim. 6:4–5). From time to time, visitors stop by a church or telephone with theological questions. Most of them want to be instructed, but there are a few who just want to argue. In that case, the best thing a minister can do is agree to disagree and politely send them on their way. The church is not a debating society. Indeed, few things are more distracting to God's work than quarrelsome leaders. David Dickson observed the same problem more than a century ago: "Men of points and pugnacity are very annoying in a session or congregation, and they may rise to the terror of presbyteries and other church courts. They may love the truth at heart—and we believe they often do—but they love fighting too. . . . A carping, censorious spirit is to be watched and prayed against in all of us: it is often the precursor or companion of backsliding in doctrine or life."[13]

An argumentative man is the worst kind of man to have on a board of elders. When overseers discuss the ministry of the church, they need to express their opinions clearly and charitably because the best decisions emerge from lively discussion. On occasion, it is even appropriate for objections to be raised. But this must never be done with a contentious spirit.

Nor must an elder be "a lover of money" (1 Tim. 3:3). Avarice, as the sin is sometimes called, comes up often in Paul's first letter to Timothy. Indeed, most of chapter 6 is taken up with issues of wealth and poverty. Issues related to money also come up often in the history of the church. Since the days of

12. E. K. Simpson, quoted in Donald Guthrie, *The Pastoral Epistles*, Tyndale New Testament Commentaries (Downers Grove, IL: InterVarsity, 1957), 81.

13. Dickson, *Elder*, 32.

the apostles, some men have tried to use the ministry for financial gain (see 1 Tim. 6:5). Greed led to the corruption of the medieval church. Closer to our own times, the love of money contributed to the decline of many large churches in American cities. Televangelists are so obsessed with it that Christians have become infamous for asking for money.

It is a grave mistake to consider wealth a credential for spiritual leadership. Being rich does not disqualify a man from the eldership, but it does not recommend him for it, either. What matters is how he uses his money, and especially how much affection he has for it. An overseer must not be a money-lover. The same vice is mentioned in Hebrews 13, along with the contrasting virtue: "Keep your life free from love of money, and be content with what you have" (Heb. 13:5). The antidote for greed is contentment. People who are greedy are always thinking about what they lack, whereas those who are content lack nothing. In a way, since they have everything they need, they are as wealthy as if they possessed the entire world. This is the kind of contentment a man must have to serve as an elder in the church. As far as money is concerned, he can take it or leave it.

The Elder's Duties

Most of the qualifications on Paul's list explain who elders *are* rather than what they *do*. This is because "the usefulness of an elder will depend in the long run more on his character than on his gifts and knowledge."[14] But there are two requirements here that show us something about the duties of an elder. The first of these requirements is that elders are to be "hospitable" (1 Tim. 3:2). Overseers are to have open homes as well as open hearts. Literally, they are to show "love for strangers" (*philoxenon*).

Hospitality has always been among the highest Christian virtues. Anyone who welcomes a stranger is like Abraham, who entertained angels (see Gen. 18; Heb. 13:2). All Christians are to be good hosts. In the days of the early church, however, hospitality was necessary for the spread of the gospel: "For in those days there were no hotels comparable to those we are familiar with, and roadside inns were scarce, dirty, unsafe and unsavoury."[15] Naturally,

14. Ibid., 34.

15. John Stott, *Guard the Truth: The Message of 1 Timothy and Titus* (Downers Grove, IL: InterVarsity, 1996), 95.

people involved in Christian work needed a good place to stay. In requiring hospitality as a qualification for eldership, Paul was pointing "beyond the normal hospitality he should display as head of a household to the hospitality he should extend on behalf of the church."[16] This kind of hospitality remains useful for Christian work to this day. As they have opportunity, elders should entertain missionaries and other Christian workers. The underlying principle is that elders must make a personal commitment to the worldwide work of the gospel.

There are many other important reasons for contemporary Christians to practice hospitality. One is for evangelism. The dinner table is one of the best places to talk about spiritual things with non-Christian friends. Hospitality is also necessary for the well-being of God's family. One of the great evils of contemporary culture is the fragmentation of the family. As Christians, we need to find our primary identity as brothers and sisters in Jesus Christ. One of the best places to establish these family ties is around the dinner table. Consider the brother who was invited to join a Christian family for Christmas dinner. He was cautious because he did not want to intrude on any "family time." This was thoughtful; families do need to spend time together. But if we are brothers and sisters in Jesus Christ, then any time we are together is "family time." Elders, especially, need to make sure we spend quality time together as a family.

This brings us to the qualification that lies closest to the heart of an overseer's work. He must be "able to teach" (*didaktikon*). In other words, he must be "qualified by education and moral power to impart the sound Christian teaching in opposition to the many false teachers."[17] An elder must have wisdom, said Calvin, "in knowing how to apply God's word to the profit of the people."[18]

As far as teaching is concerned, most Presbyterian churches follow 1 Timothy 5:17 in making a distinction between teaching and ruling elders: "Let the elders who rule well be considered worthy of double honor, especially those who labor in preaching and teaching." All the elders direct the affairs of the church; some concentrate on teaching and preaching. Typically, the

16. Jouette M. Bassler, *1 Timothy, 2 Timothy, Titus* (Nashville: Abingdon, 1996), 67.

17. William M. Ramsay, *Historical Commentary on the Pastoral Epistles*, ed. Mark Wilson (Grand Rapids: Kregel, 1996), 71.

18. Calvin, *Second Epistle of Paul*, 79.

principal work of the minister is to teach the Word of God. A minister may do many other things as well. He may use his gifts in administration, leading worship, discipleship, counseling, and so forth. But first and foremost, the minister is a Bible teacher, and thus in some way he exercises the ministry of God's Word in every aspect of his calling.

Ministers are not the only ones who must be able to teach, however. This qualification is for ruling elders as well. Their teaching takes place in a variety of contexts, such as Sunday school classes and home Bible studies. They also teach whenever they disciple, evangelize, or make pastoral visits. And for all these duties, ruling elders must be able to teach.

The Elder's Family

A man does not become an overseer overnight. Eldership is a job that requires prior experience. The most important place for an elder to get this experience is at home: "He must manage his own household well, with all dignity keeping his children submissive" (1 Tim. 3:4). The family life of an elder must be exemplary. The same must be true of a man's relationships at work, or in other areas of public involvement. (Here it is important to understand that many households in the ancient world extended beyond a person's immediate family, and thus required the head of the household to provide effective leadership for servants and other laborers.) Leadership in these arenas is especially important for bachelor elders, who do not have the full benefit of family relationships as a proving ground for ministry.

The Greek word for "manage" (*proistamenon*) has two primary meanings. One is to supervise, and the other is to nurture or to be concerned. Fatherhood brings both aspects together. The father is the leader who governs the household, but the way he does this is by caring for the needs of each family member. Elders do the same thing in the household of God: they exercise their spiritual authority both by governing and by caring.

What does it mean for the overseer to "keep his children submissive" (1 Tim. 3:4)? It almost sounds as if the man is supposed to rule his family by force. But of course obedience can never be coerced because it is a matter of the heart, and thus ultimately it is a gift of God's grace. So how can a father encourage his children to be obedient? Here Paul gives us a hint: "with all dignity" (1 Tim. 3:4). The word "dignity" means respect or reverence, and it may well refer to the way the children treat their father. Certainly parents have the right to demand respect from their children. But "dignity" also describes the way the father relates to his children: he treats them like people made in the very image of God, and therefore he promotes a relationship of mutual respect. The best way to grow obedient children is not to control or manipulate them, but to respect them. This means being fair, consistent, sympathetic, and merciful. A father who treats his children respectfully will earn their respect. By contrast, a man whose angry temper and inconsistent discipline exasperates his children and exacerbates their rebellion is not qualified to serve as a spiritual father in the church.

To turn this around, a man whose children respect him must be a good father, which is exactly what the church is looking for. A man who cares for his own children well is ready to care for all God's children. He already knows how to instruct, nurture, discipline, and deal patiently with rebellion. The Puritans loved to say that the family is a little church. This was especially true in the days of the first Christians, when most congregations met in people's homes. But it always will be true. The *Book of Common Prayer* poses this question to candidates for ordination: "Will you be diligent to frame and fashion your own selves, and your families, according to the doctrine of Christ, and to make both yourselves and them, as much as in you lieth, wholesome examples and patterns to the flock of Christ?"[19]

The importance of an elder's family life is obvious: "If someone does not know how to manage his own household, how will he care for God's church?" (1 Tim. 3:5). The question is rhetorical. Obviously, a man has to have his own house in order before he can keep God's house in order. Sadly, most Christians know teaching and ruling elders who do not know how to manage their families very well at all. But many other fathers do know how, and they make the very best elders and pastors.

The word "manage" (*epimeleomai*) is rich in its practical implications. It appears one other time in the New Testament, for Jesus used it when he told how a man on his way to Jericho was mugged and left for dead: "But a Samaritan, as he journeyed, came to where he was, and when he saw him, he had compassion. He went to him and bound up his wounds, pouring on oil and wine. Then he set him on his own animal and brought him to an inn and

19. *The Book of Common Prayer* (New York: Protestant Episcopal Church, 1945), 542–43.

took care of him (*epimeleomai*)" (Luke 10:33–34). The Samaritan is a beautiful example for fathers and elders. Taking care of people always demands sacrifice. It includes pity, healing, and embrace. Doubtless the Samaritan had his own busy schedule with a long list of things he needed to get done. But good neighbors—like good fathers and good elders—are willing to be inconvenienced by other people's problems.

The Elder's Experience

The last two qualifications are not simply for the good of the church, but also for the good of the elder himself: "He must not be a recent convert, or he may become puffed up with conceit and fall into the condemnation of the devil" (1 Tim. 3:6). This qualification has to do with spiritual maturity. Paul calls a newly baptized Christian a *neophyte*, which means something like "new growth," or "newly planted."

To illustrate Paul's point, consider the unfortunate mistake that groundskeepers made one summer at Wheaton College in Illinois. After leveling the soccer field, they sowed new grass seed improperly and it all washed away. By the end of August the playing surface was still a dirt patch. New seed was planted and sprang up immediately. All through the autumn the grass grew lush and green. It looked beautiful, but it was not ready to be played on. If it had been used in a soccer match, giant chunks of turf would have come up with every kick. The grass needed to weather the storms of winter before it was ready for use. In the same way, a new Christian is not yet ready to oversee the church. He has not yet endured the winter of spiritual difficulty. The eldership is no place for beginners. As Paul will later say, "do not be hasty in the laying on of hands" (1 Tim. 5:22). It is much better to be short an elder or two than to have a novice on the session.

In examining a man for eldership, a church should count his spiritual age, not his biological age. One young man was interviewed for a position as a senior pastor when he was still in his twenties. The question of his tender years naturally came up in the interview process. However, a young woman from the church rightly pointed out that since the candidate had known the Lord from childhood, he was hardly a recent convert: he had been a Christian for decades. Similarly, when former Dallas Cowboys' star Deion Sanders became a professing Christian in 1997, he wanted to get up and start preaching right away. But in a televised interview he explained that first he wanted to take a month to study the Bible, "or however long it takes." Mr. Sanders underestimated how difficult it is to master the Bible, but he had the right instinct. Although a new convert is full of zeal, he is not ready to be a pastor.

The Greek word for being "puffed up" (*typhōtheis*) originally referred to something that was filled with smoke. It is sometimes taken to mean "puffed up with conceit." New converts grow so fast in the Christian life that they may be tempted to look down on others. Yet pride is the most dangerous of character traits in a minister, who must be the servant of all. There is another way to understand the reference to smoke, however. The danger may be that a new convert will become clouded in his judgment.[20] The smoke of false doctrine can be blinding. In all likelihood, one of the problems with the false teachers in Ephesus was that they were new believers, which helps explain why Paul gave this qualification for elders. A church governed by neophytes will probably end up in a theological fog.

The Elder's Reputation

The last requirement for an elder is that "he must be well thought of by outsiders, so that he may not fall into disgrace, into a snare of the devil" (1 Tim. 3:7). This qualification is a reminder that the church is in the world, and that in the ordination of overseers, some consideration must be given to the non-Christian public. This may explain why so many of the qualifications Paul gives for overseers represent the highest virtues of pagan culture. An elder must have excellent references outside as well as inside the church.

People's impressions of Christ are partly based on his ministers. Ministers have a public role in the community. Unless their lives speak for themselves, no one will ever listen to what they have to say. If people do not think highly of a church's leaders, they will not think highly of the church. The church has enough critics and detractors already without putting scandalous men into the pastorate. John Chrysostom, the great preacher of Constantinople, made an excellent observation about this verse. He pointed out that

20. Bassler, *1 Timothy*, 68.

although Paul and the other apostles were often persecuted, they were never brought up on morals charges. Quite the opposite: "They were slandered as deceivers and impostors, on account of their preaching, and this because they could not attack their moral characters and lives. For why did not one say of the Apostles, that they were fornicators, unclean, or covetous persons, but that they were deceivers, which relates to their preaching only? Must it not be that their lives were irreproachable?"[21]

The way the apostles lived made the message—not the messenger—the issue. This is an example for every believer. How easy it would be to win the world for Christ if every believer behaved like a Christian. As it is, we find ourselves having to defend the followers of the gospel as often as we defend the gospel itself.

Beware of the Devil

The qualifications Paul gives for elders end on an ominous note, with two references to God's archenemy, Satan. If new converts are rushed into office, they may "fall into the condemnation of the devil" (1 Tim. 3:6). Or an elder with a bad reputation may "fall into disgrace, into a snare of the devil" (1 Tim. 3:7).

When the church makes a poor choice of elders, there is always the danger of their falling into devilish behavior. Like Satan, an elder may become proud. Then, like Satan, he would be subject to God's curse on the arrogant and rebellious. Or an elder may fall into a trap set by Satan. Like an unwary bird, he may wander into the fowler's snare.

These warnings lead us to an obvious conclusion: Satan is out to get the elders of the church. This is basic military strategy. Truly, it is the oldest trick in the book. Satan has been using it since the days of Adam. The best way to defeat an army is to attack its command and control. What better way to frustrate God's plans for the church of Jesus Christ than to overthrow the elders he has appointed to lead it?

Consider how effective Satan has been in recent years at damaging the office of elder. First, many ministers have fallen into grievous sin. When a

21. John Chrysostom, "Homilies on the Epistles of St. Paul the Apostle to Timothy, Titus, and Philemon," trans. and ed. Philip Schaff, *Nicene and Post-Nicene Fathers*, First Series, 14 vols. (Peabody, MA: Hendrickson, 1994), 13:439.

minister is disgraced, his ministry is disgraced. Indeed, the entire church of Jesus Christ is brought into disrepute whenever a minister commits a scandalous sin. Second, the eldership has become a battleground for gender rights. The effect of this—besides bringing division—has been to distract the church from the ministry of the Word. Third, many Christians feel they have the right to complain about their elders. Too often, Christians grumble that their elders ought to be doing this or are not doing that. If a teaching or ruling elder is guilty of sin, he is to be disciplined according to the instructions Paul gives in chapter 5. If his ministry can be improved, then pray for him, or, better yet, volunteer to help him with some duty. But complaining about spiritual leaders is what Satan wants people to do, so be careful not to do it!

By making mention of the devil, Paul reminds overseers to be on their guard. Watch out for temptation. Live above reproach. Use good judgment. Practice hospitality. Defend sound doctrine. Be peaceable. Take care of your family. Resist the devil. At the same time, Paul's warning is a reminder to every Christian to pray urgently for the elders of the church, who are subject to the most intense spiritual warfare of all.

I will never forget the way one mature Christian described how he prays for me. He said, "I want you to know I pray for you every day. I feel as if I must do this so that the chain will remain unbroken. I don't have the same sense of urgency with anyone else, but I feel as if we have to gather around you in prayer to protect you from Satan's attacks." These are the words of a man who understands what the devil is up to, and what the elders of the church are up against. Pray accordingly.

9

Qualifications for Deacons

1 Timothy 3:8–13

Deacons likewise must be dignified, not double-tongued, not addicted to much wine, not greedy for dishonest gain. They must hold the mystery of the faith with a clear conscience. . . . For those who serve well as deacons gain a good standing for themselves and also great confidence in the faith that is in Christ Jesus.
(1 Tim. 3:8–9, 13)

Some years ago, a pastoral assistant conducted training for deacons at an urban church. As part of her preparation she telephoned the director of the Philadelphia Restaurant School and asked, "What qualities are you looking for in a waiter?" The director explained that, above all else, a good waiter is someone who notices what people need and gives it to them even before they ask.

It may seem strange to compare deacons to restaurant personnel, but the connection is biblical. The first deacons in Jerusalem were appointed to serve meals:

> Now in these days when the disciples were increasing in number, a complaint by the Hellenists arose against the Hebrews because their widows were being

> neglected in the daily distribution. And the twelve summoned the full number of the disciples and said, "It is not right that we should give up preaching the word of God to serve tables. Therefore, brothers, pick out from among you seven men of good repute, full of the Spirit and of wisdom, whom we will appoint to this duty. But we will devote ourselves to prayer and to the ministry of the word." (Acts 6:1–4)

The word the apostles used for "serving tables" is the Greek word for "deaconing" (*diakonein*). Deacons are the waiters of the church. So the seven men chosen by the apostolic church to serve food were the first deacons.

The election of the first deacons explains the primary difference between elders and deacons. There is a practical division of labor between the only two ordained offices in the church of Jesus Christ (see Phil. 1:1). Like the apostles, elders devote themselves to prayer and the ministry of the word (Acts 6:4). They labor in the spiritual work of intercession and proclamation. Meanwhile, as their title indicates, deacons serve. They take care of people's material needs in a spiritual way. "The office of deacon is not one of rule," says one book on church government, "but rather of service both to the physical and spiritual needs of the people."[1] According to Martin Luther, the diaconate is a ministry "for distributing the Church's bounty to the poor, in order that the priests might be relieved of the burden of temporal concerns."[2] So deacons mainly assist God's people in tangible ways. They "wait on tables," according to one use of the biblical term, which explains why a restaurant school might have something to teach a board of deacons.

A Dignified Life

An even better place to turn for the qualifications of deacons is Paul's first letter to Timothy, where the Bible teaches that a deacon must have a dignified life (1 Tim. 3:8), a sound doctrine (1 Tim. 3:9–10), and a stable family (1 Tim. 3:11–12).

1. *The Book of Church Order of the Presbyterian Church in America*, 5th ed. (Atlanta: Committee for Christian Education and Publications, 1997), 7–2.

2. Martin Luther, *De captivitate Babylonica* (1520), in *D. Martin Luthers Werke* (Weimar edition), 6.566.34–567.5.

The apostle begins by saying a deacon's life must be worthy of respect: "Deacons likewise must be dignified, not double-tongued, not addicted to much wine, not greedy for dishonest gain" (1 Tim. 3:8). This is not the way the world usually chooses its leaders. The virtues listed here have little to do with talents or abilities. They are not the kinds of credentials that show up on most résumés. Instead, the biblical qualifications have to do with a person's morals. God is more concerned with who deacons are than what they do.

The Bible's emphasis on character gives churches some flexibility in deciding what deacons do, as long as their ministry is charitable and compassionate. Calvin preached that "it is certain, that God will have this rule to be observed and kept in his Church, that is to say, that the poor be cared for: and not only that every private man for his own behalf alone by himself do help them which are poor, but that there be a public office, and men appointed to have care of them that are in necessity, that things may be ordered as they ought."[3] In most churches the ministry of deacons includes feeding the poor, caring for the sick, visiting the elderly, and handling cases of benevolence. In some churches they offer transportation, collect the offering, or manage the finances. In an urban neighborhood they may help keep the building secure. Whatever deacons do, the Bible leaves the church to decide; the Bible only dictates how they are to behave.

First, a deacon's life must be "dignified," or worthy of respect. This has to do with diaconal deportment, and is similar to the guideline that elders must be "above reproach" (1 Tim. 3:2). Deacons are to carry themselves with dignity and gravity. They must be respectable both inside and outside the church.

Deacons must not be "double-tongued" (*dilogous*; 1 Tim. 3:8). John Bunyan may have had this verse in mind when he named one of the parsons in *Pilgrim's Progress* "Mr. Two Tongues." Deacons must not engage in double-talk. The word of a deacon ought to be one of the strongest guarantees in the church. People both inside and outside the church must be able to take deacons at their word. Writing in the fifth century, Theodoret thought that being two-tongued meant saying one thing to one person and another thing to someone else.[4] Alternatively, it means saying one thing and then doing

3. John Calvin, *Sermons on the Epistles to Timothy & Titus* (London, 1579; repr. Edinburgh: Banner of Truth, 1983), 297.

4. A. T. Hanson, *The Pastoral Epistles*, New Century Bible Commentary (Grand Rapids: Eerdmans, 1982), 79.

another. Jesus told a parable about people like that: "A man had two sons. And he went to the first and said, 'Son, go and work in the vineyard today.' And he answered, 'I will not,' but afterward he changed his mind and went. And he went to the other son and said the same. And he answered, 'I go, sir,' but did not go" (Matt. 21:28–30). The point of the parable is that *doing* is more important than saying. But neither one of the man's sons would have made a good deacon. Deacons must do what they say they will do. They cannot be two-faced.

One reason deacons must be careful what they say is that they know so much about people's private affairs. In his *Historical Commentary on the Pastoral Epistles*, Sir William Ramsay described the temptations that can arise:

> Now there can be no doubt that the work of deacons was more closely connected with the indoor and family life of members of the congregation than the work of presbyters. The deacons had more intimate duties in the administration of charity and help where it was needed. They had to find out the needs of individuals, to go about among the members of the congregation, and to converse and to sympathize with them. There was great temptation to say too much to one person or in one family, and thus to be betrayed into inconsistency and self-contradiction in speaking to another. Nothing is easier than for a person to slip into the fault of double-tonguedness when he is trying to accommodate himself to various families in one congregation.[5]

Since I serve as a pastor in the city, people regularly approach me for financial assistance. Often, after we pray together, I say, "This is a matter for the deacons. May I explain your situation to one of them?" When I share the need, I love to hear a deacon say, "I will take care of this." I take the deacon's word for it; the problem will be resolved—unless, of course, it is only double-talk, which is why deacons must be sincere.

Deacons must not be "addicted to much wine" (1 Tim. 3:8). As usual, the Bible puts things in just the right way. Deacons are not forbidden to drink wine altogether, because God permits Christians to drink some wine (e.g. 1 Tim. 5:23). But he does want his people—especially his officers in his church—to be sober.

5. William M. Ramsay, *Historical Commentary on the Pastoral Epistles*, ed. Mark Wilson (Grand Rapids: Kregel, 1996), 79.

The next qualification is fiscal. Deacons are not to be "greedy for dishonest gain" (1 Tim. 3:8). Like their elders, they must not be in love with money (see 1 Tim. 3:3). The reason for this is obvious. Deacons handle some of the finances of the church, often in secret. Since the days of the early church, deacons have collected and distributed alms for the poor. To this day, many churches collect offerings for diaconal work immediately following the Lord's Supper. This is a good way for Christians to show their gratitude to God for salvation in Christ, and also a good way to care for the poor. Deacons hold the money they receive from such offerings in sacred trust. It would be an outrageous sin to use it for personal advantage. By definition, a deacon is someone who serves, not someone who helps himself. In the use of money, as in the use of words and alcohol, a deacon must lead a dignified life.

A Sound Doctrine

Qualifications for service begin with conduct, but that is not where they end. Deacons must have sound doctrine as well as dignified lives: "They must hold the mystery of the faith with a clear conscience" (1 Tim. 3:9). In other words, deacons must be orthodox in their theology.

When the New Testament speaks of "mystery," it is not referring to things the church is still trying to figure out. The gospel is not a theological "whodunit." Rather, a mystery is something long hidden but now revealed. It refers to "the secret thoughts, plans, and dispensations of God that are hidden from the human reason, as well as from all other comprehension below the divine level, and hence must be revealed to those for whom they are intended."[6] The mystery of all mysteries is the eternal plan of salvation that God has revealed in Jesus Christ. Perhaps the best example of this way of talking about salvation comes at the end of Romans, where Paul speaks of "my gospel and the preaching of Jesus Christ, according to the revelation of the mystery that was kept secret for long ages but has now been disclosed and through the prophetic writings has been made known to all nations, according to the command of the eternal God, to bring about the obedience of faith" (Rom.

6. William F. Arndt and F. Wilbur Gingrich, *A Greek-English Lexicon of the New Testament and Other Early Christian Literature*, 2d ed. (Chicago: University of Chicago Press, 1979), 530.

16:25–26). The mystery Paul was writing about is not something that we don't know; it is something we *do* know for our salvation.

What are some of the mysteries or deep truths of the faith? They are the basic doctrines of Christianity: That one God exists in three persons—Father, Son, and Holy Spirit. That God created everything there is out of nothing. That humanity sinned against God and has thereby come under judgment. That out of his great love, God the Father sent God the Son into the world to save sinners. That Jesus Christ is both God and man. That Jesus gave his life as an atoning sacrifice when he died on the cross for sins. That everyone who believes in the Son by the power of the Spirit receives eternal life. And that these mysteries are revealed in the Bible, which is the infallible Word of God. Deacons must believe and defend these basic principles of the Christian faith.

The reason deacons have to be sound in their doctrine is their influence in the church. Deacons do not have the same kind of teaching authority elders have. Notice one difference between the qualifications for these two offices: only the elders must be "able to teach" (1 Tim. 3:2). In fact, the reason deacons were appointed in the first place was so that elders could devote themselves "to prayer and to the ministry of the word" (Acts 6:4). Nevertheless, deacons are teachers. As William Ramsay explained, "That the deacon should have proved himself apt to teach is not required; but this does not mean that teaching was outside of his sphere of duty."[7]

What are some of the ways that a deacon may teach? When deacons visit prisoners or the sick, they bring spiritual encouragement. Often they teach people how to manage their personal affairs in a biblical way, especially their finances. Deacons also teach others how to serve. They do not have to accomplish all of the mercy ministry themselves, but they are responsible to make sure that it all gets done. So by word and by example they teach the church how to serve. In the words of one manual for diaconal service, "It is their duty to develop the grace of liberality in the members of the church."[8] Then deacons must be ready to evangelize. The first deacons, like Stephen and Philip (Acts 7–8), were great evangelists. So whenever deacons help the poor, they do it in the name of Jesus Christ, with a testimony of his saving power.

7. Ramsay, *Historical Commentary*, 78.
8. *Book of Church Order*, 9–2.

Otherwise, the church becomes just another social service. To carry out their ministry of discipleship and evangelism, deacons must hold on to the deep truths of the faith.

They are to do this with a good conscience (unlike the false teachers in Ephesus who rejected "faith and a good conscience"; see 1 Tim. 1:19). Deacons must not be dubious in their doctrine. Instead, they must know the fundamentals of the faith, and if they ever begin to doubt them, they ought to seek the help and correction of their elders. This is why, when they are ordained in the Presbyterian Church in America, deacons answer the following question in the affirmative:

> Do you sincerely receive and adopt the *Confession of Faith* and the *Catechisms* of this Church, as containing the system of doctrine taught in the Holy Scriptures; and do you further promise that if at any time you find yourself out of accord with any of the fundamentals of this system of doctrine, you will, on your initiative, make known to your Session the change which has taken place in your views since the assumption of this ordination vow?[9]

The best way to find out if deacons are sound in their doctrine is to examine them before they take office: "And let them also be tested first; then let them serve as deacons if they prove themselves blameless" (1 Tim. 3:10). Similarly, when the first seven deacons were chosen by the church in Jerusalem, they were "men of good repute, full of the Spirit and of wisdom" (Acts 6:3). No accusation could justly be brought against them.

The fact that deacons must be tested proves that their role in the church was official. The New Testament uses the word "deacon" (*diakonos*) loosely to describe anyone who serves. Paul even uses it to describe his own ministry as an apostle (see 2 Cor. 6:4). But at least by the end of Paul's ministry, "deacon" had become a recognized office in the church.

The Bible gives freedom by not specifying how such officers are to be examined. Scrutiny is mandatory, according to the standards listed in this passage. How the scrutiny takes place is left to the discretion of the church. Often, deacons prove their worth by serving in other ministries. This is a universal principle of Christian ministry: the way to prepare for greater

9. *Book of Church Order*, 24–4.

service is to be diligent in some lesser service. Faithful ministry is both rewarded by God and recognized by the church. At one annual congregational meeting new candidates for the office of deacon were to be presented to the church. However, when it was time for them to be introduced, they were nowhere to be found. They were finally discovered in the kitchen, busily washing the dishes from the congregational dinner. Of course! Where else would one expect to find future deacons?

Most churches have a procedure for identifying and ordaining deacons. In Presbyterian churches deacons are nominated by members of the church, examined by their elders, and then elected by the congregation. But however it is done, a deacon's life and doctrine must be approved. Deacons may serve in the church only if their soundness and respectability are beyond question.

A Stable Family

The rest of the qualifications for deacons are domestic. If they are married, deacons must have stable families: "Their wives likewise must be dignified, not slanderers, but sober-minded, faithful in all things. Let deacons each be the husband of one wife, managing their children and their own households well" (1 Tim. 3:11–12).

More will be said about these wives in a moment, but the reason they are addressed at all is the privacy of diaconal work. Marvin Vincent wisely observes that a deacon's wife "would sustain an active relation to his office, and by her ministries would increase his efficiency, and by frivolity, slander, or intemperance, would bring him and his office into disrepute."[10] Presumably some men should not be ordained as deacons because their wives are not suitable for them to serve as officers in the church.

The deacon himself must be "the husband of one wife" (1 Tim. 3:12). This standard has to do with marital fidelity. It does not mean that bachelors are ineligible for the office of deacon, but it does mean that a deacon is a one-woman man. If he is unmarried, he must maintain sexual purity. If he is married, he must be monogamous. Obviously, polygamists are not allowed

10. Marvin R. Vincent, *Word Studies in the New Testament*, 2d ed., 4 vols. (1888; repr. Peabody, MA: Hendrickson, n.d.), 4:236.

to serve as deacons. Nor can a man serve who has divorced on anything except biblical grounds (see Matt. 5:32; 19:9). However, this qualification is also positive. A deacon must really be a husband to his wife, physically, spiritually, and emotionally. He must love her and serve her. He must give himself to her the way Christ gave himself to the church (Eph. 5:25–28). How can he serve the people of God if he is not serving his own wife?

In addition to being a good husband, a deacon must be a good father. Again, this does not mean that men without children may not serve as deacons. It does mean that deacons are to discipline their children with love. Since households included servants in those days, this verse also touches upon a man's working relationships. How can a deacon be respectable in the church if he is not respectable in the marketplace?

The reason for these high standards is that the church is "the household of God" (1 Tim. 3:15). Therefore, one of the best ways to tell if a man is ready to be a deacon is to see how he conducts his own household. Is he devoted to his wife? Does he nurture his children? Does he care for his colleagues? Is the name of Jesus Christ exalted in his home and at his workplace? A man who cannot manage his own household well will bring disorder to God's house.

What about Deaconesses?

More needs to be said about the "wives" of deacons (1 Tim. 3:11). The Greek word that Paul uses here is *gynaikas*, which can mean either "wives" or "women" (as it is translated several times in 1 Timothy 2:9–12). Some scholars suggest, therefore, that in verse 11 *gynaikas* does not refer to wives but to deaconesses, or female deacons. So the question arises whether women served as deaconesses in the New Testament church.

The strongest reason for thinking that these women were deaconesses is the way they are introduced. Both verse 8 and verse 11 contain the word "likewise" (*hōsautōs*), which sounds as if it introduces a new office. Furthermore, these women are to be "dignified" (1 Tim. 3:11), which is the same phrase used to describe deacons (1 Tim. 3:8). Both of these verses are grammatically dependent on the main verb in verse 2, which strengthens the connection between them. Taken together, these parallels make it sound as if the women Paul had in mind were to fulfill a separate but equal office in the church. Furthermore, if the Bible meant "wives," we might expect it to say "*their* wives" so as to eliminate any possibility of confusion.

Nevertheless, there are several reasons for thinking that "wives" may be the better translation. The first is that if Paul meant deaconesses he would have said so. The word "woman" is such a common term that it hardly seems sufficient to designate an office in the church.[11] Furthermore, the word *gynaikas* appears in the very next verse (1 Tim. 3:12; cf. 3:2), where it clearly means "wife." It would make perfect sense, therefore, for Paul to have the same women in view in both verses. Then there is the fact that the instructions for these women (or wives) are very brief. One short verse hardly seems adequate to cover the qualifications for deaconesses, especially since it is embedded within the qualifications for deacons.

We are bound to conclude that by itself, 1 Timothy 3:11 is not sufficient to prove that women should serve in the office of deaconess. Indeed, the very fact that these women are singled out from the deacons shows that the ministry of these women must not be identical to that of the deacons. Donald Guthrie gives a balanced summary: "The reference is too general to postulate with certainty a distinct order of deaconesses, but some feminine ministration was necessary in visitation. . . . For such work certain moral qualities would be essential whether for deacons' wives or for deaconesses in their own right."[12] Since the meaning is not certain, perhaps it is best to translate the word *gynaikas* as "women helpers." Indeed, it is possible to argue that these women were neither deacon's wives, nor deaconesses, but women who assisted the deacons.

If the office of deaconess is not established in 1 Timothy 3, the diaconal ministry of women is certainly present elsewhere in the Bible. New Testament women frequently carried out diaconal ministry, in the broad sense of the word. Consider Dorcas, who was "full of good works and acts of charity" (Acts 9:36). Or Lydia, who clothed the Philippians in purple (16:11–15). Or Tryphena and Tryphosa, women described as "workers in the Lord" (Rom. 16:12). Or especially Phoebe, who was "a patron of many" and is identified as "a servant of the church at Cenchreae"—literally, "a deaconess"

11. Philip H. Towner, *1–2 Timothy and Titus*, IVP New Testament Commentary Series (Downers Grove, IL: InterVarsity, 1994), 91.

12. Donald Guthrie, *The Pastoral Epistles*, Tyndale New Testament Commentaries (Downers Grove, IL: InterVarsity, 1957), 85.

(Rom. 16:1–2). To summarize, many New Testament women carried out diaconal ministry and one, at least, was called a "deaconess," even if she was not ordained as an officer of the church. The obvious conclusion is that, whatever title they are given, women must be deeply involved in the mercy ministries of the church.

It is helpful to recognize that deaconesses have been a longstanding tradition in the church. In Egypt during the second century they "provided nursing mothers who sat in the public squares, often under pagan statues, while other women went up and down the streets to collect the unwanted babies abandoned in the night. They brought them, nursed, bathed and raised them."[13] Such ministry was characteristic of women throughout the Christian world, at least by the third century. In his survey of the women's ministry in the early church, J. M. Ross shows that deaconesses served as doorkeepers, visited the sick, helped when women were baptized, and cared for orphans.[14] In the fourth century, John Chrysostom described the order of deaconesses to be "necessary and useful and honorable in the Church."[15]

Closer to our own times, Benjamin Breckinridge Warfield was a strong proponent of women deacons. Warfield taught at Princeton and was among the leading conservative evangelicals at the turn of the twentieth century. He based his argument for deaconesses partly on the example of Phoebe, and partly on a letter from the Roman governor Pliny to the Emperor Trajan. The letter, which was written around AD 112, referred to women as holding a servant office in the church. Warfield's conclusion was that these women "constituted a female diaconate similar to and of like standing with the board of deacons which, in the New Testament, we find in every church."[16]

The church of Warfield's day did not ordain women to serve as deaconesses, but Warfield himself recognized the need for putting the gifts of women into service. He believed that returning women to the ministry of deaconess would restore order in the church. To that end, he quoted his colleague Dr. Alexander McGill approvingly: "If the people of a particular church would simply elect

13. Ray Bakke, *A Theology as Big as the City* (Downers Grove, IL: InterVarsity, 1997), 192.

14. J. M. Ross, "A Reconsideration of the Diaconate," *Scottish Journal of Theology* 12 (1959): 153.

15. John Chrysostom, "Homilies on the Epistles of St. Paul the Apostle to Timothy, Titus, and Philemon," trans. and ed. Philip Schaff, *Nicene and Post-Nicene Fathers*, First Series, 14 vols. (Peabody, MA: Hendrickson, 1994), 13:441.

16. Benjamin Breckinridge Warfield, "Presbyterian Deaconesses," *Presbyterian Review* (1889), 286.

women as well as men to the office of deacon, making one board or two separate boards, at their pleasure, of course ordained with the same vows and responsible to the same authority . . . the order is restored."[17]

The practice of the Presbyterian Church in America may come close to what the Bible teaches. Only men are ordained to the office of deacon, in keeping with the view that the women in 1 Timothy 3:11 are wives rather than deaconesses (or else that they are women who assist the deacons). Yet the elders are encouraged to "select and appoint godly men and women of the congregation to assist the deacons in caring for the sick, the widows, the orphans, the prisoners, and others who may be in any distress or need."[18] The church thus permits congregations to commission women to the ministry of diaconal service, whatever that ministry may be called.

If women are to serve, they must be qualified. Therefore, they should display the characteristics described in 1 Timothy 3:11. As the proverb says, "What's good for the goose is good for the gander." In this case, what is good for the deacon is good for the deaconess. Thus the biblical instructions for the women echo what has already been said to the men. The wives of deacons (or deaconesses) are to be "dignified, not slanderers, but sober-minded, faithful in all things" (1 Tim. 3:11).

According to 1 Timothy 3:11, the women who serve in diaconal ministry must be "dignified" or respectable. They must be women who are held in high regard both inside and outside the church. They must not be "slanderers" (*diabolous*)—a word for malicious talk or false accusation that is sometimes used of the devil himself (e.g. Rev. 12:9–10). The reason for this qualification has been mentioned already. Diaconal work often involves personal matters. The private affairs of a house should remain private, except insofar as they require the spiritual care of church officers. Women who serve must not be gossips. To give a further qualification, they must be "sober-minded." This refers not simply to alcohol, but to self-control in every area of life. The wives of deacons (or deaconesses) must not be self-indulgent in their use of food, clothing, or possessions. They must be stable emotionally. And these women must be trustworthy, "faithful in all things." They must be utterly reliable and completely dependable.

17. Ibid., 287.

18. *Book of Church Order*, 9–7.

The ministry of such women is vital to the health of the church. If the problem with feminist theology has been its failure to submit to divine order, the traditional church has often failed to employ the gifts of women to their full biblical extent. Here are B. B. Warfield's last words on the subject: "A living church cannot do without Deaconesses as its organs for doing good. Deaconesses cannot do without the church as the appointed organization for doing good in the world."[19] Whether they are called deaconesses or not, women should exercise servant ministry to the glory of God. They should "minister to those who are in need, to the sick, to the friendless, and to any who may be in distress."[20]

A Deacon's Reward

Diaconal work is very demanding. The standards of the office are high. The duties of the office are difficult. Sometimes deacons and deaconesses get tired of meeting the same needs over and over again. Other times they are perplexed about what mercy means in a particular situation. Over time, they may become discouraged in their service.

Perhaps because of the difficulty of the office, the biblical qualifications for deacons end with an encouraging promise: "Those who serve well as deacons gain a good standing for themselves and also great confidence in the faith that is in Christ Jesus" (1 Tim. 3:13). Although much of a deacon's work is done in private, it is noticed and commended by God.

The word for "standing" (*bathmos*) is a word for a degree, rank, or grade. It is hard to know exactly what that means in this case. It might mean that the best deacons will be promoted to the office of elder, but that is doubtful. Deacons are not elders-in-training. The diaconate is a separate office, having its own dignity and requiring its own gifts. Some deacons may well become elders as they mature in the faith, but some of the best deacons should remain deacons for life because that is what they are called and gifted to do. Another possibility is that "good standing" refers to one's reputation. Thus, deacons who serve well gain spiritual influence in the

19. Benjamin Breckinridge Warfield, "The Deaconess as a Part of the Church," *Our Church Work* (1903), in Ronald G. Lutjens, "B. B. Warfield on Women Deacons," *Presbyterian Journal* (May 15, 1985), 8.

20. *Book of Church Order*, 9–2.

church. Or it may even refer to their standing before God. God gives honor to worthy deacons, in both this life and the life to come. Either way, it is an encouraging prospect.

To this is added a second promise. Deacons who serve well gain "great confidence in the faith that is in Christ Jesus" (1 Tim. 3:13). This confidence (*parrēsian*) is boldness or assurance. It might mean that deacons become bold in their Christian testimony. More probably, it refers to boldness before God. For those who sometimes doubt their salvation, this is an important lesson to learn. Assurance of faith does not come through introspection, but through service. Those who labor for the Lord most actively love him most confidently.

What use should be made of the biblical qualifications for deacons? First, they are a guide for the church. They help Christians know what to look for when it comes time for deacons to be nominated or elected. Second, these qualifications are the divine standard for deacons. They are a reminder of how God expects them to behave and what he expects them to believe. They would be good for a deacon (or deaconess) to post by the mirror or paste to the inside of a Bible. Finally, these qualifications are a worthy goal for anyone who might eventually become an officer in the church. Make yourself available to serve the Lord. Ask the Holy Spirit to make your life dignified, your doctrine sound, and your family stable. Even if you never become a deacon, your time will not have been wasted. The qualifications for deacons are simply the virtues of a Christian exercised to a supreme degree.

It will always be something of a disappointment to me that I never became a deacon. At the end of my senior year in college I was asked to serve as a deacon in the church, but I was shortly to leave for seminary, and thus could not stand for election. To this day, I feel a sense of loss, because to wait on tables in the name of Christ is one of life's highest callings. The diaconate is the ecclesiastical office that most closely resembles the servanthood of Jesus Christ. In fact, Jesus sometimes used the word "deacon" (*diakonos*) to describe his own ministry: "Whoever would be great among you must be your deacon, and whoever would be first among you must be slave of all. For even the Son of Man came not to receive diaconal care, but to serve as a deacon, and to give his life as a ransom for many" (author's paraphrase of Mark 10:43–45; cf. Luke 22:27; Rom. 15:8).

Deacons serve because Jesus first served them. As T. F. Torrance has written:

> It is only in this Jesus that we learn what *diakonia* really is, the loving service in mercy that looks for no reward beyond the knowledge that we do what is commanded of us and looks for no thanks from those to whom mercy is extended, but it is only because this Jesus has made our cause His very own, sharing our existence in servitude and sharing with us His own life of love, that we may and can engage in this kind of *diakonia* in Him.[21]

21. T. F. Torrance, "Service in Jesus Christ," in *Service in Christ*, ed. James I. McCord and T. H. L. Parker (London: Epworth, 1966), 3.

10

The Great Mystery of Godliness

1 Timothy 3:14–16

He was manifested in the flesh,
vindicated by the Spirit,
seen by angels,
proclaimed among the nations,
believed on in the world,
taken up in glory. (1 Tim. 3:16)

The truth is not as true as it used to be. Sometimes it may even be falsehood. During one White House scandal, a prominent lawyer was asked if his client was telling the truth. "Tell us what the truth is," the reporter demanded. "The truth is what is in that deposition," answered the lawyer, "unless we make a deal with the prosecutor and say something else." In other words, "the truth" is something that may or may not actually be true. It is something to manipulate for personal gain.

Sadly, lawyers and politicians are not the only ones who do not know the difference between truth and falsehood. In his book *No Place for Truth, or,*

Whatever Happened to Evangelical Theology? David Wells argues that the church is weak because it has "exchanged the sensibilities of modern culture for the truth of Christ."[1] If Wells is right, then the church is no longer the church. For in the process of explaining his purpose for writing to Timothy, the apostle Paul defines the church by its relationship to the truth: "I hope to come to you soon, but I am writing these things to you so that, if I delay, you may know how one ought to behave in the household of God, which is the church of the living God, a pillar and buttress of truth" (1 Tim. 3:14–15).

Order in the House

Paul was planning to visit Ephesus before long. But in case he was detained—by an arrest, perhaps, or yet another shipwreck—he wanted Timothy to know how to carry out his pastoral duties in the meantime. Since 1 Timothy was a public letter, it seems he also wanted to remind the Ephesians to support their pastor by behaving themselves in the household of God. From what we have seen in 1 Timothy so far, the kind of conduct the apostle has in mind includes proper doctrine (1 Tim. 1:1–20), proper gender relations (1 Tim. 2:1–15), and proper spiritual leadership (1 Tim. 3:1–13) in the church.

It is not certain precisely how this letter fits with Paul's itinerary in the book of Acts. Nor is it known if his travels ever brought him back through Ephesus after all. But in the providence of God, Paul's uncertainty led him to write this letter, and the Holy Spirit has used it ever since to tell Christians all over the world "what kind of conduct befits a member of God's household" (1 Tim. 3:15 NAB). "Household" is an image that comes up repeatedly in 1 Timothy and throughout the New Testament (e.g. Gal. 3:26–4:7; 1 Tim. 3:4–5). The members of the true church are sons and daughters of God the Father. Having been born again through faith in God's Son, we have been adopted into his family by the Holy Spirit. Therefore, we are brothers and sisters in Christ. Each and every one of us has a place of fellowship and service in God's household.

Second, the church is God's residence—what Paul calls "the church of the living God" (1 Tim. 3:15; cf. Josh. 3:10). In other words, the church is not

1. David F. Wells, *No Place for Truth, or, Whatever Happened to Evangelical Theology?* (Grand Rapids: Eerdmans, 1993), 217.

simply God's household; it is also his house. "There are good reasons why God should call the Church His House," writes Calvin, "for not only has He received us as His sons by the grace of adoption, but He Himself dwells in the midst of us."[2] Here Paul may well have been reminding the Ephesians what he told them in an earlier letter: "In him you also are being built together into a dwelling place for God by the Spirit" (Eph. 2:22; cf. 2 Cor. 6:16). The church is the house that God built.

The promise that God makes his home in his church must have been of special encouragement to the Ephesians, who worshiped within the shadow of the temple of the goddess Diana. Diana's temple in Ephesus was one of the Seven Wonders of the Ancient World. But however impressive it seemed from the outside, it was utterly devoid of life. The goddess in the temple was nothing more than a dead idol. By contrast, Paul wanted to remind the Ephesians that the church of Jesus Christ is the *real* temple. The living God does not dwell in temples built by human hands (cf. Acts 17:24). He lives among his people, especially in their public worship. Whenever Christians gather for prayer and praise, for Word and sacrament, God takes up residence among them. To put it in the vernacular, God is in the house.

This is why Christian worship properly begins with a prayer of invocation. In the invocation, a church invites the Holy Spirit to enter its house of worship with power. If the church is true to God's Word, the Spirit will always make his presence known. Whenever visitors enter a church where the Spirit of God is present with the people of God in worship, they say, "Surely God is in this place!"

THE PILLAR OF TRUTH

The church is not only a home for God and for his people; it is also a home for God's truth. Paul continues his temple imagery with a third definition of the church: it is "a pillar and buttress of truth" (1 Tim. 3:15). Roman Catholic theologians often use this verse to argue against the Reformation doctrine of *sola scriptura*. "See," they say, "the *church* is the foundation for the truth. Therefore, Scripture is not the only rule of faith and practice, as

2. John Calvin, *The Second Epistle of Paul the Apostle to the Corinthians and the Epistles to Timothy, Titus and Philemon*, trans. T. A. Smail, Calvin's Commentaries (Edinburgh: Oliver & Boyd, 1964), 231.

Protestants say. We must obey church tradition as well as the Bible. The truth rests upon the church, and not the other way around."

One problem with the Catholic view of this verse is that it forgets Paul's previous letter to the Ephesians: "You are fellow citizens with the saints and members of the household of God, built on the foundation of the apostles and prophets, Christ Jesus himself being the cornerstone" (Eph. 2:19–20). The ultimate bedrock foundation of the church is the Word of God spoken by the prophets of the Old Testament, written by the apostles of the New Testament, and made incarnate by God's own Son. How can the church be the foundation of the truth if the truth is the foundation of the church?

Notice further that one of the words Paul uses to describe the church in 1 Timothy 3:15 is the word "buttress" (*hedraiōma*). A buttress is not a building's foundation, but part of its supporting structure. To be specific, a buttress helps to stabilize the walls and pillars of a large building. In the same way, the church of Jesus Christ helps to hold the truth steady. The people of God are people of the truth. In opposition to every form of false teaching, they support truth in the world.

The other word Paul uses to describe the relationship between the church and orthodoxy is the word "pillar" (*stylos*). The architectural function of pillars is well known: they hold up the roof. So to say that the church is the pillar (and buttress) of the truth is to say that it lifts up the truth for all the world to see. As John Stott says, "The purpose of pillars is not only to hold the roof firm, but to thrust it high so that it can be clearly seen even from a distance. . . . Just so, the church holds the truth aloft, so that it is seen and admired by the world. Indeed, as pillars lift a building high while remaining themselves unseen, so the church's function is not to advertise itself but to advertise and display the truth."[3] Thus the truth that the church is a "pillar of the truth" is not so much a doctrinal truth as it is a practical truth.[4] Over against the Roman Catholic view that the church *determines* the truth, the Bible teaches that the church *displays* the truth.

It may be significant that the Greek omits the definite article: verse 15 reads "*a* pillar" rather than "the pillar." Every Christian congregation is one

3. John Stott, *Guard the Truth: The Message of 1 Timothy and Titus* (Downers Grove, IL: InterVarsity, 1996), 105.

4. This insight comes from a 1998 Bible exposition workshop that London's Dick Lucas taught at College Church in Wheaton, Illinois.

pillar of truth. The Ephesians were reminded of this every time they saw the temple of Diana, which had more than one hundred Ionic columns in all, each six stories high. So many pillars were needed because the entire roof was made of marble. Without all of these pillars the temple would collapse, rather than remaining visible for miles around. Similarly, every church is a pillar that helps to bolster the truth of Jesus Christ by holding it up for the world.

A GREAT MYSTERY

If the church is a pillar and buttress of the truth, it needs to know what the truth is, and the truth is a great mystery: "Great indeed, we confess, is the mystery of godliness" (1 Tim. 3:16). When the Bible uses the word "mystery" it is not referring to something that is unsolved, but to something long hidden that has now been revealed (cf. Rom. 16:25–26; 1 Tim. 3:9). In the Bible, a mystery is the secret plan of redemption which is no longer secret because God has divulged it.

The mysteries concerning Jesus Christ are profound; they are "great beyond all question" (1 Tim. 3:16 REB). The greatness of the mysteries of the gospel is demonstrable and "undeniable."[5] There is no doubt about it. The mysteries of the gospel are great by common consent. Almost certainly, this was another attack on the goddess Diana. During Paul's first visit to Ephesus, the silversmiths felt threatened by his missionary work, so they sent the city into an uproar. As many as twenty thousand people crowded into the theater at Ephesus, where "they all cried out with one voice, 'Great is Artemis of the Ephesians!' " (Acts 19:34). They shouted this slogan so long and so loud that their words were still ringing in Paul's ears when he wrote this letter. Paul knew the meaning of true greatness, however, so he wrote: "Great indeed, we confess, is the mystery of godliness" (1 Tim. 3:16). His very phrasing helps convey the glory and grandeur of the gospel, for the mystery is Jesus himself. This is the truth that the church is called to uphold in the world: the saving mystery of the gospel of Jesus Christ.

5. Walter Bauer, *A Greek-English Lexicon of the New Testament and Other Early Christian Literature*, 2d ed., ed. by William F. Arndt, F. Wilbur Gingrich, and Frederick W. Danker (Chicago: University of Chicago Press, 1979), 569.

The mystery of Jesus Christ is described in six lines that sound like part of an early creed, confession, or catechism. Because the lines are rhythmic, and because their first words all rhyme, it is often thought that this verse formed part of an early Christian hymn:

> He was manifested in the flesh,
> vindicated by the Spirit,
> seen by angels,
> proclaimed among the nations,
> believed on in the world,
> taken up in glory. (1 Tim. 3:16)

In order to capture their liturgical quality, Walter Lock has put these lines into English verse:

> In flesh unveiled to mortals' sight,
> Kept righteous by the Spirit's might,
> While angels watched him from the sky:
> His heralds sped from shore to shore,
> And men believed, the wide world o'er,
> When he in glory passed on high.[6]

These lines deserve careful study, especially since scholars disagree about how they should be divided. One suggestion is to separate the creed into two stanzas, each three lines long. The first stanza refers to the earthly ministry of Jesus Christ (he was "manifested," "vindicated," and "seen"), while the second stanza refers to the work of Jesus Christ after his ascension (he was "proclaimed," "believed on," and "taken up").

Walter Lock, who follows this two-part structure, calls the first stanza "The Life of the Incarnate Lord" ("as seen on earth, as watched from heaven") and the second stanza "The Life of the Ascended Lord" ("as preached on earth, as lived in heaven").[7] Gordon Fee describes the difference between them like this: "The first stanza sings Christ's earthly ministry, concluding

6. Walter Lock, *A Critical and Exegetical Commentary on the Pastoral Epistles (I & II Timothy and Titus)*, International Critical Commentary (Edinburgh: T & T Clark, 1924), 42.

7. Ibid., 45.

with a word of triumph and glorification. Similarly, the second stanza sings the ongoing ministry of Christ through his church, concluding again with the theme of glorification. In a certain sense both stanzas reflect the theme of humiliation and exaltation."[8]

Other scholars point out that the lines come in pairs or couplets. In each case, there is a contrast between earth and heaven: "flesh" and "Spirit," "angels" and "nations," "world" and "glory." This suggestion may also have some merit, although the contrast between "angels" and "nations" seems somewhat forced.

Since it is not certain how to subdivide the verse, perhaps it is better not to try. This hymn—if it is a hymn—is a short history of Jesus Christ. It contains the gospel truth about his work of salvation in outline form. Each line describes a different period or event in his life and ministry. Therefore, it seems best to understand these statements in chronological order.

He Appeared in a Body

Paul begins by saying, "He was manifested in the flesh" (1 Tim. 3:16; cf. 2 Tim. 1:10). The best and oldest manuscripts say "Who" rather than "He," but the meaning of the verse is the same in either case: God was manifested in physical form.[9]

God the Son had lived in all the splendor of his deity from eternity past (cf. Phil. 2:6–8). Then he became a man, identical to us in his physical body. This is the mystery of the incarnation: God the Son became the God-man. By taking upon himself human flesh and blood, he became one person with two natures: a divine nature and a human nature. Calvin described his epiphany like this:

> Thus is Jesus Christ true God, in so much as he was the wisdom of God before the world was made, and before all everlastingness. Now it is said, that he was made manifest in the flesh. By this word *flesh*, Saint Paul giveth us to understand that he was true man, and put upon him our nature. But

8. Gordon D. Fee, *1 and 2 Timothy, Titus*, New International Biblical Commentary (Peabody, MA: Hendrickson, 1988), 94.

9. See Bruce M. Metzger, *A Textual Commentary on the Greek New Testament*, corr. ed. (Stuttgart: United Bible Societies, 1975), 641.

> yet he showeth by this word, *manifested*, that there are two natures in him. And yet we may not imagine, that there is one Jesus Christ which is God, and another Jesus Christ which is man: but we must know him only God and man.[10]

Since God the Son appeared as a man, everything he did on this earth he did in a real human body. The events of the passion of Jesus Christ were physical events. His cheek was kissed by his betrayer. His face was spit upon. His body was struck and slapped. His back was flogged. His brow was pierced by thorns. His head was struck with a staff. As the Scripture says, "Christ suffered in the flesh" (1 Peter 4:1).

Christ even died in the flesh. It was a real body that was nailed with real nails to a cross of real wood. It was a real body that was punished for sin: "He himself bore our sins in his body on the tree" (1 Peter 2:24). Then it was a real body—a corpse—that was taken down from the cross, wrapped in linen, and laid in a tomb. God the Son did not just appear in a body; the body in which he appeared was crucified, dead, and buried.

Vindicated by the Spirit

God the Son did not remain in the grave, however; he was "vindicated by the Spirit" (1 Tim. 3:16). In other words, the Holy Spirit confirmed and proved that Jesus Christ is God's own Son and the Savior of the world by raising him from the dead.

Some scholars think that this part of the creed refers again to the incarnation. In that case, the word "spirit" would refer to the human spirit of Jesus. However, although it is true that Jesus Christ had a spirit as well as a body, what is emphasized here is that he was *vindicated* by the Spirit.

When was Jesus vindicated? The Holy Spirit proved Jesus was who he claimed to be throughout his earthly ministry. The Spirit proved it at Jesus' baptism, when he descended upon him from heaven like a dove (Matt. 3:16). He proved it by preserving Jesus from sin throughout his earthly ministry. He proved it whenever he performed miracles, especially when he drove out

10. John Calvin, *Sermons on the Epistles to Timothy & Titus* (London, 1579; repr. Edinburgh: Banner of Truth, 1983), 325.

demons. "But if it is by the Spirit of God that I cast out demons," Jesus said, "then the kingdom of God has come upon you" (Matt. 12:28).

The Spirit vindicated the Son in all these ways, but most of all he did it through the resurrection. When Christians think about the resurrection, we usually think first of God the Son, who was raised up from the grave. We may even remember that it was God the Father who raised him. But Easter Sunday is also a day to praise God the Holy Spirit. The resurrection was such an important event that it required the work of each and every member of the Trinity. God the Father raised God the Son from the dead by the power of God the Holy Spirit: "Christ died for sins once for all, the righteous for the unrighteous, to bring you to God. He was put to death in the body but made alive by the Spirit" (1 Peter 3:18 NIV; cf. Rom. 8:11). Although Jesus laid down his life to take it up again (see John 10:18), he did not raise himself by himself. He was raised from the dead by his Father (e.g. Acts 2:24; Rom. 10:9), but this was done through the Spirit. The Holy Spirit was the one who gave life and glory to the dead body of Jesus Christ.

When the Holy Spirit raised Jesus from the dead, he confirmed that everything Jesus ever said or did was true. Although Jesus Christ was rejected by the world, he was approved by the Spirit. The Spirit vindicated the Son by raising him from the dead. The word for "vindication" is also the word for "justification," which is why the King James Version says Jesus was "justified in the Spirit" (1 Tim. 3:16). Justification is a legal declaration. In this case, it means that by his resurrection Jesus was declared to be the Son of God and the Savior of the world. As the apostle Paul explained on another occasion, Jesus "was declared to be the Son of God in power according to the Spirit of holiness by his resurrection from the dead" (Rom. 1:4). The resurrection was the Holy Spirit's verification that Jesus is the Christ.

Seen by Angels

After Jesus was "vindicated by the Spirit" he was "seen by angels" (1 Tim. 3:16). The word "angels" (*angelos*) usually means what it says. It refers to the principalities and powers of the unseen world, especially those glorious, supernatural creatures who worship God in heaven and serve him on earth—the angels.

We know from the Gospels that some of the angels were witnesses of the incarnate Christ. Angels sang at his birth (Luke 2:13–14). They attended to him in the wilderness (Mark 1:12–13). An angel even appeared in the Garden of Gethsemane to strengthen Jesus for the work of the cross (Luke 22:43). But the angels were also witnesses of the risen Christ. They were the first to tell the disciples that Jesus was alive (Matt. 28:1–7; cf. Luke 24:23), but how could they give such testimony unless they had seen his resurrection body for themselves? Then, finally, angels witnessed the ascension of Jesus into heaven (Acts 1:9–11). To summarize, "These ministering spirits sang at his birth, ministered in the hour of his temptation, guarded his sepulcher, attested his ascension, and expected his return."[11]

The reason for mentioning the angels here is to show that the mystery of godliness is known in heaven as well as on earth. Although the angels themselves are not saved by grace, they glorify God for our salvation, as they are doing this very moment. The Bible teaches that Jesus Christ "has gone into heaven and is at the right hand of God, with angels, authorities, and powers having been subjected to him" (1 Peter 3:22).

There is, however, another possible meaning for this line of Paul's hymn. The word "angel" simply means "messenger," which makes it an appropriate word for God's heavenly messengers. But it can also refer to his earthly messengers, meaning the apostles. What Paul says about these messengers in 1 Timothy 3:16 was certainly true of the apostles: they saw Jesus. The apostles were eyewitnesses of his life and work, and especially of his resurrection. In fact, the Greek word Paul uses here for seeing (*ōphthē*) is the same word he uses when he tells the Corinthians that the risen Christ "appeared" to Peter and the rest of the apostles, including Paul himself (1 Cor. 15:5–7).

When the first Christians confessed that Jesus was seen by messengers, therefore, they may have been referring to the apostles. This possibility has been dismissed by many commentators, but without sufficient reason, because it is in keeping with the logic of the hymn. The next thing Jesus did after he appeared in a body and was vindicated by the Spirit was to show himself to Peter, John, and the rest of the disciples, including Thomas. Here is the sequence of Paul's hymn: first, the incarnation; second, the resurrection; third, the presentation.

11. Thomas C. Oden, *First and Second Timothy and Titus*, Interpretation (Louisville: John Knox, 1989), 45.

The postresurrection appearances of Jesus were essential to the plan of salvation. In order for the apostles to know that Jesus was the Christ, they had to see his glorious resurrection body. Otherwise, they would not have been able to testify that he had won the victory over the grave. Without their eyewitness testimony, we ourselves would never believe in the resurrection, and the church of the living God would not be able to stand as a pillar and buttress to the gospel truth. The same cannot be said of the angels and their testimony. They glorified God when they saw the resurrection of Jesus Christ. But our faith rests upon Jesus' presentation to the apostles, not to the angels.

Preached among the Nations

There is another reason for thinking that "messengers" may refer to the apostles. Notice what comes next: Jesus was "proclaimed among the nations," meaning all the Gentile peoples of the world. This clearly refers to the apostolic preaching of the gospel. After the presentation came the proclamation. Having seen the risen Christ, the apostles preached the risen Christ.

The apostles received the commission to do this from Jesus himself. Before he ascended into heaven, he said to them, "All authority in heaven and on earth has been given to me. Go therefore and make disciples of all nations, baptizing them in the name of the Father and of the Son and of the Holy Spirit, teaching them to observe all that I have commanded you" (Matt. 28:18–20). The apostles began to fulfill this commission at Pentecost. While they waited in Jerusalem, they were anointed by the Holy Spirit and began to speak in foreign tongues. The Bible emphasizes that the people who heard them were "from every nation under heaven" (Acts 2:5). When Peter stood up and addressed the crowd that day, he was preaching Jesus Christ among the nations.

Pentecost was only the beginning of the worldwide work of the gospel. Jesus Christ was preached, not only in Jerusalem, but in Judea, and Samaria, and to the uttermost parts of the earth. Paul himself preached Christ in Ephesus (Acts 19), and once they came to Christ, the Ephesians began to take the gospel to the nations, especially by praying for missions (see 1 Tim. 2:1–4). Jesus is preached among the nations to this very day. This is part of the great mystery of godliness. What the church is doing at this moment in history is essential to God's plan for the redemption of the world. The gospel is going to the nations as the good news about Jesus Christ is proclaimed to every tribe, people, and language.

Believed On in the World

Wherever Jesus Christ is proclaimed, he is "believed on in the world" (1 Tim. 3:16). The first to believe were the first eyewitnesses of the resurrection. John believed even before he saw the risen Christ. When he heard the tomb was (almost) empty, he "outran Peter and reached the tomb first. And stooping to look in, he saw the linen clothes lying there, but he did not go in" (John 20:4–5). As John stood in the doorway, he saw the burial cloth, still intact, and tried to figure out what it all meant. Finally, he went inside, where "he saw and believed" (John 20:8). On the evidence of the burial clothes, he believed that Jesus had been raised from the dead.

John was only the first to believe. Mary Magdalene believed and told the disciples, "I have seen the Lord" (John 20:18). They were afraid at first, and some doubted, but when Jesus appeared to them, they also believed (Matt. 28:17). Eventually, even Thomas believed, in spite of all his initial doubts (John 20:24–29).

As soon as the apostles began to preach the gospel to the nations, others began to believe as well. Nearly three thousand people believed on the day of Pentecost alone (see Acts 2:41). As the first church in Jerusalem continued to preach the gospel, "the Lord added to their number day by day those who were being saved" (Acts 2:47). It has been that way ever since. It is doubtful whether a single day has gone by since the day Jesus rose from the tomb without people coming to him in faith, giving their lives to him.

The global mission of Jesus Christ is a global success. He is still believed on in the world. The week that I write this I have received news of dozens of conversions. The mother of a church member—an eighty-eight-year-old Jewish woman—prayed to receive Jesus as her Messiah. A boy in a neighborhood Bible club asked how he could pray to receive Jesus into his heart. A former church member wrote to say that his daughter started a Good News club for her friends; all nine of them have made a commitment to Christ. Then there was the news from overseas. The church received an e-mail from the Middle East, where missionaries reported seeing more Muslims believe the gospel and repent of their sins in recent weeks than ever before. Another report, this one from the Far East, told the story of a man who received a Bible from a missionary hospital. The next time he needed medical care he returned to the hospital. It was thirty years (!) since his previous visit, and he had been reading his Bible ever since, having long since come to faith in Jesus Christ.

The confession in 1 Timothy 3:16 makes a historical claim: "he was believed on in the world." But this statement is for the present as well as the past because God is still making history. He will continue to bring men, women, and children to salvation in Christ until history comes to an end. In fact, if you trust in Jesus Christ for your salvation, then this verse is about you as well. You are in the world. You believe on him. Therefore, your faith is one proof that Jesus is believed on in the world.

Taken Up in Glory

The only real problem with taking Paul's hymn about the mystery of godliness in chronological order is the last phrase: he was "taken up in glory" (1 Tim. 3:16). This line seems to refer to the ascension. In fact, the same verb (*analambanō*) is used in the book of Acts to describe the way Jesus ascended to heaven. After he appeared to his disciples, "as they were looking on, he was lifted up, and a cloud took him out of their sight" (Acts 1:9; cf. 1:2, 22; Mark 16:19). The problem is that this seems to be out of sequence: Jesus was "taken up in glory" before he was "proclaimed among the nations" or "believed on in the world."

One possible solution is that this last phrase refers to the second coming of Jesus Christ. When Jesus returns to this earth he will come the way he left, trailing clouds of glory, to gather all his people to himself. The reason this is put in the past tense is that it is such a certainty. Jesus has promised to come again in power and glory, and he will undoubtedly do so.

The important thing, in any case, is that Jesus has become the glorified Christ. "Glory" (*doxa*) is the word the Bible uses to describe "brightness, splendor, or radiance." It "denotes in particular the glory, majesty, and sublimity of God."[12] By virtue of his resurrection, Jesus is exalted and enthroned.

12. George Knight, *The Pastoral Epistles*, New International Greek Testament Commentary (Grand Rapids: Eerdmans, 1992), 186.

He radiates the glory of God. What better way to end a hymn than with the glorious praise of the glorious Christ? Epiphanius had this glory clearly in mind when he composed his "Second Creed"—a confession of praise that strikes a joyous chord in every believer's soul: "The Word became flesh; the same suffered in the flesh; rose again; went up to heaven in the same body, sat down gloriously at the right hand of the Father; is coming in the same body in glory to judge the quick and the dead."[13]

The Godliness of the Mystery

The truth that the church holds out to the world is the mystery of the incarnation ("manifested in the flesh"), resurrection ("vindicated by the Spirit"), presentation ("seen by angels"), mission ("proclaimed among the nations"), reception ("believed on in the world"), and glorification ("taken up in glory") of Jesus Christ. The only thing left to say about this mystery is that it is a mystery "of godliness" (1 Tim. 3:16; cf. 2:2; 4:8). In other words, this hymn or confession contains practical truth. It promotes the worship of God and encourages the exercise of true religion.

John Chrysostom understood well that the mystery of Christ is for godliness. When he preached this mystery at his church in Constantinople, he brought his sermon to the point of practical application: "Great indeed was it. For God became Man, and Man became God. A Man was seen without sin! A Man was received up, was preached in the world! Together with us the Angels saw Him. This is indeed a mystery! . . . . But let us live in a manner worthy of the mystery."[14] This is good pastoral counsel. The truth about Jesus Christ demands a response.

What does it mean to live worthily of the mystery of godliness? Since Jesus "was manifested in the flesh," let us glorify him with our bodies. Let us use our hands to help, our lips to bless, and our minds to serve. Since Jesus was "vindicated by the Spirit," let us pray that we ourselves will be vindicated on the day of judgment. Let us ask God to prove that we belong to him by giving

13. Epiphanius, "Two Creeds of Epiphanius: Second Formula (AD 374)," in Philip Schaff, *Creeds of Christendom*, 3 vols. (Grand Rapids: Baker, 1983), 2:37.

14. John Chrysostom, "Homilies on the Epistles of St. Paul the Apostle to Timothy, Titus, and Philemon," trans. and ed. Philip Schaff, *Nicene and Post-Nicene Fathers*, First Series, 14 vols. (Peabody, MA: Hendrickson, 1994), 13:442.

us glorious resurrection bodies. Since Jesus was "seen by messengers," let us join the angels and the apostles in their worship around his throne. Since Jesus was and is "proclaimed among the nations," let us testify to his grace, declaring the gospel to everyone we love and sharing in the worldwide work of missions, so that all peoples might praise him. Since Jesus was and is "believed on in the world," let us believe on him with all our hearts for salvation as well as for everything else we need. Last of all, since Jesus was "taken up in glory," let us await his soon return with eager expectation, longing for the day when we will see the great mystery for ourselves.

11

Where Bad Theology Comes From

1 Timothy 4:1–5

Now the Spirit expressly says that in later times some will depart from the faith by devoting themselves to deceitful spirits and teachings of demons, through the insincerity of liars whose consciences are seared. (1 Tim. 4:1–2)

The world is full of bad theology. On television a preacher of prosperity says, "Be healed! Jesus died for your disease on the cross!" On the radio a teacher presents such a distorted view of Calvinism that it would cause the most stable Christian to doubt his or her salvation. In the magazines leading evangelicals are confused about whether justification comes by faith alone or not. Then add all the errors of non-Christian religion: the fanciful speculations of the New Age; the dangerous views about Jesus in the cults; the mindless, godless philosophies of the consumer culture. The world is full of untrue, unsound, unbiblical theology. Where does it all come from?

Apostasy Ahead

Having explained the mystery of godliness (1 Tim. 3:16), Paul explains the mystery of ungodliness, telling Timothy and the church to expect bad theology: "Now the Spirit expressly says that in later times some will depart from the faith" (1 Tim. 4:1). This is not simply Paul's analysis of the church; it is a prophecy of the Holy Spirit.

Paul does not specify when the Holy Spirit said this. This unhappy news may have been revealed to Paul as he wrote to Timothy. More likely, the apostle was referring to some earlier prophecy, perhaps one uttered by a prophet in the early church. Similar prophecies do appear elsewhere in the New Testament. Paul may even have been recalling the words of Jesus Christ: "And then many will fall away and betray one another and hate one another. And many false prophets will arise and lead many astray" (Matt. 24:10–11). The parallel with 1 Timothy is close because Jesus speaks of people "falling away." Or the apostle may simply have been reminding the Ephesians of the warning he gave their elders when he said farewell to them at Miletus: "I know that after my departure fierce wolves will come in among you, not sparing the flock; and from among your own selves will arise men speaking twisted things, to draw away the disciples after them" (Acts 20:29–30).

The living voice of the Holy Spirit testifies in no uncertain terms that although Christians may be saddened by false theology, they should never be surprised by it. Timothy was well acquainted with the dangers of unsound doctrine. He knew, for example, that Hymenaeus and Alexander had made a shipwreck of their faith (1 Tim. 1:19–20). At that very moment, he was contending against false teachers in the Ephesian church. Like Timothy, the church can take the Spirit's word for it: "in later times some will depart from the faith" (1 Tim. 4:1).

The technical theological term for abandoning the faith is "apostasy," which comes from the Greek noun *apostasia*. Here the related verb appears: to "depart from the faith" is to apostatize (1 Tim. 4:1). One scholar defines such apostasy as "the serious situation of becoming separated from the living God after a previous turning towards him, by falling away from the faith."[1] Apostasy does not mean that believers who have saving faith can lose it. This would

1. W. Bauder, in Colin Brown, ed., *The New International Dictionary of New Testament Theology*, 3 vols. (Grand Rapids: Zondervan, 1975–78), 1:608.

be an impossibility, since every sinner who receives the gift of saving faith is preserved by the Holy Spirit until the day of Christ (see John 10:28; Phil. 1:6).

What apostasy does mean, however, is that someone who once claimed to be a Christian has renounced the gospel. Here again, as he does throughout this epistle, Paul refers to Christianity as "the faith." He has in mind those central doctrines that rest on the solid foundation of Holy Scripture and are necessary to saving faith: the sovereignty of God the Father, the deity of God the Son, the reality of God the Holy Spirit, and redemption through the death and resurrection of Jesus Christ, received by faith. Sad to say, some who profess to believe these doctrines later deny them. Indeed, one of the distinguishing marks of the later times is that people who call themselves Christians will forsake the Christ of authentic Christianity.

Since human beings are curious about the future, we are bound to ask, "When will these later times be?" There is an important clue in this passage. In verse 1 the Holy Spirit speaks about the future: "in later times some will depart from the faith." Yet by verse 3 the apostle is speaking in the present tense about things happening in the Ephesian church at that very moment. This indicates that the later times of the final age have already begun.

The same shift from the future to the present occurs in 2 Timothy 3:1–5, where Paul warns Timothy that "in the last days there will come times of difficulty" (2 Tim. 3:1). He then proceeds to explain how people will behave in the end times: they will be insolent, violent, and arrogant. Thus he warns Timothy to "avoid such people" (2 Tim. 3:5). In other words, Timothy himself knew some of the wicked people of the last days. They were already living in Ephesus!

When someone asks, therefore, "Do you think we are living in the last days?" the answer is always, "Yes!" These are the later times. These are the last days, which, as John Wesley said, "extend from our Lord's ascension till His coming to judgment."[2] George Knight helpfully defines them as "the days inaugurated by the Messiah and characterized by the Spirit's presence in power, the days to be consummated by the return of Christ."[3] The end times thus encompass the whole Christian era from the resurrection of Jesus Christ to his second coming in power and glory.

2. John Wesley, *Explanatory Notes upon the New Testament* (London: Epworth, 1954), 57.

3. George Knight, *The Pastoral Epistles*, New International Greek Testament Commentary (Grand Rapids: Eerdmans, 1992), 188.

If these are the later times, then apostasy is to be expected. From time to time Christians will hear news of former church members who have abandoned the faith. Some will fall into grievous sin. Others will gradually drift away from the church. Still others will reject Reformation truth for the falsehoods of other faiths. As sad as these things are, they should not surprise us. When someone abandons orthodox Christianity it should not throw our faith into question. Rather, it proves the truth of Scripture "that in later times some will depart from the faith" (1 Tim. 4:1).

DIABOLICAL DOCTRINE

The Scripture goes on to explain that such apostasy comes from bad theology. In verses 3 through 5 Paul will proceed to explain what the false doctrines are. First, however, he explains where they come from. Bad theology has two sources, the first of which is positively diabolical. Those who abandon the faith do so "by devoting themselves to deceitful spirits and teachings of demons" (1 Tim. 4:1). Bad theology comes from seductive spirits and deceptive demons. The Revised English Bible thus identifies their teachings as "demon-inspired doctrines."

There are two errors to avoid when thinking about demons. The first is to give the devil more than his due. Some Christians think there are demons lurking behind every door. They assume they are under spiritual attack every time they get a headache or miss the bus. Others attribute most of their own sins to demonic activity. Still others become so obsessed with demons that they live in unholy fear. But the truth is that Jesus Christ defeated the devil and all his lackeys on the cross of Calvary. The Son of God became a man so that "through death he might destroy the one who has the power of death, that is, the devil, and deliver all those who through fear of death were subject to lifelong slavery" (Heb. 2:14–15). On occasion, God may allow fallen angels to manipulate the physical universe or to tempt human beings to commit sin. But demons do not and cannot have control over anyone who is filled with the Holy Spirit.

The opposite error is to deny that demons exist. As Baudelaire once said, "The devil's cleverest ruse is to make men believe that he does not exist."[4]

4. Charles Baudelaire, quoted in Donald Grey Barnhouse, *The Invisible War* (Grand Rapids: Zondervan, 1965), 156.

But the devil *does* exist. Spiritual warfare is as real today as it was in the days of Jesus Christ. We continue to "wrestle against the rulers, against the authorities, against the cosmic powers over this present darkness, against the spiritual forces of evil in the heavenly places" (Eph. 6:12). This struggle will continue until the day of judgment, which is why the Lord Jesus instructs his disciples to pray every day for deliverance from the evil one (see Matt. 6:13).

The main reason Christians need daily spiritual protection is the deceitfulness of the devil. Jesus called Satan "a liar and the father of lies" (John 8:44). Elsewhere Paul speaks of his schemes (2 Cor. 2:11; Eph. 6:11) and bewitchments (Gal. 3:1). His work is said to be "displayed in all kinds of counterfeit miracles, signs and wonders" (2 Thess. 2:9 NIV; cf. Rev. 13:14). Believers are thus warned not to believe every spirit, but to test the spirits "to see whether they are from God, for many false prophets have gone out into the world" (1 John 4:1).

Satan was a deceiver from the very beginning. When he came to Eve in the form of a serpent, his appearance was deceptive, and he asked a deceptive question: "Did God actually say, 'You shall not eat of any tree in the garden'?" (Gen. 3:1). Satan was putting words in God's mouth because God had said nothing of the kind. Then he made a deceptive claim: "You will not surely die" (Gen. 3:4). Satan told one lie after another. This is his *modus operandi*, his standard operating procedure. When he hinted to Eve that God was stingy, he was denying God's goodness. When he told Eve that she would not die, he was denying God's justice. Satan was the first liberal theologian. It is his particular aim to persuade people that true theology is false and false theology is true.

In addition to lying about creation, the devil also lies about redemption. Consider the words of Martin Luther:

> When God's holy Word arises, it is always its lot that Satan opposes it with all his might. At first, he rages against it with force and wicked power. If that promises no success, he attacks it with false tongues and erring spirits and teachers. What he is unable to crush by force he seeks to suppress by cunning and lies. This was his strategy at the beginning. When the Gospel first came into the world, he launched a mighty attack against it through Jews and Gentiles, shed much blood, and filled Christendom with martyrs. When this did not succeed, he raised false prophets and erring

> spirits and filled the world with heretics. . . . And we must be prepared for this, and by no means allow it to disturb us, for so it must be.[5]

If Satan's favorite strategy is deception, it follows that the church is in real danger of being fooled by false doctrine. Some theology is so bad it can be spotted a mile off. But most false doctrines contain enough truth to resist detection. The most dangerous heresies often sound the most like authentic Christianity. Consider a few examples. The distortions of the signs and wonders movement hide behind the truth of the need for people to make a personal commitment to Jesus Christ. The distortions of Roman Catholicism hide behind the truth of the value of good works. The lies of Mormonism hide behind the truth of family values. The lies of the International Church of Christ hide behind the truth of the necessity of baptism. Every false doctrine tries to find some truth to hide behind.

The deceptiveness of false doctrine teaches every Christian to be wary. A man once told me that after he committed his life to Christ he listened to every program on Christian radio. As he matured in the faith, he learned what a mistake that can be. The discerning Christian does not listen to every so-called Christian radio program, read every so-called Christian book, or enter every so-called Christian church, but is wary enough to be on guard against diabolical deceptions.

Through Lying Leaders

If bad theology comes ultimately from demons, it comes more immediately through human beings. It comes, in fact, "through the insincerity of liars whose consciences are seared" (1 Tim. 4:2). This is the second source of bad theology. It comes from lying leaders as well as deceptive demons.

This is not to say that every theological error comes from someone who is demon-possessed. However, false doctrine is transmitted from false angels through false teachers. The word the Holy Spirit uses to describe such a teacher is "hypocrite" (*hypokritēs*)—a word that comes from the Greek theater. It means to assume a role in a dramatic production, to play a part.

5. Martin Luther, *What Luther Says*, ed. Ewald Plass (St. Louis: Concordia, 1959), 395–96.

Hypocrisy explains why heresy is so deceptive. Many false teachers are good actors. They know how to play the part of a Christian. This, too, is part of Satan's master plan: "Satan disguises himself as an angel of light. So it is no surprise if his servants, also, disguise themselves as servants of righteousness" (2 Cor. 11:14–15). Or as Hamlet put it, "The spirit that I have seen / May be the devil: and the devil hath power / To assume a pleasing shape."[6] False teachers often play the part of Christians, pretending to be followers of Jesus Christ. They call themselves Christians. They seem to be committed and sincere. They are thoroughly convinced of their orthodoxy. They go to church, and they may even preach from a pulpit. Heresy always wears the mask of Christianity.

It is all a lie, however. False teachers are sincere all right: sincerely wrong! Neither they themselves nor their doctrines are true. There may even be something intentional about the way they distort the gospel. John Stott says that "hypocrisy is a deliberate pretence and a lie a deliberate falsehood."[7] There is a grave warning here for Christians who try to seem more godly than they actually are!

Eventually, liars start to live their own lies. They do not even realize they are lying any more, for their "consciences are seared" (1 Tim. 4:2). There is some disagreement about what Paul means by this expression (*kaustēriazō*). Some take it to refer to the branding of cattle or slaves to establish ownership, in which case the point is that false teachers are tools of the devil. It may be better, however, to take this expression in its medical sense, of coagulating live tissue with a burning instrument to stop bleeding. Sometimes when skin is burned it becomes insensitive, almost as if anesthetized. Once the nerves have been deadened, the skin is no longer able to feel pain. The same thing can happen to the human conscience. It can become cauterized by sin. The more a soul sins, the less painful sin seems, until finally the conscience becomes dead to all feeling (cf. Eph. 4:18–19). At that point, it is no longer able to warn the soul against sin.

To use a different analogy, the conscience is like an alarm clock. The first time a man commits a particular sin the alarm bells ring all over his

6. William Shakespeare, *Hamlet, Prince of Denmark*, Act 2, Scene 2, lines 648–50.

7. John Stott, *Guard the Truth: The Message of 1 Timothy and Titus* (Downers Grove, IL: InterVarsity, 1996), 111.

conscience. But the next time he commits the same sin, it is not nearly as alarming. "This isn't so bad," he says to himself. "I've done this once or twice before." The man carefully locates the snooze button on his conscience so that next time he is able to disarm it more quickly. Eventually, he unplugs his conscience altogether and slumbers unto death.

Unless Christians are careful, this self-destructive pattern can be repeated anywhere:

> The grim sequence of events in the career of the false teachers has now been revealed. First, they turned a deaf ear to their conscience, until it became cauterized. Next, they felt no scruple in becoming hypocritical liars. Thirdly, they thus exposed themselves to the influence of deceiving spirits. Finally, they led their listeners to abandon the faith. It is a perilous downward path from the deaf ear and the cauterized conscience to the deliberate lie, the deception of demons and the ruination of others.[8]

Apostasy is the inevitable result of hypocrisy. So do not wound your conscience by committing outrageous sins or by excusing lesser ones. Guard your conscience so that it remains sensitive to the least offense against the holiness of God.

By now it should be obvious why Paul so frequently reminds Timothy to keep his conscience clear. His goal is for Timothy to have love which comes from "a pure heart and a good conscience and a sincere faith" (1 Tim. 1:5). He urges him to keep "holding faith and a good conscience" (1 Tim. 1:19). Similarly, he tells deacons to "hold the mystery of the faith with a clear conscience" (1 Tim. 3:9). In short, Paul wants every Christian to be as conscientious as he himself was. For as the apostle later testified to Timothy, he served God "with a clear conscience" (2 Tim. 1:3), and as he told Felix, "I always take pains to have a clear conscience toward both God and man" (Acts 24:16). One reason Paul was such a good theologian was that he was such a holy Christian.

A clear conscience is always highly to be prized, but is most necessary of all for the pastors and teachers of the church. A theologian who grows comfortable with sin is well on his way to becoming a heretic, while a tender conscience preserves orthodoxy.

8. Ibid., 112.

The Ascetic Life

Up to this point, Paul has been speaking about bad theology in general terms. In verse 3 he finally starts to get specific by telling us that the false teachers in Ephesus believed that celibacy and vegetarianism were necessary for salvation: they "forbid marriage and require abstinence from foods that God created" (1 Tim. 4:3). Given what Paul has said in the previous two verses, this surely is a surprising summary of what the false teachers were saying. We might well have expected the apostle to say that these men were denying the deity of Jesus Christ, or adding works to faith as the basis for justification, or advocating some other heretical doctrine. But before talking about their theology, Paul first locates their heterodoxy in two areas of everyday practice.

There is nothing wrong, in principle, with being a single, or a vegetarian, or both. God calls some individual Christians to remain unmarried or to refrain from certain foods for a time. In fact, the apostle Paul himself was called to both. He himself was a bachelor, and he encouraged other Christians to value singleness (1 Cor. 7:8). He also followed the biblical practice of fasting with prayer (e.g. Acts 14:23).

The trouble comes when these or other matters of relative indifference are treated as essentials of the gospel. This legalistic mindset is often a problem in the church. A group of Christians discover something that helps them grow in the Christian faith. They rediscover a forgotten doctrine, take up some political cause, follow a new method for family life, or commit themselves to a ministry, which is all well and good. But then they decide that what is good for them ought to be mandatory for others. Soon they go around trying to get everyone to adopt one style of Christianity. They assume that anyone who does not do what they do is less spiritual than they are.

This is exactly what the false teachers in Ephesus were doing. They had committed themselves to one particular diet and one particular lifestyle. Fine. There is nothing wrong with remaining single or with fasting. Nor is there anything wrong in principle with private vegetarianism (although Romans 14:2 hints that this lifestyle may come from spiritual weakness). The trouble came when the false teachers decided that what was good for them was good for everyone. They tried to require every Christian to adopt their practices for abstaining from sex and food.

Apparently, these false teachers taught that meat and marriage were inherently sinful. This passage mentions "foods" without specifying what they were. Perhaps this is a reference to Jewish dietary customs which came from the Mosaic law. Yet elsewhere—especially in Rome (Rom. 14:2, 21) and in Corinth (1 Cor. 8:13)—the controversy in the church concerned eating meat. Whatever the precise practices may have been, the single best word to describe this kind of theology is "ascetic." According to the *Oxford English Dictionary*, an ascetic is "a person who practices severe self-discipline and abstains from all forms of pleasure, especially for religious or spiritual reasons." By forbidding marriage and changing their diet, some members of the Ephesian church were denying the pleasures of sex and food, and at the same time saying that physical self-denial was essential to a person's standing before God.

What lies behind forbidding meat and marriage is the Gnostic idea that there is something sinful about the body. According to this line of thinking, the physical universe is a hindrance to spiritual life. Souls are all that matter, and physical appetites only lead to sin. John Stott explains the ascetic mindset like this: "From the beginning of church history some teachers . . . have argued that sex and hunger are themselves unclean appetites, that the body itself is a nasty encumbrance (if not actually vile), and that the only way to holiness is abstinence, the voluntary renunciation of sex and marriage, and, since eating cannot be given up altogether, then at least the renunciation of meat."[9]

Asceticism has a long history. The Essenes who wrote the Dead Sea Scrolls refused to marry. So did the Manichaeans, who lived in the east from the third to the tenth centuries. Similarly Irenaeus reports that the Encratites of his day "preached against marriage, thus setting aside the original creation of God, and indirectly blaming him who made them male and female for the propagation of the human race. Some of those reckoned among them have also introduced abstinence from animal food, thus proving themselves ungrateful to God, who formed all things."[10] There has long been an ascetic tendency in Roman Catholicism. This explains the existence of

9. Ibid., 112–13.

10. Irenaeus, *Against Heresies*, I.28.1, ed. Alexander Roberts and James Donaldson, *Ante-Nicene Fathers*, 10 vols. (Peabody, MA: Hendrickson, 1994), 1:353.

monasteries and why Catholic priests are forbidden to marry. It is also the reason why orthodox Catholics refuse to eat meat during Lent.

A more contemporary example of asceticism is the Straight Edge movement, which takes its name from a 1981 punk song by Ian MacKaye and Minor Threat: "I'm a person just like you / But I've got better things to do / Than sit around and smoke dope. . . . I've got a straight edge."[11] As the song suggests, Straight Edgers refuse to smoke or use drugs—so far, so good. However, they are equally opposed to marriage. Sex, they say, is only for having children. It is immoral for human beings to eat anything that comes from an animal, including dairy products. Straight Edgers are willing to use physical violence against people who disagree with their views. Thus, even to the present day, there are people "who forbid marriage and require abstinence from foods" (1 Tim. 4:3).

The Ingratitude of Asceticism

What is wrong with a little asceticism? After all, John the Baptist lived on honey and locusts (Mark 1:6). Jesus had nowhere to lay his head (Matt. 8:20). Paul even talked about disciplining his body to "keep it under control" (1 Cor. 9:27). Besides, sex and food so easily lend themselves to sins of the flesh.

One problem with self-denial is that it is often used as a way to become self-righteous. Calvin accuses the false teachers in Ephesus of trying "to acquire righteousness for themselves by abstaining from those things which God has left free. The only reason why consciences are burdened by such laws is that perfection is being sought apart from the law of God."[12] Another problem with ascetic Christianity is that it rejects God's good gifts. When they are used in a lawful way, both food and sex are meant for joy. God himself created them "to be received with thanksgiving by those who believe and know the truth" (1 Tim. 4:3).

Consider marriage. Paul spends less time defending that institution here, perhaps because family life receives positive mention elsewhere in this epistle (see 1 Tim. 3:2, 12; 5:14). Remember, too, that Paul's other letter to the

11. In Gene Edward Veith, "Being Bad to Do Good," *World* (Jan. 24, 1998), 22.

12. John Calvin, *The Second Epistle of Paul the Apostle to the Corinthians and the Epistles to Timothy, Titus and Philemon*, trans. T. A. Smail, Calvin's Commentaries (Edinburgh: Oliver & Boyd, 1964), 238.

Ephesians included a good bit of teaching about marriage (Eph. 5:22–33). But what the Bible teaches about marriage is that it is a divine gift, ordained by God the Father (Gen. 2:24) and blessed by God the Son (Matt. 19:4–6). Therefore, marriage is to be received with thankful joy. Chastity in marriage is no less holy than virginity in singleness.

The Puritans offer many good examples of how to appreciate the gift of marriage. Contrary to popular opinion, they were not puritanical about sex. They prized marriage, including its sexual aspect. In his *Book of Matrimony*, the Puritan Thomas Becon defined marriage as the

> high, holy and blessed order of life, ordained not of man, but of God . . . wherein one man and one woman are coupled and knit together in one flesh and body in the fear and love of God, by the free, loving, hearty, and good consent of them both, to the intent that they two may dwell together as one flesh and body, of one will and mind, in all honesty, virtue and godliness, and spend their lives in equal partaking of all such things as God shall send them with thanksgiving.[13]

Like marriage, food is one of God's good gifts. Christians are allowed to eat whatever foods they please. Paul's reasoning is very straightforward: what God has made, we may eat. This is one very practical consequence of the doctrine of creation: "everything created by God is good" (1 Tim. 4:4). Throughout the first chapter of Genesis, God describes everything he made as very good; among other things, what God has made is good to eat.

The proper way to receive the good gifts of creation is "with thanksgiving" (*eucharistias*), which is Paul's favorite term to express gratitude to God. Gratitude is so important that it is mentioned twice in three verses: God created these things "to be received with thanksgiving by those who believe and know the truth. For everything created by God is good, and nothing is to be rejected if it is received with thanksgiving, for it is made holy by the word of God and prayer" (1 Tim. 4:3–5).

There are two important qualifications here. The first comes from the doctrine of redemption: followers of Christ must be the most grateful people of all. Christians are here defined as "those who believe and know the truth"

13. In Leland Ryken, *Worldly Saints: The Puritans as They Really Were* (Grand Rapids: Zondervan, 1986), 49.

(1 Tim. 4:3). To believe is to believe that Jesus Christ is the Son of God and the Savior of the world. It is to trust in his death on the cross and resurrection from the grave for salvation. True gratitude is a response to saving grace. It begins with thanksgiving for the gift of eternal life through Jesus Christ. The other qualification comes from the doctrine of creation. Paul does not say that everything is good; he says that "everything created by God is good" (1 Tim. 4:4). What God made is good, but there is always the danger of corrupting what God has made. Christians are to enjoy life to the fullest, but it is not "anything goes!" Although the right use of food and sex have God's blessing, lechery and gluttony fall under God's curse.

One way to test if God's gifts are being used properly is to ask this question: "Can I thank God for what I am doing right now without being ashamed of myself?" A sensitive Christian will find it impossible to thank God for gross excess. Furthermore, true gratitude always leads to generosity. Christians who keep their food to themselves—or keep the benefits of family life to themselves, for that matter—are not receiving God's gifts with thanksgiving at all.

When Paul speaks about thanksgiving, he may be referring to the practice of saying grace before meals. One way to receive food with thanksgiving is to do what the Lord Jesus did: offer a prayer of thanksgiving before and/or after eating it. In the Gospel of Mark we overhear Jesus giving thanks for the loaves and the fish (Mark 6:41; 8:6), as well as for the bread and the wine of the Last Supper (Mark 14:22–23). This was also the practice of the apostle Paul, who speaks of sitting down to his meals "with thankfulness" (1 Cor. 10:30). The way to receive any gift is with a word of thanks. The Scripture further describes giving thanks for food as a consecration: "it is made holy by the word of God and prayer" (1 Tim. 4:5). Praying before a meal does not make the food any more holy than it already is, but saying grace is a way of acknowledging that daily bread is a sacred gift. According to Calvin, "the only recompense we can make to God for His liberality is a testimony of our thanks."[14]

It is hard to say for certain what Paul means here by "the word of God" (1 Tim. 4:5). Various commentators have suggested that it refers to the gospel message (Paul sometimes equates "the word of God" with the gospel), or to

14. Calvin, *Second Epistle of Paul*, 240.

the Lord's Supper, or even to the first chapter of Genesis, where God said over and over again that everything he created was very good (an interpretation that fits in well with Paul's emphasis on creation in these verses). Still others point out that the Jews often used Scripture when they said grace. The last suggestion is a good one. Breakfast, lunch, and dinner may all be consecrated to God. Every meal is a dialogue with heaven. As Fairbairn says, the Bible is "God's word to man warranting him to use the creation gift," while saying grace is "man's word to God, acknowledging the gift, and asking his blessing on it."[15] Christian singles and families ought to dedicate their meals to God through prayer and the reading of Scripture. Table devotions have been the standard practice of God's people throughout history. The fact that they have gone out of fashion in some Christian circles today makes them all the more necessary.

Giving thanks, however, is not just for mealtimes. Gratitude is a whole way of life. Christians ought to give thanks to God for every good thing. G. K. Chesterton wrote something helpful about this in one of his personal notebooks. Chesterton was an English essayist and biographer. He was also a Catholic, but not of the ascetic kind, as one can tell from what he wrote:

> You say grace before meals.
> All right.
> But I say grace before the play and the opera,
> And grace before the concert and pantomime,
> And grace before I open a book,
> And grace before sketching, painting,
> Swimming, fencing, boxing, walking, playing, dancing;
> And grace before I dip the pen in the ink.[16]

Chesterton's point is that God is to be praised for everything he has created. I am in a good position to appreciate this because I am writing these words one fine spring morning. As I walked the streets of Philadelphia early in the day I saw a starling in a tree. Starlings are not the most attractive birds. They

15. Patrick Fairbairn, *Commentary on the Pastoral Epistles* (Edinburgh, 1874; repr. Grand Rapids: Zondervan, 1956), 176.

16. G. K. Chesterton, quoted in Dudley Barker, *G. K. Chesterton: A Biography* (New York: Stein and Day, 1973), 65.

lack the bright colors of song birds and they have trouble carrying a tune. Yet the starling I saw was almost melodic. He was inspired, no doubt, by the fresh buds on the tree and the bright sun in the sky. As I paused to look and to listen, I joined him in grateful praise to the God who made us both. Everything God made is good and is to be received with thanksgiving. Even starlings.

A Grateful Theology

The last thing to be said about the origins of bad theology is that gratitude is essential to sound theology. Thanksgiving is so important to daily Christian life that anyone who rejects God's good gifts runs the risk of abandoning the faith.

A good example of the way sound theology depends upon a grateful heart comes from the early days of the Swiss Reformation. Shortly before Easter in 1522, several printers scandalized the city of Zurich by eating meat during the traditional Catholic fast for Lent. The printers decided to do this for two reasons. One was practical. They performed such hard physical labor that they felt they needed to eat meat to keep up their strength. But the other reason was theological. The printers wanted to eat meat in order to make a public declaration of their commitment to the doctrines of the Reformation.

To understand this, it helps to know that the Lenten fast in Zurich had become a form of works-righteousness, a way of earning favor with God through self-denial. But the printers knew where bad theology comes from—and where it leads. They believed that they were saved by grace, not by works. They also understood that "everything created by God is good, and nothing is to be rejected if it is received with thanksgiving" (1 Tim. 4:4). Therefore, they ate their meat to the glory of God, which of course is the way every believer ought to do everything.

12

Minister in Training

1 Timothy 4:6–10

If you put these things before the brothers, you will be a good servant of Christ Jesus, being trained in the words of the faith and of the good doctrine that you have followed. (1 Tim. 4:6)

The funeral of Charles Hodge was a momentous occasion. The professor of systematic theology at Princeton Seminary was not only a learned scholar and a champion of Reformation orthodoxy, but he was also a beloved teacher and friend. On the day of his funeral, all the shops in Princeton were closed. After the worship service ended at the First Presbyterian Church, a great procession formed at the seminary and moved slowly to the cemetery. Of all the tributes given to Hodge on that solemn day, perhaps the most fitting was given by Professor William Paxton: "When due allowance is made for his intellect and his learning, after all his chief power was in his goodness. Christ enshrined in his heart was the centre of his theology and his life. The world will write upon his monument GREAT; but we, his students, will write upon it GOOD."[1]

1. In David B. Calhoun, *Princeton Seminary*, 2 vols. (Carlisle, PA: Banner of Truth, 1996), 2:56.

A minister of the gospel can receive no higher praise. The epitaph that Paxton gave to Hodge is essentially the same epitaph Paul wanted Timothy to deserve when he came to the end of his ministry. The apostle did not encourage Reverend Timothy to aspire to greatness; he simply wanted him to become "a good servant of Christ Jesus" (1 Tim. 4:6).

The Good Teaching

What makes a minister good? Paul tells Timothy three things that it takes to become a good minister: good teaching (1 Tim. 4:6), godly training (1 Tim. 4:7–9), and a global task (1 Tim. 4:10). Good teaching, godly training, and a global task are not exclusively for ministers, however. The Bible hints at this when it refers to Timothy, not as a minister, but as a good "servant" or "deacon" (*diakonos*) of Christ. A deacon is simply a servant, and "servant" is a word that ought to describe every minister. But of course servanthood is not just for ministers. Any Christian who puts these verses into practice is a good servant of Jesus Christ (cf. Matt. 25:21).

First comes good teaching: "If you put these things before the brothers, you will be a good servant of Christ Jesus, being trained in the words of the faith and of the good doctrine that you have followed" (1 Tim. 4:6). The word "brothers" is a reminder that the church is God's family—"the household of God" (1 Tim. 3:15). The words "these things" refer generally to all of 1 Timothy, and more specifically to the opening verses of chapter 4, in which the Holy Spirit explained where bad theology comes from. Deceptive demons and lying leaders will cause some to abandon the Christian faith (1 Tim. 4:1–2). Against the asceticism of false teachers who forbid people to eat meat or to marry, the Scripture teaches a grateful, receptive attitude toward everything God has made. This is what Timothy must teach. These are the things that he must "put before the brothers," the truths that he must point out. A minister is like a merchant who sets out his wares in the marketplace. He displays biblical truth. And if the opening verses of this chapter are any indication, showing the truth includes showing up error.

A good minister, therefore, is a defender of the faith. Yet opposing false doctrine can be a thankless job. Most Christians desire to have the truth explained, but not all are willing to have error exposed. If a minister says, "Jesus is the way to salvation," all the people say "Amen!" But suppose he says, "Jesus is the *only* way to salvation," and then proceeds to deny the saving power of other religions. This is bound to stir up controversy. Or consider another example. Suppose that in addition to saying that salvation comes by grace, a minister names the religious movements that teach salvation by works. "Well, that's a bit narrow-minded," some will say. "I wish he wouldn't be so negative." Standing up for sound doctrine will never meet with universal approval. But it *will* meet with divine approval, for God's Word states that a minister who puts these things before the brothers is a good minister.

A good minister seeks to please God rather than men, and Paul had every reason to hope that Timothy would become a good minister. For one thing, he had been trained on good teaching. To put the Greek term more accurately, Timothy was "nourished" (*entrephomai*) in the truths of the faith (1 Tim. 4:6). Since nourishment describes the care and feeding of young children, this partly refers to Timothy's upbringing. His grandmother Lois and his mother Eunice had nurtured him in the faith (see 2 Tim. 1:5). He had been instructed in the law of God. He had memorized portions of the Old Testament. He had been catechized in the attributes of God, the history of salvation, and the promises of the coming Messiah. Timothy was born and bred to be a good minister.

All of this shows the necessity of good teaching in the home. A good upbringing is worth years of seminary. It prepares the sons and daughters of the church to become good servants in every walk of life. It will make them good neighbors, citizens, artists, professionals, laborers, schoolteachers, parents, missionaries, and ministers.

Timothy's upbringing also included the theological training that he received from the apostle Paul. The "words of the faith" are the essentials of the gospel, although this expression might refer to the words of Jesus himself. The "good doctrine" is the apostolic doctrine about Jesus Christ (cf. 1 Tim. 6:3). Timothy was trained in these words and doctrines during his internship with the apostle Paul (Acts 16:1–4).

A good upbringing, however, is only the beginning. Being trained in the faith is not just for childhood; it is for a whole lifetime. Since the Greek verb for training is in the present tense, the implication is that Timothy continues to be trained in biblical truth. He is a lifelong student of Christian doctrine. He still follows the good teaching he received at home and in the church.

The best Bible teachers never lose their passion for Bible study. I saw this firsthand when I spent several months with William Still, a Presbyterian pastor who preached for more than fifty years at the same church in Aberdeen, and whose ministry led to a recovery of evangelical faith in the Church of Scotland. Mr. Still was well into his eighties at the time I met him, and still preaching twice every Sunday. As we sat in his sitting room every morning I would ask him questions about piety, ministry, and theology. Often we hit upon a line of inquiry which merited further investigation. We would pull out our Bibles, or he would dash off to the next room to get a book off the shelf. In the thrill of the chase, Mr. Still would exclaim, "We're still learning, aren't we, Philip? We're always learning!" Every good servant of Christ draws continual nourishment from the Word of God.

The Godly Training

There is more to becoming a good minister than earning a degree in theology. In fact, Paul warns Timothy against becoming the wrong kind of theologian: "Have nothing to do with irreverent, silly myths" (1 Tim. 4:7). Paul has warned Timothy about this kind of thing before. At the beginning of his letter he spoke out against those who "devote themselves to myths and endless genealogies" (1 Tim. 1:4). "Irreverent myths" may refer to the gods and goddesses of pagan mythology. Timothy preached in Ephesus, remember, where Diana was queen. The mention of mythology may also refer to Jewish fables about the lives of the Old Testament saints.

"Silly myths" are superstitious beliefs—any kind of folk wisdom that smacks of superstition: the crystals in the spirit shop, the horoscope in the daily newspaper, the prayer flags of the Hindus, or what have you. God is not in any of these things; they are God-less. Therefore, Timothy is to stay away from them. The general principle is that good Christians, and especially good ministers, do not speculate about matters not taught in Scripture. They refuse to become distracted by the trivial ideas of the day. They do not allow controversies in politics, sports, education, or even religion to distract them from solid biblical truth.

Instead of wasting time with idle speculation, Christians must exercise themselves unto godliness. It takes godly training as well as good teaching to make a good minister. So the Scripture says, "train yourself for godliness"

(1 Tim. 4:7). Of all the things Paul wanted to say to Timothy, this must have been the most important. The word "godliness" (*eusebeia*) occurs fifteen times in the New Testament, but nine of them are in this epistle. If someone had asked Timothy what Paul's letter was about, he might well have said, "Well, I suppose it was mostly about the life in God's household, but the thing that impressed me was my personal need for godliness." For all its concern about a minister's doctrine, this letter has a profound concern for a minister's life.

The word "godliness" means reverence. It denotes the respect that the believer owes to God—what one scholar describes as "that mingled fear and love which together constitute the piety of man toward God."[2] Such godliness comes from the awareness that all of life is lived before the face of God. Calvin thus called godliness "the beginning, middle and end of Christian living."[3] The godly person places God at the center of every activity and endeavor. God is in the sleeping and the waking, the eating and the drinking, the coming and the going. The godly person walks with God at home, at work, at church, at school, and at play. Godliness includes godly thoughts, godly speech, and godly behavior. It is the attitude toward life that David expressed when he said, "I have set the LORD always before me" (Ps. 16:8). Godliness comes from a God-centered life.

Above all else, God wants his people and his ministers to be godly. This is why Paul did not give Timothy seven steps to boost church attendance, or helpful tips about becoming a better administrator, or a thorough critique of his preaching style. Instead, he gave him the most practical instruction of all: a good minister is a godly minister. One group of Christians who understood this well was the Puritans, who typically defined the ideal minister as "godly and learned." Yet these men also recognized that, in the words of Richard Bernard, "common people respect more a preacher's life than his learning."[4] And rightly so! Given the choice between a gifted man and a godly man, whom would you want in your pulpit?

2. R. C. Trench, *Synonyms of the New Testament*, 8th rev. ed. (New York, 1876), 167.

3. John Calvin, *The Second Epistle of Paul the Apostle to the Corinthians and the Epistles to Timothy, Titus and Philemon*, trans. T. A. Smail, Calvin's Commentaries (Edinburgh: Oliver & Boyd, 1964), 244.

4. Richard Bernard, *That Faithful Shepherd*, in William Haller, *The Rise of Puritanism* (New York: Columbia University Press, 1938), 138.

A good illustration of the importance of godliness comes from the ministry of Lorne Sanny, who formerly served as president of the Navigators. One Sunday morning, a woman in Sanny's church discovered that she had a flat tire. As soon as he noticed her difficulty, Sanny stripped off his coat and tie to put on the spare. He later discovered that this single act of kindness was remembered long after all the sermons he preached in that church had been forgotten. Actions do not always speak louder than words, but they do have a way of turning up the volume. Sanny's life confirmed the truth of his doctrine.

Godliness does not happen automatically. It requires difficult, diligent training. In this respect, taking care of the soul is much like taking care of the body. Paul made this connection when he told Timothy, "bodily training is of some value" (1 Tim. 4:8). From this and other statements the apostle made, it is apparent that he was something of a sports fan. Paul's letters contain references to boxing, wrestling, track and field, and various kinds of athletics. To judge from the Greek word he often uses, the apostle had been to the *gymnasium*.

Paul knew, therefore, that great athletes are also made, and not just born. Most Olympians have extraordinary natural abilities, but they also make a total life commitment to improving their speed, strength, and athletic technique. Competing at a world-class level requires many years of strenuous daily training. For example, when the American skier Picabo Street had her first career-threatening knee injury, she had to learn how to ski all over again. It took one year of one hundred percent commitment to stretching, lifting, running, and skiing before she was ready to win a gold medal in downhill skiing at the Winter Olympics. Or consider a different kind of physical training. One of my friends is an aspiring opera singer. At the time of this writing, he is working to correct a flaw in the way his body produces sound. It has something to do with gaining better control over the opening in his throat, and it will take perhaps a year of painstaking vocal work for him to progress to the next level of expertise. At this stage his voice lessons slowly proceed note by note.

If such thorough training is necessary for the body, why should the soul be any different? We must do our spiritual exercises. We must train ourselves to be godly. No one else can do this for us, so we must become fitness freaks, spiritually speaking.

When it comes to physical conditioning, it usually helps to have a trainer. These days, if people want to get their bodies in top condition, they hire a personal trainer. The trainer's job is to set up a schedule of exercises to get the client into shape. There is a sense in which every Christian has a personal trainer: the Holy Spirit, speaking in Scripture. The Spirit of God uses the Word of God to produce the life of God in the soul. What makes people godly is reading, hearing, studying, and meditating on the Bible. As John Stott points out, "We cannot become familiar with this godly book without becoming godly ourselves."[5]

One man discovered the truth of this statement shortly before he became a Christian. On the recommendation of a friend, he had been reading through the New Testament epistle of 1 Peter every day. He hardly understood what he was reading, and he was not trying to study it; he was just reading. Nevertheless, by the end of his first week of reading, some of his friends noticed a significant change taking place in his life and asked him to explain it. Eventually, the man figured out that there was a connection between what he was reading and how he was living. The Word of God was training him to be godly.

The Word of God itself suggests many other ways to get spiritual exercise, starting with prayer. Prayer is the God-centered conversation that fuels the God-centered life. With prayer goes fasting, which is perhaps the most neglected of spiritual disciplines. These days fasting has gone the way of the medicine ball that athletes once used for fitness training down at the YMCA: nobody uses it any more. However, fasting was a regular part of the spiritual life for Jesus and his disciples (see Matt. 6:16–18). Fasting strengthens the work of prayer and reminds the Christian of his or her utter dependence on God for life and strength. Partaking in the sacrament of the Lord's Supper is another good form of spiritual exercise. The bread and the wine of communion are nourishment for the Christian life. Then there are tithes and offerings, which are exercises in generosity, and also deeds of mercy: feeding the hungry, clothing the naked, welcoming the stranger, visiting the prisoner, helping the aged.

All of these spiritual duties help train the Christian to be godly, and all of these duties are to be done. Every athlete knows the importance of balanced training. Doing twenty chin-ups a day is great for the biceps, but it does not

5. John Stott, *Guard the Truth: The Message of 1 Timothy and Titus* (Downers Grove, IL: InterVarsity, 1996), 117.

do much for the hamstrings. No one goes down to the health club simply to skip rope for an hour. A good workout is a complete workout. In the same way, every healthy man or woman of God ought to be a spiritual cross-trainer—nourished by the Word, vital in prayer, generous in giving, and active in mercy.

The result of all this godly training will be a godly life. By themselves, acts of Christian devotion do not guarantee godliness, which is a matter of the heart. But Scripture reading, prayer, the sacraments, and charity are the drills that God has appointed for our spiritual training. By faith and the Holy Spirit, these spiritual exercises produce spiritual fruit.

The Value of Godliness

For all of their similarities, there is one great difference between training the body and training the soul: "While bodily training is of some value, godliness is of value in every way, as it holds promise for the present life and also for the life to come. The saying is trustworthy and deserving of full acceptance" (1 Tim. 4:8–9).

Physical exercise has its place. It is good to have a healthy body, and thus it is appropriate for Christians to play sports or work out at the gym. Physical training has value. Notice, however, that it only has "some value." Bodily exercise has its limits. Here Paul may have been making a dig at the false teachers. They were the ones, remember, who put so much emphasis on what people did with their bodies (1 Tim. 4:3). Almost certainly, the apostle was taking a swipe at the sports craze in Ephesus. The Ephesians spent a great deal of time and money training young athletes to perform at pagan festivals.[6] But although the sporting life has its place, its benefits are strictly temporary. Bodily exercise has value only for this life, not for the life to come. William Shakespeare made the same point more poetically in his *Sonnet 146*: "Why so large cost, having so short a lease / Dost thou upon thy fading mansion spend?" It is a fair question. Eventually a man's lease on life will run out. Even if he continues to play tennis into his eighties, he cannot take his tennis racket with him to heaven. All the benefits of physical training expire at death.

6. George Knight, *The Pastoral Epistles*, New International Greek Testament Commentary (Grand Rapids: Eerdmans, 1992), 201.

Godliness, on the other hand, "is of value in every way" (1 Tim. 4:8). Here J. N. D. Kelly offers a helpful paraphrase: "while bodily training is beneficial up to a point, sound religion is beneficial all the way."[7] Incidentally, most commentators agree that verse 8 (rather than verse 10) contains the "trustworthy saying" that is mentioned in verse 9.[8] Either interpretation is possible, but verse 8 sounds more like a popular saying. Perhaps it came from Greek philosophers who worried that athletics were crowding out academics. If so, Paul was giving an ancient proverb the apostolic seal of approval. To return to Paul's argument, godliness is valuable in all kinds of situations. As the New Revised Standard Version puts it, "godliness is valuable in every way." It is valuable in the home, the church, and the marketplace. It is valuable both in times of trouble and in times of prosperity. It helps a person deal with enemies as well as friends. Godliness is never superfluous. It guides the believer in every situation.

As useful as it is for the present life, godliness holds even more promise for the future. Christians have the best of both worlds: "godliness is of value in every way, as it holds promise for the present life and also for the life to come" (1 Tim. 4:8). When it comes to Christian character, you really *can* take it with you! Godliness is the one thing a person can take from this life to the next; it lasts forever. This makes spiritual training much more valuable than physical training. Paul used a similar analogy to make a similar point when he wrote to the Corinthians: "Every athlete exercises self-control in all things. They do it to receive a perishable wreath, but we an imperishable" (1 Cor. 9:25). Not every athlete who trains for the Olympics wins a medal (or a laurel wreath, as champions wore in Paul's day). But everyone who trains to be godly will gain an eternal crown of glory.

To put this in doctrinal terms, there is a connection between sanctification in this life and glorification in the life to come. Sanctification is the work that the Holy Spirit does in this life to make the believer godly. Glorification is the work that the Holy Spirit will do in the next life to make the believer *gloriously* godly. These two works of the Holy Spirit—sanctification and glorification—cannot be separated (cf. Rom. 8:30). The godliness begun in

7. J. N. D. Kelly, *The Pastoral Epistles: Timothy I and II, Titus*, Harper's New Testament Commentaries (San Francisco: Harper and Row, 1960), 99–100.

8. See Knight, *Pastoral Epistles*, 198.

this life will be perfected in the next. Sanctification is the root of glorification; glorification is the fruit of sanctification. And this is why "godliness holds promise for the present life and also for the life to come" (1 Tim. 4:8).

The Global Task

Mentioning eternal life leads Paul to remind Timothy why he entered ministry in the first place: "For to this end we toil and strive, because we have our hope set on the living God, who is the Savior of all people, especially of those who believe" (1 Tim. 4:10). The final thing it takes to become a good servant of Christ is commitment to the global task of world evangelization.

This verse explains what Christian ministry is all about. It is honest about the difficulty of ministry. The work of the gospel is a struggle. It is full of toil and strife. Somehow it doesn't seem surprising that the English word "agony" comes from the Greek word for "striving" (*agonizomai*)—a term that continues the idea of strenuous training and hints at the sufferings of ministry. But all this work is worth the effort. "No pain, no gain" was one of Paul's principles for effective ministry. The agony is ecstasy because the church has the message of salvation in Jesus Christ.

Paul and Timothy received this saving message for themselves when they set their hope on the living God (1 Tim. 4:10). Every believer has this same hope. We know that Jesus Christ has risen from the dead and is seated at the right hand of God the Father. We know that God will save us on the day of judgment. Having this assurance, we make every possible effort to share that message with everyone else. We labor and strive to see men, women, and children receive eternal life. We have a burden for the global task of saving lost souls. Evangelism lies at the heart of every truly Christian ministry. The church will not rest until every last person on this planet has heard the good news of salvation from sin and deliverance from death in Jesus Christ, "who is the Savior of all people, especially of those who believe" (1 Tim. 4:10).

This is the second time that Paul has described Jesus as the Savior of all men. The first instance came in the second chapter: "For there is one God, and there is one mediator between God and men, the man Christ Jesus, who gave himself as a ransom for all, which is the testimony given at the proper time" (1 Tim. 2:5–6). As we have seen, the context of those verses made it clear that Paul did not mean that Christ died for each and every human being who ever lived, but that he died for all sorts of people. In case there is any misunderstanding, however, Paul is careful to clarify what he means. To say that Jesus is the Savior of all men might imply that all men will be saved. But Paul was no universalist. So here in chapter 4 he goes on to say that Jesus is the special Savior of those who believe. Salvation from sin thus comes by grace through faith.

The word "especially" does not mean there are two kinds of salvation: general and special. Recent scholarship demonstrates that the word "especially" (*malista*) means "to be precise," or "in other words."[9] Thus the verse should read as follows: "God is the Savior of all men—that is to say, he is the Savior of those who believe." The apostle "is not saying that God saves believers more than he saves others; he is simply modifying his general statement that God is the Savior of all men by adding the limitation that you cannot be saved unless you believe."[10] This is why, when Christians share the gospel, we insist on the absolute necessity of trusting in Jesus Christ for eternal life. If you do not believe in Jesus, then you are not saved; it is as simple as that. Jesus Christ is a Savior only for those who truly believe.

Faith in Christ can be compared to the sinner's passport to heaven. Every country requires newcomers to present a valid passport, as I learned one summer when I traveled to Haiti. The man in front of me at the Customs Office was denied entrance in Port-au-Prince, because when the customs officer ran her fingers over his papers, she could not feel the embossed seal that would prove his documents were official.

Or consider a more chilling example—a scene from the film *The Killing Fields* in which a reporter from New York tries to help his Laotian assistant escape from war-torn Cambodia. The foreigners assemble in a compound near Phnom Penh, anxiously awaiting permission to leave the country under French protection. Since he is an educated man, the assistant will almost certainly be killed by the Khmer Rouge if he is left behind. The man's only hope is a false passport. So the reporter feverishly assembles the proper-looking documents, develops a photograph, forges the proper signatures, and hands his friend a fake passport. Unfortunately, when it comes time for

9. See T. C. Skeat, "'Especially the Parchments': A Note on 1 Tim. 4.13," *Journal of Theological Studies*, ns 30 (1979): 173–7.

10. A. T. Hanson, *The Pastoral Epistles*, New Century Bible Commentary (Grand Rapids: Eerdmans, 1982), 92.

the foreigners to have their documents examined, there is a rainstorm. All the foreigners line up in the pouring rain to have their documents examined. As the soldiers approach, the Laotian man looks down to check his passport. He opens it to find, to his horror, that instead of seeing his own face, he sees only an inky black square. His photograph has disintegrated in the rain, and he is doomed to go to the killing fields.

If proper identification is required, what passport will you present at the immigration office to heaven? There every passport will be carefully checked. It is sad, but solemnly true: anyone holding a forgery will be thrown "into the eternal fire prepared for the devil and his angels" (Matt. 25:41). The only acceptable passport to heaven is faith in Jesus Christ. He is the Savior of all men. That is to say, he is the Savior of those who *believe*! On the day when every creature is gathered before the judgment seat of God, your only hope is to have the proper passport: one that is given to you by the Holy Spirit who gave you the gift of faith, that is embossed with the cross where Christ died for your sins, and that has your own name and picture inside it because you have set your hope in the living God.

13

A Portrait of the Minister as a Young Man

1 Timothy 4:11–16

Command and teach these things. Let no one despise you for your youth, but set the believers an example in speech, in conduct, in love, in faith, in purity. . . . Keep a close watch on yourself and on the teaching. Persist in this, for by so doing you will save both yourself and your hearers. (1 Tim. 4:11–12, 16)

John Bunyan's famous book *The Pilgrim's Progress* tells the story of Christian's journey to the Celestial City. Early in his travels, Christian comes to the house of Interpreter, who shows him a portrait: "Christian saw the Picture of a very grave Person hung up against the wall; and this was the fashion of it. It had eyes lifted up to Heaven, the best of Books in his hand, the Law of Truth was written upon his lips, the World was behind his back. It stood as if it pleaded with men, and a Crown of Gold did hang over his head."

Christian asks the obvious question: Who is this man, and what does his picture mean? Interpreter explains the riddle:

> The Man whose Picture this is, is one of a thousand; he can beget children, travel in birth with children, and nurse them himself when they are born. And whereas thou seest him with his eyes lift up to Heaven, the best of Books in his hand, and the Law of Truth writ on his lips, it is to shew thee that his work is to know and unfold dark things to sinners; even as also thou seest him stand as if he pleaded with men; and whereas thou seest the World as cast behind him, and that a Crown hangs over his head, that is to shew thee that slighting and despising the things that are present, for the love that he hath to his Master's service, he is sure in the world that comes next to have Glory for his reward.[1]

What Christian saw at Interpreter's house was the portrait of a gospel minister. He was a man who helped sinners become the children of God, who kept a firm grip on God's Word, and who turned his back on everything the world had to offer. The apostle Paul wanted Timothy to become the same kind of minister, with "the World behind his back" and "the best of Books in his hand." In the closing verses of 1 Timothy 4 he paints a portrait of the minister as a young man.

An Exemplary Life

The sketch for Paul's portrait comes at the beginning of verse 16: "Keep a close watch on yourself and on the teaching." Or, as the King James Version has it, "Take heed unto thyself, and unto the doctrine." Timothy must keep a careful eye on both his behavior and his teaching. If he fails in either one he will fail in the ministry. As Matthew Henry commented, "Those who teach by their doctrine must teach by their life, else they pull down with one hand what they build up with the other."[2]

The vital connection between life and doctrine is beautifully expressed in "The Windows," a poem written by the seventeenth-century English writer George Herbert. Herbert—who was a country pastor—compares the preacher to a stained-glass window, who will shine brightly only if the work of Christ is etched into his life.

1. John Bunyan, *The Pilgrim's Progress*, ed. Charles W. Eliot, Harvard Classics (Danbury, CT: Grolier, 1988), 32–33.

2. Matthew Henry, *Matthew Henry's Commentary on the Whole Bible*, 6 vols. (New York: Revell, n.d.), n.p.

Lord, how can man preach thy eternal word?
  He is a brittle crazy glass:
Yet in thy temple thou dost him afford
  This glorious and transcendent place,
  To be a window, through thy grace.

But when thou dost anneal in glass thy story,
  Making thy life to shine within
The holy Preacher's; then the light and glory
  More rev'rend grows, and more doth win:
  Which else shows wat'rish, bleak, and thin.

Doctrine and life, colours and light, in one
  When they combine and mingle, bring
A strong regard and awe: but speech alone
  Doth vanish like a flaring thing,
  And in the ear, not conscience ring.[3]

First life, then doctrine—the order is important. Timothy cannot defend the Christian faith until he lives the Christian life. To quote the famous Puritan Richard Baxter, "There are too many men who are ministers before they know how to be Christians." Since Paul wanted Timothy to be a Christian first of all, he begins by telling his young protégé to lead an exemplary life: "Command and teach these things. Let no one despise you for your youth, but set the believers an example in speech, in conduct, in love, in faith, in purity" (1 Tim. 4:11–12).

The Greek word for "command" (*parangelle*) means "to direct" or "to give orders." It is a reminder that a teaching elder has true spiritual authority. It is his responsibility to teach—even to command, in God's name—his congregation to trust and obey the doctrine he has received from the apostles. Why did Paul need to remind Timothy of his God-given authority? Maybe because Timothy was timid. In his next missive, Paul will write, "God gave us a spirit not of fear but of power and love and self-control" (2 Tim. 1:7; cf. 1 Cor. 16:10). Whether Timothy was timid or not, he was

3. George Herbert, "The Windows," *George Herbert and the Seventeenth-Century Religious Poets* (New York: Norton, 1978), 30.

still a youngster, relatively speaking. Paul feared that his authority as a minister might be undermined by his tender years. So he said, "Let no one despise you for your youth" (1 Tim. 4:12).

There were two classes of grown men in those days: young men (*neoi*) and elders (*gerontes*). In Ephesus, each group had its own social association, with its own funds, officers, events, and athletic facilities.[4] Timothy belonged in the younger category, which included men up to the age of forty. Given the date when he first joined Paul (AD 49–50; cf. Acts 16:1–3) and the date of this letter (c. AD 62–64), he may have been in his thirties at the time. It was a relatively young age to bear full pastoral responsibility for an important church. Certainly it was no time to be immature or irresponsible. Timothy needed to be wise beyond his years.

At the same time, the Christians in Ephesus needed to respect Timothy's office. The command not to let anyone look down on him was intended for their ears as well as his own. Paul wanted to make sure that no one discriminated against Timothy on the basis of his age. Despite the young man's inexperience, they needed to treat him like a "Timothy," not like a "Timmy."

The Puritan Herbert Palmer faced the same difficulty when he went to preach to a French-speaking congregation in Canterbury, England. Not only was Palmer short in stature, he was fresh out of Cambridge University. As he mounted the pulpit steps to preach for the first time, an elderly French lady said in a loud voice, "Alas! what shall this child say to us?"[5] I can understand how Palmer felt. One Sunday, shortly after I arrived at Tenth Presbyterian Church at the tender age of twenty-eight, the elders were joined by C. Everett Koop for their morning prayers. Although Dr. Koop had moved from Philadelphia when he became United States surgeon general, he was still an elder of the church. As he sat down for prayer, he took one look at me and said, "The elders of this church are getting younger all the time!"

How can a young minister gain the respect of his elders? Not by demanding it, obviously, or by throwing his weight around, but only by setting a godly example. The way to stop people from looking down on you is to make sure they look up to you, and the way to do that is to lead by example. This

4. William M. Ramsay, *Historical Commentary on the Pastoral Epistles*, ed. Mark Wilson (Grand Rapids: Kregel, 1996), 117.

5. This account of Herbert Palmer's ministry comes from William S. Barker, *Puritan Profiles* (Fearn, Ross-shire: Christian Focus, 1996), 32.

is what Herbert Palmer did at the French church in Canterbury. In fact, once the suspicious old woman heard his reverent prayers and faithful preaching, she lifted her hands and praised God for his ministry. The same thing needed to happen in Ephesus. For better and for worse, to a greater or lesser extent, congregations are made in the image of their pastors. Paul himself often told people to follow his example. To the Corinthians he said, "Be imitators of me, as I am of Christ" (1 Cor. 11:1), and when he said farewell to the Ephesian elders, he reminded them of the manner of his ministry (Acts 20:18–21). Similarly, Timothy needed to be the very model of a Christian. "People would not despise his youth if they could admire his example,"[6] especially "in speech, in conduct, in love, in faith, in purity" (1 Tim. 4:12).

Start with the minister's conversation. His *speech* is to be seasoned with grace. He is to converse naturally and forcefully about spiritual things. He is to tell the truth. He is not to be argumentative (cf. 1 Tim. 6:4–5). He is not to use humor to tear others down. Even his words of rebuke are to be covered with affection, like the medicine in a spoonful of jam.

Such godly speech is one part of godly *conduct*, which is what Paul mentions next. The word refers to a minister's general behavior, to the way he lives. Conduct and speech go together. Richard Baxter warned ministers to watch how they live, "lest you may unsay with your lives that which you say with your tongues."[7] What a minister's life ought to say is that he is God's man, all the time: at home, at church, at the grocery store, on the freeway, on the playground, at the barber shop . . . everywhere.

The minister also sets an example in *love*, the virtue of all virtues. He is to keep both of the great commandments, loving God with all his heart and his neighbor as he loves himself (Matt. 22:37–40). He is to have a passionate concern for the spiritual condition of the lost. He is to have a special place in his heart for the people God has placed under his spiritual care. He shares in their joys and in their sorrows. He cares most for those who are most difficult to care for.

With tender love goes bold *faith*. An exemplary minister has strong faith in God, complete confidence in his Master. He believes in the power of God

6. John Stott, *Guard the Truth: The Message of 1 Timothy and Titus* (Downers Grove, IL: InterVarsity, 1996), 120.

7. Richard Baxter, *The Reformed Pastor* (Edinburgh: Banner of Truth, 1974), 67.

to save sinners. He seeks divine wisdom for the uncertainties of the future. He lives, studies, teaches, and preaches by faith. Indeed, the minister ought properly to be the boldest believer in the church.

Last, but not least, the minister sets an example by his *purity*. The Greek term for purity (*hagneia*) can describe general moral conduct, but the Greeks more often used it to refer to sexual behavior. An exhortation to sexual purity seems particularly appropriate for a young man like Timothy (cf. 2 Tim. 2:22). In these sex-obsessed times the church must insist on the necessity of chastity, especially in the ministry. A 1988 study by *Leadership* magazine discovered that 30 percent of Protestant clergy had engaged in sexual contact with someone other than a spouse.[8] Sadly, the week that I write this, I have received news that three ministers in the same presbytery committed adultery. Sexual sin has the inevitable result of destroying a man's ministry, damaging a church's reputation, and dishonoring the name of Jesus Christ.

The people of God must pray for the purity of their ministers. Young men preparing for pastoral ministry must not wait until they get married (or until they go to seminary, or until they get ordained) before they become sexually pure. They must begin immediately to apply the gospel of faith and repentance to any areas of sexual sin, and to practice godly discipline in what they look at, what they think about, what they say, and what they touch. As for men who are already in ministry, they must heed all the warnings in the Proverbs about the mortal danger of lust:

> Let not your heart turn aside to her ways;
>   do not stray into her paths,
> for many a victim has she laid low,
>   and all her slain are a mighty throng.
> Her house is the way to Sheol,
>   going down to the chambers of death. (Prov. 7:25–27)

To summarize, a pastor must set an example in every way. If he does, then his people will know how to live the Christian life. One is reminded of the famous words of Robert Murray M'Cheyne: "My people's greatest need is my personal holiness." These words are all the more appropriate when it is

8. Cited in Kenneth L. Woodward, "Sex, Morality and the Protestant Minister," *Newsweek* (July 28, 1997), 62.

remembered that they were uttered by a minister who died when he was only thirty. M'Cheyne understood, as Paul wanted Timothy to understand, that even as a young man, "he was to excel in those very qualities in which youth is wont to be deficient—gravity, prudence, consideration for others, trustworthiness, mastery over the passions."[9]

A man who lacks any one of these biblical virtues is unsuitable for pastoral ministry. Imagine a minister who is a gossip, or a liar. Imagine a loveless minister, with little or no compassion for the weak. Imagine a man who relies on his own strength to minister, rather than pastoring by faith. Or imagine a minister who is morally or sexually impure. With Calvin, we may say that sound biblical teaching "will be of little worth if there is not a corresponding uprightness and holiness of life."[10]

The Biblical Doctrine

Upon scanning this portrait of a young minister, Timothy may have been tempted to ask, with the psalmist, "How can a young man keep his way pure?" The psalmist says to his God, "By guarding it according to your word" (Ps. 119:9). Paul gave Timothy the same answer: "Until I come, devote yourself to the public reading of Scripture, to exhortation, to teaching" (1 Tim. 4:13). The implication is that Paul will resume some of these duties himself when he returns to Ephesus (cf. 1 Tim. 3:14). Until such time, however, Timothy must teach the biblical doctrine.

Teaching the Bible begins with *reading* the Bible. This applies to private study, of course, but the Greek word used here for reading (*anagnōsei*) refers to the public reading of Scripture. This held a central place in early Christian worship. It was one of the practices the first Christians carried over from Jewish worship. When Jesus visited the synagogue in Nazareth, for example, he read the Isaiah scroll before he began to teach (Luke 4:16–21). By the time Paul was writing to Timothy, public readings included not only the scrolls of Moses and the Prophets, but also the letters of the apostles. For example, Paul's

9. E. F. Scott, *The Pastoral Epistles*, The Moffatt New Testament Commentary (1936), in Donald Guthrie, *The Pastoral Epistles*, Tyndale New Testament Commentaries (Downers Grove, IL: InterVarsity, 1957), 97.

10. John Calvin, *The Second Epistle of Paul the Apostle to the Corinthians and the Epistles to Timothy, Titus and Philemon*, trans. T. A. Smail, Calvin's Commentaries (Edinburgh: Oliver & Boyd, 1964), 248.

first letter to the Thessalonians closes with the charge to "have this letter read to all the brothers" (1 Thess. 5:27; cf. 2 Cor. 3:14; Col. 4:16; Rev. 1:3).

The public reading of Scripture was necessary in the early church because books and parchments were scarce. For many Christians, public worship was the only opportunity to hear the Word of God. This is how Justin Martyr described a worship service from the second century: "On the day called Sunday, all who live in cities or in the country gather together to one place, and the memoirs of the apostles or the writings of the prophets are read, as long as time permits; then, when the reader has ceased, the president verbally instructs, and exhorts to the imitation of these good things."[11]

Subsequent history shows that the work of the gospel flourishes wherever the Bible is read.[12] This is why the disappearance of Scripture reading from some evangelical worship services is so alarming. It is good for churches to read from both the Old and the New Testaments, and to have a reading from the Gospels, or perhaps a reading from the Psalms. But however it is done, the Word of God from the Old and New Testaments is still to be read in all the churches.

The Scripture is not only to be read, but it is also to be explained, as it was in the days of Justin Martyr. Thus Paul commands Timothy also to devote himself to the exhortation and teaching of the Word of God (1 Tim. 4:13; cf. 1 Tim. 6:2). The first term the apostle uses (*paraklēsis*) is the word for exhortation. It means to encourage or to persuade, but it refers to Bible exposition, as can be seen from Paul's visit to Pisidian Antioch: "On the Sabbath day they went into the synagogue and sat down. After the reading from the Law and the Prophets, the rulers of the synagogue sent a message to them, saying, 'Brothers, if you have any word of exhortation for the people, say it' " (Acts 13:14–15; cf. Rom. 15:4). Paul proceeded to preach salvation in Jesus Christ from the Old Testament Scriptures (Acts 13:16–41). What the Bible means by a "word of exhortation" is a sermon (see also Heb. 13:22).

The second term the apostle uses (*didaskalia*) is the word for teaching or instruction. Timothy was to catechize God's people in Christian doctrine.

11. Justin Martyr, *First Apology*, I. 67, in *Ante-Nicene Fathers*, ed. Alexander Roberts and James Donaldson, 10 vols. (1885; repr. Peabody, MA: Hendrickson, 1994), 1:186.

12. See especially Hughes Oliphant Old's history of homiletics (and notice the first term in the title): *The Reading and Preaching of the Scriptures in the Worship of the Christian Church*, 7 vols. (Grand Rapids: Eerdmans, 1998-).

This may have included private instruction, but it also refers to the public explanation of apostolic teaching. Hughes Oliphant Old explains, on the basis of 1 Timothy 4:13, that "early Christian preaching had a strong didactic flavor. Preachers were supposed to move the heart and will, but they were also supposed to teach. . . . The reading and exposition of Scripture, the admonishing of the congregation, and the teaching of the Christian way of life were all integral parts of the ministry of the Word."[13]

Bible exposition is essential to the health of the church. Paul did not tell Timothy to replace the sermon with a drama, or to give the Ephesians five steps to a happier life. He told him to teach the Scriptures. This is because Bible exposition has always been at the heart of biblical worship, at least since the days of Ezra (see Neh. 8:1–8). Timothy, and all Christian ministers everywhere, must follow the same pattern. First the Bible is to be read; then it is to be explained and applied. The systematic exposition of Scripture remains the most effective means for the conversion of sinners and the confirmation of the saints. It is the most effective means because it is God's chosen means. Indeed, it must be doubted whether worship which does not preserve a central place for preaching and teaching the Bible is proper Christian worship at all.

Teaching biblical doctrine is what Timothy had been ordained to do, and his ordination to gospel ministry is mentioned explicitly in verse 14: "Do not neglect the gift you have, which was given you by prophecy when the council of elders laid their hands on you." Paul refers to the same event in 2 Timothy 1:6, where he reminds Timothy to "fan into flame the gift of God, which is in you through the laying on of my hands." Paul is speaking here about ordination, which may be defined as "the authoritative admission of one duly called to an office in the Church of God, accompanied with prayer and the laying on of hands."[14] Although it is not a sacrament, the laying on of hands is "an outward sign of an inward gift for ministry."[15] The practice itself goes back to the blessings of the Old Testament. For example, it is said that when Moses commissioned Joshua, his successor "was full of the spirit

13. Ibid., 1:247.

14. *The Book of Church Order of the Presbyterian Church in America*, 5th ed. (Atlanta: Committee for Christian Education and Publications, 1997), 17–2.

15. Thomas C. Oden, *First and Second Timothy and Titus*, Interpretation (Louisville: John Knox, 1989), 125.

of wisdom, for Moses had laid his hands on him" (Deut. 34:9). Much later, Judaism "developed a rite in which the teacher would pass on his authority to his students at the end of their course of studies by laying his hands on their heads."[16] It was natural, therefore, for the first Christians to commission missionaries and pastors through the laying on of hands. This is the way Paul and Barnabas were set apart for missionary service by the church in Antioch (Acts 13:3; cf. 6:6). In much the same way, Timothy was ordained for the gospel ministry at the hands of the Ephesian elders, including the hands of Paul himself (cf. 2 Tim. 1:6).

One special feature of Timothy's ordination was a prophecy. This may have been a word from the Lord telling the church to ordain him (cf. Acts 13:2), or perhaps it was a prophecy about what would happen through his ministry (cf. 1 Tim. 1:18). In any case, Timothy was called to the ministry by the Holy Spirit. No man should ever invite himself to become a pastor. Instead, a true minister is called by the Holy Spirit, working through the desires of his heart and the wisdom of the church. This spiritual call is essential for enduring the hardships of ministry. In one of his pastoral letters, John Newton wrote that "the man who is once moved by the Spirit of God to this work, will prefer it, if attainable, to thousands of gold and silver; so that, though he is at times intimidated by a sense of its importance and difficulty, compared with his own great insufficiency, yet he cannot give it up."[17]

Timothy was not only called by the Spirit, but he was also gifted by the Spirit. When the elders laid their hands on him, he received supernatural help for gospel ministry. This shows that the Holy Spirit is powerfully present in the ordination of teaching and ruling elders. The Bible does not say what Timothy's gift was. He may have received some unique spiritual endowment for ministry. More likely, "the gift" refers generally to the talents needed for pastoral ministry and especially to the tasks mentioned in the previous verse: reading, preaching, and teaching. Timothy was a gifted minister, equipped by the Holy Spirit.

Since the Greek term for gift is *charisma*, one may say that Paul wanted Timothy to have a charismatic ministry, in the proper sense of the word. A pastor does not minister in the strength of his natural ability, but by the

16. Jouette M. Bassler, *1 Timothy, 2 Timothy, Titus* (Nashville: Abingdon, 1996), 87.
17. John Newton, *Letters of John Newton* (Edinburgh: Banner of Truth, 1960), 54.

power of the Holy Spirit. Where there is no Spirit, there can be no effective ministry. And since the gift for ministry comes from God, it must not be neglected. Timothy must not be like the foolish man who buried his talent in the ground and gave the Lord a poor return on his investment (Matt. 25:14–30). Instead, he must fulfill his ordination vows by actively employing his pastoral gifts in the service of Christ.

The Church's Salvation

Timothy's continuance in the ministry is a matter of life and death, for Paul closes his instructions by saying, "Practice these things, devote yourself to them, so that all may see your progress. Keep a close watch on yourself and on the teaching. Persist in this, for by so doing you will save both yourself and your hearers" (1 Tim. 4:15–16). Timothy must persevere for the salvation of the church (not to mention his own salvation).

Paul first tells the young minister to "practice" (*meleta*) his life and doctrine (1 Tim. 4:15). The New English Bible puts it like this: "Make these matters your business," while the New International Version says, "Be diligent." "Practice" is perhaps the best translation, and it calls to mind Paul's earlier comments about training oneself to be godly. When it comes to ministry, practice makes perfect.

Next comes an unusual phrase: "Devote yourself to them," or as the New International Version has it, "Give yourself wholly to them." More literally, Timothy is "to be in these things." To put this into contemporary English, a minister lives for preaching. One can almost imagine Timothy walking around Ephesus wearing a trendy Christian T-shirt that expressed his passion for his calling: "Pastoral ministry is life . . . the rest is just details."

The command to give oneself to ministry comes as a comfort as well as a challenge. Pastoral ministry *is* my life. When I am deep in thought, my wife will sometimes ask what I am thinking about. Unless I am reviewing the batting order of the St. Louis Cardinals, I usually have to admit that I am trying to resolve a pastoral problem or thinking through a biblical text. Not that ministers should live warped or unbalanced lives! If a pastor is married, his family life has priority, as Paul has already explained (1 Tim. 3:4). Physical exercise also has its place (1 Tim. 4:8). Nevertheless, pastoral ministry is a total life-commitment.

If Timothy makes that commitment, then he will make the kind of "progress" that everyone will be able to see (1 Tim. 4:15). This instruction may have been another attack on the false teachers, who seem to have used the idea of progress as one of their slogans (cf. 2 Tim. 3:9). But the mention of progress was also intended to keep Timothy from getting discouraged. If he was like most young ministers, there were times when he wondered if he would ever become the minister God wanted him to become. There must have been occasions when he was disappointed with his preaching or discouraged about his evangelism. After all, the man who set the standard for pastoral ministry in Ephesus was none other than the apostle Paul! A man does not become a minister all at once, however. There is always room for improvement. Even if Timothy was not yet the minister he would become, at least he could make visible progress in life and doctrine.

This last sentence of 1 Timothy 4 is sometimes considered a difficult one: "Persist in this, for by so doing you will save both yourself and your hearers" (1 Tim. 4:16). Everywhere else, the Bible teaches that salvation comes through Jesus Christ alone (cf. 1 Tim. 1:15). Yet here the Scripture seems to give Timothy the power of salvation, both for himself and his congregation.

Some have tried to handle this difficulty by saying that the word "save" means something besides salvation from sin and death. This interpretation is possible, because the Greek word for salvation (*sōzō*) was often used to mean something like "safekeeping." We speak the same way in English, where the word "saving" can be used for something as simple as saving leftovers. On this interpretation, Timothy's persistence in personal godliness and the faithful teaching of God's Word will preserve both himself and his congregation from spiritual harm.

However, it is also possible that Paul is thinking of salvation in the gospel sense of the word. What this verse acknowledges is that ministers of the gospel have a crucial role in the salvation of sinners. Salvation comes only by faith in the death and resurrection of Jesus Christ. But "faith comes from hearing, and hearing through the word of Christ" (Rom. 10:17), and the word of Christ, in turn, comes by the preaching of the gospel. Therefore, Christian ministers are indispensable to God's plan for the salvation of the world. There is even a sense in which they can be said to "save" their hearers (cf. 1 Cor. 9:22), not by their own merits, but by the proclamation of

Jesus Christ. The spiritual destiny of any church is tied up with the spiritual destiny of its minister and his faithful proclamation of the gospel.

It was the saving importance of the gospel ministry that led Interpreter to show Christian a portrait of a gospel minister in *Pilgrim's Progress*:

> Now, said the *Interpreter*, I have showed thee this Picture first, because the Man whose Picture this is, is the only man whom the Lord of the place whither thou art going, hath authorized to be thy guide in all difficult places thou mayest meet with in the way; wherefore take good heed to what I have showed thee, and bear well in thy mind what thou hast seen, lest in thy Journey thou meet with some that pretend to lead thee right, but their way goes down to death.[18]

Sound preaching can mean the difference between life and death, and acknowledging its vital role in salvation does not detract in any way from the grace God gives in the gospel. Calvin explains it like this: "It is indeed true that it is God alone who saves and not even the smallest part of His glory can rightly be transferred to men. But God's glory is in no way diminished by His using the labor of men in bestowing salvation. . . . This ministry is itself entirely God's work, for it is He who makes men good pastors and leads them by His Spirit and blesses their work so that it may not be in vain."[19]

Paul wanted to be sure that Timothy's work was not in vain, as it would have been if he were to give up and quit before it was finished. Souls perish for the lack of sound ministry. On the other hand, ministers who continue in God's grace have the assurance of their own salvation and the joy of leading others to Christ. As John Stott observes, "Perseverance is not the meritorious cause, but rather the ultimate evidence, of our salvation."[20]

When it comes to persevering to the very end, it is hard to think of a better example than Thomas Boston. In the last months of his life, that faithful Scottish minister from the eighteenth century was confined to his bed by a serious illness. Yet Boston continued to preach. His little congregation would gather around the window of the manse, from which he

18. Bunyan, *Pilgrim's Progress*, 33.
19. Calvin, *Second Epistle of Paul*, 248–49.
20. Stott, *Guard the Truth*, 124.

would read, preach, and teach God's Word on the Lord's Day. Boston's last sermon was called "The Necessity of Self-Examination."[21] In it he challenged his beloved congregation to remain in the faith. He begged them to make sure of their eternal salvation, to "bend all their endeavors and attention to gain a blessed and happy eternity."[22] Every pastor who fits the biblical portrait begs his people to do the same thing: to believe in the Lord Jesus Christ unto salvation.

21. Thomas Boston, *The Complete Works of the Late Rev. Thomas Boston, Ettrick* (London, 1853; repr. Wheaton, IL: Richard Owen Roberts, 1980), 2:497–510.

22. Ibid., 2:503.

14

House Rules

1 Timothy 5:1–8

Do not rebuke an older man but encourage him as you would a father. Treat younger men like brothers, older women like mothers, younger women like sisters, in all purity. Honor widows who are truly widows. (1 Tim. 5:1–3)

A man from my childhood church traveled to a Latin American country on a mission trip. He stayed with a Christian family that was desperately poor. Their only possessions were the clothes on their backs, a tiny one-room shelter, and a chicken. As the mission trip drew to a close, the host family held a dinner in my friend's honor, at which soup was served for the main course. To the man's astonishment, there was meat in the soup. He wondered what kind of meat it could be. Suddenly he realized that he must be eating chicken soup.

My friend was so overwhelmed by the generosity of these Christians that tears began streaming down his cheeks. He marveled that the family had offered up their only chicken for him. Yet to the father of the household, this sacrifice seemed like the most natural thing in the world. They were willing to share everything they had with the missionary. After all, he was a brother in Christ, and therefore virtually a member of their own family.

The Family of God

The New Testament tells Christians to find their personal and family identity in Jesus Christ: "To all who did receive him, who believed in his name, he gave the right to become children of God" (John 1:12). Therefore, everyone who believes in Jesus Christ belongs to the same family.

Consider some of the ways in which the church is a family. Every Christian has the same father: the God and Father of our Lord Jesus Christ. When we say our family prayers, we begin with the words, "Our Father" (Matt. 6:9). Christians all became members of this family the same way, for God has adopted us all by his Holy Spirit: "in love he predestined us for adoption through Jesus Christ, according to the purpose of his will" (Eph. 1:5). Or, to look at the same relationship from a different point of view, we were all born-again into God's family—"born, not of blood nor of the will of the flesh nor of the will of man, but of God" (John 1:13).

Once we become members of God's family, we enter into a close relationship with our Father. Unlike some fathers, he is not distant, absent, or malevolent. Just the opposite: "For all who are led by the Spirit of God are sons of God. For you did not receive the spirit of slavery to fall back into fear, but you have received the Spirit of adoption as sons, by whom we cry, 'Abba! Father!' The Spirit himself bears witness with our spirit that we are children of God" (Rom. 8:14–16). Since we are God's children, we eat around the family dinner table at the sacrament of the Lord's Supper. We even plan to attend the same family reunion in heaven. Belonging to this family is so wonderful that it calls for double exclamation marks: "How great is the love the Father has lavished on us, that we should be called children of God! And that is what we are!" (1 John 3:1 NIV).

Now that God has made us his sons and daughters through Jesus Christ, the church is the Christian's first family. It takes precedence even over one's biological or nuclear family. Blood may well be thicker than water, but the Spirit is thicker than blood. The family God has established through Jesus Christ is the Christian's first family. Consider the example of Jesus Christ, when he was teaching in a house in Galilee:

> And his mother and his brothers came, and standing outside they sent to him and called him. And a crowd was sitting around him, and they said to him, "Your mother and your brothers are outside, seeking you." And he answered them, "Who are my mother and my brothers?" And looking about at those who sat around him, he said, "Here are my mother and my brothers! Whoever does the will of God, he is my brother and sister and mother." (Mark 3:31–35)

If anyone understood the family of God, it was Paul. It seems, as one reads through the New Testament, that the apostle had the largest extended family in the Roman world. He was forever mentioning brothers like Quartus and Sosthenes or sisters like Phoebe and Apphia. In fact, there are more than one hundred references to brothers and sisters in the writings of Paul. The apostle's first letter to Timothy is no exception, for it contains numerous references to the family business. Timothy himself is called Paul's "true child in the faith" (1 Tim. 1:2; cf. 1:18). The Ephesians are referred to as his "brothers" (1 Tim. 4:6). The church itself is God's "household" (1 Tim. 3:15). In other words, Timothy's congregation is not just *like* a family; it *is* his family.

Family Matters

In an orderly family, each person is treated with respect, according to his or her age and gender. God's household is no exception: "Do not rebuke an older man but encourage him as you would a father. Treat younger men like brothers, older women like mothers, younger women like sisters, in all purity" (1 Tim. 5:1–2). Each and every member of the family should be treated in the proper way.

Showing respect for one's elders is not simply a cultural convention; it is the will of God. Even the minister, if he is a young man, must treat older men with deference. The way to do this may vary from culture to culture. According to Old Testament law, the young should "stand up before the gray head and honor the face of an old man" (Lev. 19:32). In an Asian church, younger men obey this principle by bowing before their elders. Western Christians tend not to be as respectful, or at least not to show their respect in the same way, but they should give honor and preference to their elders any way they can. One practical implication of this principle is that children should be taught to respect their elders. It is good for them to use proper titles when they address adults. They should learn to speak when spoken to, and so forth. Being polite is a spiritual matter, especially within God's family.

Respect for elders does not mean that older men can do as they please. Sometimes Pastor Timothy will need to correct his seniors. He may not simply overlook their scandals or their heresies. In fact, Paul has already told him to "charge certain persons not to teach any different doctrine" (1 Tim. 1:3), and presumably some of these persons were older than he was. Even when a rebuke is called for, however, a young minister must not be overbearing. It is not his place to give an older man a tongue-lashing. As Towner points out, "This method of correction relies on fear and authority and is often applied when feelings of anger and insecurity are running high."[1] Instead of being harsh, a minister should deal with an older man gently and tactfully, the way he would appeal to his own father. The rebuke of an elder should be a reminder, not a reprimand.

Younger men should be treated rather differently. Timothy should not look down on them or talk down to them. Instead, he should treat them as peers: "Treat younger men like brothers" (1 Tim. 5:1). The wisdom of running a household this way is obvious. At the same time younger men are treating older men with deference, older men are treating younger men as equals. Thus dignity and intimacy are both maintained in their relationships.

The principle here is vital to the peace of the family. It is the responsibility of older Christians to bridge the generation gap to younger Christians, and not the other way around. The proper way to talk to a toddler is to get down on one's hands and knees. Similarly, the way to reach out to teenagers is to enter their world by learning their vocabulary and interests. One of the best ways to help younger Christians become mature is to treat them with a measure of equality.

Yet there is a danger here for the young. Even if older Christians treat them as equals, they should not think of themselves as equals. It might be appropriate, for example, for a younger man to continue to address an older man by his formal title, even after the older man invites him to use his first

1. Philip H. Towner, *1–2 Timothy and Titus*, IVP New Testament Commentary Series (Downers Grove, IL: InterVarsity, 1994), 114.

name. But the issue is not so much the address as it is the attitude. Older men should treat their juniors with fraternity; younger men should treat their seniors with humility.

Younger ministers, and all Christians, should relate to women as respectfully as they relate to men. Older women should be treated like mothers. They should be loved and listened to. They should be protected and cared for. There is a touching example of this from Paul's own life, when at the end of Romans he greets "Rufus, chosen in the Lord; also his mother, who has been a mother to me as well" (Rom. 16:13). To take a more contemporary example, consider the way in which the great Christian writer C. S. Lewis cared for the mother of his friend Paddy Moore. The two men had served together in World War I. Lewis agreed that if Moore died in combat, he would look after his mother. Moore was indeed killed during the war, and Lewis held up his end of the bargain. By all accounts, Mrs. Moore was a difficult woman to live with, but Lewis treated her like his own mother in his own home for some thirty years.[2]

Finally, to complete the family portrait, younger women should be treated as sisters. Within God's family, men and women ought to display tender affection toward one another, the kind of fondness that a brother has for a younger sister. But the Scripture quickly adds a warning: "in all purity" (1 Tim. 5:2). As close as a relationship between siblings may be, there must not be anything improper about it. Here the concern is frankly sexual: a minister must not compromise his commitment to Christ by having an inappropriate relationship with one of his sisters in Christ. Chastity is part of a minister's sacred trust to his congregation. Given the language that Paul uses, one might almost say that adultery among Christians is tantamount to incest. Paul said this to Timothy because he wanted to make sure that the young man's ministry was not compromised. As we shall see, not all the young women in Ephesus were discreet (1 Tim. 5:11–13), and Timothy needed to be careful in his relationships with women in the church.

One good way for a minister to preserve his purity is to avoid meeting with women completely in private. He can have conversations with women before or after church, of course. He can also arrange to meet a woman for

2. George Sayer, *Jack: A Life of C. S. Lewis* (Wheaton, IL: Crossway, 1994), 135–36, 152–54, 177–78.

spiritual counsel at the church, provided someone else is close by. But he should never go alone to a woman's house. My own rule of thumb is in keeping with this verse: I will not meet alone with any woman unless she is my wife, my sister, my daughter, or old enough to be my mother.

A Protector of Widows

The surprising thing about the house rules Paul gives Timothy is that they say so little about most family relationships and so much about widows. There are only two short verses for fathers and brothers, sisters and mothers, but fourteen verses for widows. Why is this?

Undoubtedly, the special emphasis on widows says something about the church in Ephesus. For one reason or another, the Ephesians needed help knowing how to care for their widows. Timothy may even have written to ask for Paul's guidance in this area. But the attention to detail in these instructions also says something important about God. God has a special place in his heart for single women, especially for widows. Here it should be noted that the Greek word for "widow" (*chēra*) refers to any woman without a husband, and not simply to a woman whose husband had died.[3] Kent Hughes wisely comments: "Today the application of this passage should be wider, because modern American culture has produced a category of women virtually unknown in the first century—Christian women and children who have been abandoned by their spouses and left without family support. Godly single mothers are a new class of 'widow.' And those without family and resources are the church's sacred responsibility."[4]

In the Old Testament, God is styled the "protector of widows." His affection for needy women is written into the law: "For the Lord your God is God of gods and Lord of lords, the great, the mighty, and the awesome God. . . . He executes justice for the fatherless and the widow" (Deut. 10:17–18). God's concern for widows and orphans is also written into the biblical hymnal:

3. Jouette M. Bassler, *1 Timothy, 2 Timothy, Titus* (Nashville: Abingdon, 1996), 93.

4. R. Kent Hughes, *1 & 2 Timothy: To Guard the Deposit*, Preaching the Word (Wheaton, IL: Crossway, 2000), 126.

Sing to God, sing praises to his name;
  lift up a song to him who rides through the deserts;
his name is the Lord;
  exult before him!
Father of the fatherless and protector of widows
  is God in his holy habitation.
God settles the solitary in a home. (Ps. 68:4–6)

Some of the most touching episodes in the Old Testament concern the care and feeding of widows. God fed Ruth during the barley harvest and placed a child on Naomi's lap (Ruth 1:22–2:23; 4:13–17). He spared the widow of Zarephath in the days of Elijah (1 Kings 17:7–24). He provided an abundance of oil for a widow through the ministry of Elisha (2 Kings 4:1–7). Almighty God has earned the right to be called the Protector of Widows. And not surprisingly, Jesus also took special care for widows. He brought an only son back to life for the widow of Nain (Luke 7:11–15). He commended the persistence of the praying widow (Luke 18:1–8) and the generosity of the poor woman who gave all she had at the temple (Mark 12:41–44). He also rebuked Bible scholars who "devour widows' houses" (Mark 12:40). Even on the cross, he made provision for his own mother in her widowhood (John 19:25–27).

The reason for God's concern is that widows were vulnerable in the ancient world. The learned historian William M. Ramsay wrote that given "the narrow restrictions of ancient social life, it was not easy for them to maintain their children after the earning member of the family had died, and they stood in need of special consideration and help."[5] Without the protection of a man, widows were sometimes exposed to physical danger. They lacked the economic power to provide for their needs, especially in old age. The same is often true today.

For all these reasons, God was concerned about the welfare of widows. The prophet Isaiah thus challenged God's people to "plead the widow's cause" (Isa. 1:17; cf. Ex. 22:22; Deut. 24:17; Job 29:13). God wants all his children to share their Father's heart for the fatherless and the husbandless. This means caring for widows first of all. This principle applies not

5. William M. Ramsay, *Historical Commentary on the Pastoral Epistles*, ed. Mark Wilson (Grand Rapids: Kregel, 1996), 125.

only to widows, however, but to every family member who needs special care: the sick, the elderly, the disabled, and single mothers. God knows that as long as his weakest children are protected, his whole family will be safe.

Imagine a father who leaves two children with a babysitter: a nine-year-old son and a three-year-old daughter. In all likelihood, he will leave more careful instructions about his daughter than about his son. A nine-year-old boy can almost look after himself, but a little girl requires greater care. The father's primary concern is to make sure that the babysitter knows what she needs. Our Father in heaven has a similar heart concern for all his neediest children.

Putting Religion into Practice

The early church shared God's heart for women who were alone in the world. In fact, the first ecclesiastical controversy concerned the care and feeding of widows: "Now in those days when the disciples were increasing in number, a complaint by the Hellenists arose against the Hebrews because their widows were being neglected in the daily distribution" (Acts 6:1). Under the direction of the apostles, the church in Jerusalem chose seven men to make sure all the widows got what they needed.

There are needy widows in nearly every church, of course, which is why Paul pleads their cause: "Honor widows who are truly widows" (1 Tim. 5:3). This raises the obvious question: What does it mean for a widow to be *truly* a widow? Paul's basic answer is that "a widow in need is a widow indeed," and thus he proceeds to offer several guidelines for assessing a widow's true needs.

The first qualification is that a true widow does not have independent means: "But if a widow has children or grandchildren, let them first learn to show godliness to their own household and to make some return to their parents, for this is pleasing in the sight of God" (1 Tim. 5:4). Widows who are all alone need special care from the church, whereas others can rely on family support.

In the ancient Greek world, support was related to a woman's dowry. If her husband died, she entered the household of her son or grandson. Her dowry would then pass into his possession.[6] Paul wanted to remind the

6. Bruce W. Winter, "*Providentia* for the Widows of 1 Timothy 5:3–16," *Tyndale Bulletin* 39 (1988): 83–99.

Ephesians that this custom was good Christianity—one good way to be godly. Caring for aged parents (and grandparents) is the most practical theology of all. Piety always begins at home (cf. 1 Tim. 3:5).

To make sure that Christians do their duty, the Bible gives two motivations for caring for widows. First, support is something children owe to their parents. After everything parents have done over the years, it is only fair for their children to provide for them in old age. In the economy of God, this is the way children can repay their parents. This does not necessarily mean that children need to provide all the care themselves. It is important to plan for the future, which may include carrying the proper medical and life insurance. There is also a legitimate place for professional care-givers, as well as for nursing homes, in some cases. But it is the responsibility of children to make sure that their parents receive the best possible care. Whenever possible, they should do the caring themselves, in their own homes.

Not only is family loyalty something children owe to their parents, but it is also something they owe to God. This is the second motive Paul offers: caring for family needs is "pleasing in the sight of God" (of course it is pleasing to God: he is the Protector of Widows, after all). By telling families to take care of their own needy, the apostle was not simply trying to reduce the church's budget. He wanted to make sure that Christians glorified God by loving their families.

To underscore the importance of family care, the Scripture also issues this strong warning: "But if anyone does not provide for his relatives, and especially for members of his household, he has denied the faith and is worse than an unbeliever" (1 Tim. 5:8). Even pagans have a sense of duty to their relatives, especially ones living under their own roof. Therefore, a Christian who refuses to shoulder his family responsibilities is worse than a pagan (cf. Matt. 15:4–6). This is not to say that a man must earn all or most of his family's income himself (as the verse is often mistaken to teach), but that a husband and father must bear the ultimate responsibility for his family's welfare, seeing to it that they have whatever resources they need, by whatever appropriate means God may provide (including his wife's income, for example, if her employment is in keeping with her calling as a wife and mother, and with the family's total needs). Any dereliction of this fundamental family duty is tantamount to a denial of Christ. No matter how eloquent the man's testimony may be, his life denies his Christianity.

This warning needs to be heard in our day, because we do not live in the most compassionate of times. All too often, modern society shoves the elderly out of sight and puts them out of mind. But this gives the church a wonderful opportunity to shine with the compassion of Christ. The way Christians care for parents and grandparents ought to proclaim the love of God. So should the way we care for other people's parents when, for example, we share the good news about Jesus Christ in local nursing homes. We are the children of a Father who is the Protector of Widows, and therefore we are called to be agents of his protecting and providing grace.

Anna and Her Sisters

Unfortunately, not every old woman has family who will take care of her. Some grieve for the husbands they have lost. Others have been abandoned by their families. They are all alone and may lack food, clothing, housing, medical care, or any stable source of income. They are really in need because they are destitute. But no matter what her economic status may be, if a widow belongs to God through faith in Jesus Christ, she is never alone; she always has a family. Even if no one else will help her, the church will show her mercy because the church *is* her family. This is another one of God's house rules: "Honor widows who are truly widows" (1 Tim. 5:3). Or, as the New International Version interprets the verse: "Give proper recognition to those widows who are really in need."

The word "honor" (*tima*) is a word for respect or recognition. It comes from the fifth commandment: "Honor your father and your mother, that your days may be long in the land that the Lord your God is giving you" (Ex. 20:12). The kind of honor that God has in mind means more than just respect. It means meeting a widow's emotional and material needs. Anyone who takes care of an older woman—doing her shopping, giving her rides, paying her bills, being her companion, or what have you—gives her proper recognition.

The command to honor widows implies that God himself gives them honor. Calvin thus encouraged widows "to consider what honor God does them, though they be destitute of all men's aid, yet he offers himself of his own mind, to be their protector, and to defend them. And therefore let widows comfort themselves herein and commit themselves wholly to God."[7] Calvin is right to encourage widows to commit themselves wholly to God, for that is what God himself tells them to do: "She who is truly a widow, left all alone, has set her hope on God and continues in supplications and prayers night and day" (1 Tim. 5:5). Paul has already explained how a widow physically qualifies for support: she must be destitute. Now he adds a spiritual qualification: she must be faithful. The genuine widow does not trust in the government for her welfare, or even in the church. Nor is she overwhelmed by her circumstances. Instead, like the psalmist, she puts all her hope in God (e.g. Ps. 146:5). She throws herself upon his mercy, and then she finds that she is not alone after all, because God is with her.

This verse calls Christian widows to a unique ministry of intercession, both publicly and privately (cf. 1 Tim. 2:1). Susan Hunt writes about this ministry in her book *By Design: God's Distinctive Calling for Women*:

> It seems to me that widows have entered into a dimension of dependence on God that prepares them for the ministry of intercessory prayer. The widow's mite was recognized and commended by Jesus because "she, out of her poverty, put in everything—all she had to live on" (Mark 12:44). Perhaps the widow's "might" is most mighty when these women band together as helper defenders in intercessory prayer. Older women who do not have the daily responsibilities of jobs are another power source for intercessory prayer.[8]

Perhaps the best biblical example of the praying widow is Anna, the prophetess at the temple in Jerusalem: "She was advanced in years, having lived with her husband seven years from when she was a virgin, and then as a widow until she was eighty-four. She did not depart from the temple, worshiping with fasting and prayer night and day" (Luke 2:36–37). Paul almost seems to echo this passage when he encourages widows to "continue in supplications and prayers night and day" (1 Tim. 5:5).

Every praying widow is Anna's sister. I once saw some of Anna's sisters at their prayers when I visited a Korean church in New York City. Every Friday the old women gathered in the sanctuary to pray all through the night for

7. John Calvin, *Sermons on the Epistles to Timothy & Titus* (1579; repr. Edinburgh: Banner of Truth, 1983), 463.

8. Susan Hunt, *By Design: God's Distinctive Calling for Women* (Franklin, TN: Legacy, 1994), 107–8.

God's work in their church and in their community. Anna's sisters prayed all over the Soviet Union during the dark years of communism. When one pastor visited the Ukraine after the fall of that evil empire, he saw

> how mistaken the Communists were when they allowed the older women to continue worshipping together! It was they who were considered no threat to the new order, but it was they whose prayers and faithfulness over all those barren years held the church together and raised up a generation of men and young people to serve the Lord. Yes, the church we attended was crowded with these older women at the very front, for they had been the stalwart defenders and maintainers of Christ's Gospel, but behind them and alongside them and in the balcony and outside the windows were the fruit of their faithfulness, men, women, young people, and children. We must never underestimate the place and power of our godly women.[9]

The prayers of widows give strength to the church. Calvin said that "prayer by day and night is the special privilege of widows and the childless, for they are free from the things that very properly hinder those who rule a family from doing the same."[10] As a result of their intercession, young mothers with their toddlers, ministers at their books, missionaries in their fields, men and women on their jobs all receive spiritual help for their work. If you are a widow, God is calling you to enter into deep fellowship with him through prayer. In fact, one of the praying widows in my own congregation asks that I encourage other widows to join her. Perhaps the great work of your life is only just beginning: the great work of intercessory prayer.

Paul's passionate call to prayer explains why his next words are so harsh: "But she who is self-indulgent is dead even while she lives" (1 Tim. 5:6). This "merry widow" is no woman of prayer. She has not fixed her hope on God. Instead, she takes comfort in the things of this world and lives for pleasure rather than for God. She likes to pamper herself, for the word translated "self-indulgent" (*spatalōsa*) indicates "luxurious, voluptuous indulgence."[11] It may even imply that she prostitutes herself sexually for profit. A woman

9. Glen Knecht, quoted in Hunt, *By Design*, 109.

10. John Calvin, *The Second Epistle of Paul the Apostle to the Corinthians and the Epistles to Timothy, Titus and Philemon*, trans. T. A. Smail, Calvin's Commentaries (Edinburgh: Oliver & Boyd, 1964), 253.

11. Thomas D. Lea, *1, 2 Timothy*, New American Commentary (Nashville: Broadman, 1992), 147.

who likes to "live it up" like this "is dead even while she lives" (1 Tim. 5:6). She belongs to the living dead, because although she is alive physically, she is not alive to God through faith; she is as good as dead, spiritually speaking. The contrast between the two kinds of widows is a paradox: "For one kind of life (self-indulgence) is in reality spiritual death, while one kind of death (self-denial) is in reality spiritual life."[12]

What the Scripture implies is that a widow who lives for pleasure has no right to expect any help from the church at all: "A worldly-minded, self-indulgent widow like that is dead while still alive, and therefore can have no claim on the church's alms."[13] This is a reminder that the mercy of the church is not an entitlement. The church has a responsibility to identify people's real needs and ultimate commitments. Often this means that deacons need to ask personal questions: What resources do you have? Is there anyone in your family who can help? What do you really need to get by? Are you walking with the Lord? And so forth. Then it is up to the deacons to make judgments about whom to help, and how to help them. When it comes to the mercy of the church, there is a legitimate distinction between the deserving and the undeserving poor.[14] Some people do not need any material help, especially if their families will support them. Some people do need help, but should not receive money because they are living for pleasure. However, those widows who have real needs and genuine faith have a right to receive the full help of the church.

You Will Be Like My Mother

These rules for God's household are not just for Timothy, or for ministers, but for the whole church: "Command these things as well, so that they may be without reproach" (1 Tim. 5:7). If widows do not devote themselves to prayer, or if children do not provide for their aged parents, or if the church does not

12. John Stott, *Guard the Truth: The Message of 1 Timothy and Titus* (Downers Grove, IL: InterVarsity, 1996), 131.

13. J. N. D. Kelly, *The Pastoral Epistles: Timothy I and II, Titus*, Harper's New Testament Commentaries (San Francisco: Harper and Row, 1960), 114.

14. Calvin claims that Paul is "distinguishing between the worthy and the unworthy" (*Second Epistle of Paul*, 253). See also Marvin Olasky's historical treatment of this distinction in *The Tragedy of American Compassion* (Washington, DC: Regnery, 1992).

care for its widows, then the whole church will come under reproach. In other words, outsiders will be quick to criticize the church for its failure to show mercy.

God's instructions about caring for widows are essential to genuine Christianity. Therefore, they are meant to be followed. A wonderful story about following them comes from the missionary work of Joanne Shetler, whose ministry has been mentioned already in the pages of this book. After two decades of intensive labor, Shetler saw the Balangao tribesmen of the Philippine Islands turn to Jesus Christ in faith and repentance. Tribal life was transformed as a result of biblical teaching. Although Shetler translated many parts of the Bible into Balangao, Paul's first letter to Timothy had particular influence. She tells what happened when the Balangao came to God's house rules for widows:

> We got to the end of the book where it talks about widows in need and the church's responsibility to take over for widows who have no other source of livelihood. About the same time, Forsan, one of those old women the spirits had earlier tried to kill, lost her husband. And she was a widow indeed. All of her children had long been dead. She had no relatives in Balangao. In fact, she was not even a Balangao. And in Balangao culture there is no mercy if there is no blood connection. She would have been left alone in her house with or without food until she died. One of the men who had helped me in the translation . . . went over and took Forsan by the hand with her one little pot, brought her over and said, "You will be like my mother and you will live with us in our home." And that old woman is there today, even though she is old and sickly.[15]

Once they received the grace of Jesus Christ, the Balangao became members of God's family. Every child of God must live by the rules of his house. This includes showing love to widows, because the Father of the house is the Protector of Widows.

15. Joanne Shetler, "Faithful in Obedience," in *Faithful Witness: The Urbana '84 Compendium*, ed. James McLeish (Downers Grove, IL: InterVarsity, 1985), 99–107 (p. 106).

15

Pure, Unadulterated Religion

1 Timothy 5:9–16

Let a widow be enrolled if she is not less than sixty years of age, having been the wife of one husband, and having a reputation for good works: if she has brought up children, has shown hospitality, has washed the feet of the saints, has cared for the afflicted, and has devoted herself to every good work. (1 Tim. 5:9–10)

What is the essence of true religion? The Bible gives more than one answer to this question, or at least it expresses the same answer in several different ways. The prophet Micah said that the Lord requires you "to do justice, and to love kindness, and to walk humbly with your God" (Micah 6:8). Jesus said the two greatest commandments are to love the Lord your God with all your heart and your neighbor as yourself (Matt. 22:37–40). The apostle James said something a little different, or maybe he said the same thing and made it more specific: "Religion that is pure and undefiled before God and the Father is this: to visit orphans and widows in their affliction, and to keep oneself unstained from the world"

(James 1:27). Caring for women who are alone in the world is one of the best ways to honor God and love your neighbor. It is Christianity at its finest. Taking care of widows is pure, unadulterated religion.

The List of Widows

If looking after orphans and widows in their distress is of the very essence of Christianity, this explains why Paul's letter to Timothy contains such extensive teaching about widows. The apostle has already explained what makes a widow truly a widow (1 Tim. 5:3, 5–6), and has commended true widows to the ministry of prayer (1 Tim. 5:5). He has also commanded Christians to provide for their own relatives (1 Tim. 5:4, 7–8). In the verses that follow, Paul explains how the church should treat the widows left to its care. Apparently, the early church was systematic about doing this, because he refers to a "list of widows" (1 Tim. 5:9 NIV). The Ephesians were still getting themselves organized as a newly planted church, but first things first: the church was already maintaining a roll of widows.

What was this list for? Certainly to make sure that Christian widows received their daily bread. Widows were registered so they could be helped. This is clear from the end of the passage, where the Holy Spirit instructs the church to "care for those who are really widows" (1 Tim. 5:16). The model for this was the first church in Jerusalem, which had organized a daily distribution of food from the very beginning (Acts 6:1). A church needs to keep track of who its widows are, where they live, and what they need. A good example to follow is the one set by my grandmother's old church in Pella, Iowa, which for many years sent a pastor to visit her every week in her declining years. They were practicing the kind of pure, unadulterated religion that the Ephesians practiced when they registered their widows.

There is another reason for keeping a list of widows, however. These women seem to have had some special ministry in the church. John Stott wonders if this register was "not for widows needing support, but for widows capable of offering service."[1] However, John Calvin was probably closer to the mark when he argued that the roll of widows was for both support

1. John Stott, *Guard the Truth: The Message of 1 Timothy and Titus* (Downers Grove, IL: InterVarsity, 1996), 132.

and service.[2] A good example of the position of widows in the early church comes from the ministry of Dorcas in the city of Joppa. Dorcas was exactly the kind of woman Paul goes on to describe for Timothy, a woman who was "full of good works and acts of charity" (Acts 9:36). When she died, the whole community mourned. In their grief they sent for Peter, and when he arrived, "all the widows stood beside him weeping and showing tunics and other garments that Dorcas made while she was with them" (Acts 9:39). After Peter miraculously brought Dorcas back to life, he "called the saints and widows" and "presented her alive" (Acts 9:41).

It is clear from this account that the widows had a distinctive identity within the early Christian church. There were large numbers of them, and by the third century they formed an official order in the church. These widows "gave themselves to prayer, nursed the sick, cared for the orphans, visited Christians in prison, evangelized pagan women, and taught female converts in preparation for their baptism."[3] By the Middle Ages, however, few if any churches followed the guidelines given in 1 Timothy 5. This was a source of amazement to Calvin, who had to admit that when it came to widows, even his church in Geneva was not organized along biblical lines.[4] Doubtless one reason why the contemporary church is so confused about the role of women is that this pattern for women's ministry has been neglected, or even forgotten altogether.

Widows Who Belong on the List

The main reason for thinking that these widows must have been active in some form of Christian ministry is the way they are described: "Let a widow be enrolled if she is not less than sixty years of age, having been the wife of one husband, and having a reputation for good works: if she has brought up children, has shown hospitality, has washed the feet of the saints, has cared for the afflicted, and has devoted herself to every good work" (1 Tim. 5:9–10). These qualifications would seem overly strict if a

2. John Calvin, *The Second Epistle of Paul the Apostle to the Corinthians and the Epistles to Timothy, Titus and Philemon*, trans. T. A. Smail, Calvin's Commentaries (Edinburgh: Oliver & Boyd, 1964), 256.

3. Stott, *Guard the Truth*, 133.

4. John Calvin, *Sermons on the Epistles to Timothy & Titus* (1579; repr. Edinburgh: Banner of Truth, 1983), 479.

widow had to meet all of them before she could get any help from the church. In particular, it seems unlikely that Paul would set a seemingly arbitrary age as a prerequisite for destitute women to receive benevolence.[5] Possibly the qualifications he gives are intended to serve as loose guidelines rather than strict requirements. But these requirements would perhaps make better sense as qualifications for women to serve in some form of ministry in the church.

Three requirements are given. First, maturity, or seniority: "Let a widow be enrolled if she is not less than sixty years of age" (1 Tim. 5:9). The age Paul gives may well come as a surprise to a postmodern culture, with its preoccupation on youth. In the ancient world, however, sixty was sometimes viewed as the age at which a person reached full maturity. In Plato's ideal republic, for example, sixty was the minimum age for priests and priestesses. J. N. D. Kelly summarizes by saying, "Sixty was the recognized age in antiquity when one became an 'old' man or woman, and a woman's sexual passions might be deemed to have lost their dangers then."[6] Presumably, women under the age of sixty could work to support themselves, or else remarry. However, the Bible assumes that a widow in her sixties or seventies is unlikely to marry.

The second requirement to be enrolled as a widow is fidelity. Only a widow who has been "the wife of one husband" (1 Tim. 5:9) is eligible for the list. The expression used here is the same one used earlier to describe elders and deacons (3:2, 12): the widow is to be a one-man woman. Part of what prepared her for faithful ministry was a faithful marriage.

The third requirement is charity: she must have a "reputation for good works" (1 Tim. 5:10), which Paul proceeds to list in logical order. He begins with bringing up children, because raising a family is the most important work many Christian women are given to do. But the good work of bringing up children is not limited to a woman's own children. There were a great many orphans in the ancient world, as there are today. A godly woman has pity for all God's children, and as she has the opportunity, she shows them God's loving care.

5. Donald Guthrie, *The Pastoral Epistles*, Tyndale New Testament Commentaries (Downers Grove, IL: InterVarsity, 1957), 102.

6. J. N. D. Kelly, *The Pastoral Epistles: Timothy I and II, Titus,* Harper's New Testament Commentaries (San Francisco: Harper and Row, 1960), 115.

Maternity leads to hospitality. Once a woman gets her house in order, she is ready to welcome strangers, which has always been a cardinal Christian virtue. According to Chrysostom, "the hospitality here spoken of is not merely a friendly reception, but one given with zeal and alacrity, with readiness, and going about it as if one were receiving Christ Himself."[7] Hospitality was especially important in the ancient world, where travel was inhospitable, and even dangerous. Caring for strangers "reflected God's hospitable grace, encouraged interaction between Christian communities, and facilitated the movements of traveling Christian preachers and thus the spread of the gospel."[8]

The first thing a good hostess did for her guests in the ancient world was to remove their sandals and wash their dusty feet. Hence Paul's requirement that in order to be enrolled, a widow must have "washed the feet of the saints" (1 Tim. 5:10). This gesture of humility was usually performed by slaves, but a widow known for her good deeds would do it herself. Such a woman is willing to perform humble, even menial service for her brothers and sisters in Christ.

Foot washing is a reminder that the godly widow patterns her life after the example of Jesus Christ, for on the night that he was betrayed, Jesus "rose from supper. He laid aside his outer garments, and taking a towel, tied it around his waist. Then he poured water into a basin and began to wash the disciples' feet and to wipe them with the towel that was wrapped around him" (John 13:4–5). Like a common servant, Jesus bathed the grubby feet of his disciples. The disciples could hardly believe it, and at first Peter wouldn't stand for it. Why was their Master acting like a servant? How could the Lord of glory take the place of a slave? The answer is that Jesus was showing the disciples how much he loved them (see John 13:1). He did not come into the world "to be served but to serve, and to give his life as a ransom for many" (Matt. 20:28). Washing his disciples' feet was a preview of the feature event, when Jesus would pour out his life blood for their sins on the cross.

Whenever a Christian washes the feet of the saints, or performs some other humble act of service, he or she follows the example of Jesus Christ,

7. John Chrysostom, "Homilies on the Epistles of St. Paul the Apostle to Timothy, Titus, and Philemon," trans. and ed. Philip Schaff, *Nicene and Post-Nicene Fathers*, First Series, 14 vols. (Peabody, MA: Hendrickson, 1994), 13:454.

8. Jouette M. Bassler, *1 Timothy, 2 Timothy, Titus* (Nashville: Abingdon, 1996), 97.

who said, "If I then, your Lord and Teacher, have washed your feet, you also ought to wash one another's feet. For I have given you an example, that you also should do just as I have done to you. Truly, truly, I say to you, a servant is not greater than his master, nor is a messenger greater than the one who sent him. If you know these things, blessed are you if you do them" (John 13:14–17). The widow who belongs on the church's official list is the kind of woman who has received the blessing of Jesus by following his example of loving service.

Finally, a true widow "has cared for the afflicted, and has devoted herself to every good work" (1 Tim. 5:10). This list is not meant to be exhaustive. A godly woman is godly in every way. She nurses the sick back to health, gives food to the hungry, comforts the victims of persecution, and so forth. Charity begins at home, but then it spreads all around the community. One of the reasons the church has always been a leader in mercy ministry is that Christian people—especially Christian women—have devoted themselves to all kinds of good deeds. Christians were the first to rescue abandoned babies, the first to set up schools for orphans, the first to develop nursing care, the first to establish homes for the elderly, and so forth.

To take just one example, consider the life and ministry of Elizabeth Fry. In 1813 a woman named Anna Buxton took Fry to visit London's infamous Newgate Prison. When they arrived, the two women were nearly overwhelmed by the miserable conditions in which the prisoners lived:

> Three hundred women, with their young children, were shut up together in four rooms, without sufficient clothing, absolutely without any beds but the floor, in the cold winter, with no one to guide or control them, and with nothing to do. They were allowed to receive money, and to buy as much intoxicating drink as they liked in the prison. The result was that those four rooms were like dens of wild beasts. . . . The governor of the prison dreaded to approach their cells.[9]

The two women did not know what else to do except to kneel down to pray. As they did so, the prisoners gathered around to join them. "I heard

9. Susan Hunt, *By Design: God's Distinctive Calling for Women* (Franklin, TN: Legacy, 1994), 152. Hunt's account is drawn from *Sketches of the Women of Christendom* (New York: Dodd, Mead & Company, n.d.), 303–17.

weeping," Fry would later say. "A very solemn quiet was observed. It was a very striking scene; the poor people on their knees around us, in their deplorable condition."

Fry devoted the last thirty years of her life to sharing the gospel with those women in word and deed. At first, the authorities tried to stop her because they thought the situation was hopeless. But Fry persuaded them to let her try. She began by sewing woolen garments for the prisoners. She started a school for their children. She made the prisoners agree not to swear, beg, or quarrel. She brought supplies so they could do needlework. Every morning and evening she gathered them at the sound of a bell for Bible reading and prayer. The whole character of Newgate Prison was radically transformed:

> In a few weeks the magistrates came again, and saw the results of the effort. The poor women were sitting quietly at work, and listening to reading, decently dressed, with calm and cheerful faces. The gentlemen acknowledged the change most gratefully. They felt that it is indeed the mother's heart that gives the hope and patience needed to endure and save the naughty children of the world. From this first prison, these plans of helping the female prisoners, by Christian teaching and by employment, and by all kinds of sisterly sympathy and succor, spread throughout England and throughout Christendom.[10]

This was only the beginning of Fry's work. Among many other things, she established the first "Nightly Shelter for the Homeless in London." Elizabeth Fry was exactly the kind of woman Paul described for Timothy, a woman "devoted to every good work" (1 Tim. 5:10). By the time she was sixty, she had a reputation for such works. This is because she did not wait until she was sixty to start doing them. Her work in Newgate Prison began when she was in her early thirties. What qualifies a widow to receive support from the church and to perform a service for the church is the work of a lifetime.

Younger women, especially, ought to devote themselves to all kinds of good deeds. I praise God for the charity of Christian women, especially in the city. They host Bible clubs for the children in their neighborhoods. They care for pregnant teenagers. They form friendships with people dying

10. Hunt, *By Design*, 153–54.

of AIDS. They tutor inner city children. They open their homes to guests. They pray for the work of the church. They work in the hospitals, the schools, and even on the streets of the city to show the love of Christ. The work of these women is a reminder of something once said by Libanios, the ancient pagan philosopher who taught rhetoric in ancient Antioch. One of the great scholar's pupils was John Chrysostom, who later became the famous preacher of Constantinople. Chrysostom's father died when he was young, and his mother made extraordinary personal sacrifices to ensure that her son would get the education he needed to serve the kingdom of God. When Libanios heard her story from one of Chrysostom's classmates, he remarked, "Great heavens, what remarkable women are to be found among the Christians!"[11]

Indeed.

Too Young to Make the List

Not every woman made Paul's list. Some were not eligible to serve in public ministry or even to receive financial support. Christian charity is not an entitlement, not even for Christian widows! Some did not qualify for help because they had not been faithful to their husbands or active in good works. Or they were too young: "But refuse to enroll younger widows" (1 Tim. 5:11).

What was Paul's rationale for this restriction? First, younger widows are less likely to keep their promise: "for when their passions draw them away from Christ, they desire to marry and so incur condemnation for having abandoned their former faith" (1 Tim. 5:11–12). As difficult as these verses are, it is important to realize that Paul was not opposed to marriage or sex. In the English language, "passion" and "desire" almost make it sound as if wanting to get married or share sexual intercourse is immoral! But these terms simply refer to a woman's natural sexual desire, which is given by God and finds its proper fulfillment in marital intercourse. Nor is Paul opposed to remarriage. People in the ancient world commonly believed that it was disloyal for widows to remarry. Obviously, this is not the biblical view, since verse 14 explicitly gives permission for young widows to remarry.

11. J. N. D. Kelly, *Golden Mouth: The Story of John Chrysostom—Ascetic, Preacher, Bishop* (Ithaca, NY: Cornell University Press, 1998), 7.

If Paul is not opposed to marriage in and of itself, then what is he opposed to? The word "faith" leads some scholars to think that these women have left Christianity altogether. For support they point to the instructions Paul gave to the Corinthians: "A wife is bound to her husband as long as he lives. But if her husband dies, she is free to be married to whom she wishes, only in the Lord" (1 Cor. 7:39). Possibly in their sexual desire, some of the young widows in Ephesus were marrying pagans and thus abandoning the Christian faith (cf. 1 Cor. 7:39).[12]

It is perhaps more likely, however, that "faith" is used here in the sense of "pledge" or "vow." This may be another clue that these widows had a special ministry in the church, or at least that for spiritual reasons they vowed to remain single. Presumably, women who entered this order of widows made a covenant commitment before God to remain unmarried. They dedicated themselves to Christ, almost as if they were married to him. The oath these women took was completely voluntary, but once it was made, it needed to be kept. If a young widow took a vow of celibacy and then later proceeded to remarry, she would have to break her commitment to the church—virtually breaking off an engagement to Christ himself.

In any case, the warning that Paul gives applies more generally to all single Christians, and not just to widows. It is possible for the desire to get married to outweigh someone's desire to serve Christ. Sometimes single Christians are so determined to get married that not even their relationship to Christ can stand in their way. They put their lives on hold until God provides a spouse (which he might never do, of course). Or they use poor judgment about dating relationships, even courting unbelievers. Or they rush off and get engaged without noticing all the warning signs that the person they want to marry is unsuitable. There were young widows like that in the early church, too, and they brought judgment on themselves. The reason they incurred condemnation was not that they had a sexual impulse, or even that they remarried, but that they broke their promise to Christ. It would have been better for them not to make a vow at all than to make one they were unable to keep.

Incidentally, Paul's warning shows one inherent liability in the way that orders of nuns are established in the Roman Catholic Church. Through the

12. Thomas C. Oden, *First and Second Timothy and Titus*, Interpretation (Louisville: John Knox, 1989), 157.

centuries the Catholic Church gradually lowered the age from sixty until finally even teenagers could take a vow of celibacy. They also allowed women who had never married to become nuns. But the Bible wisely restricts such a vow to widows of at least sixty, because younger women are less likely to be able to keep their promise. Whether young or old, married or single, women who aspire to godliness should dedicate themselves to deeds of mercy and seek contentment in their present situation in life without presuming on God's plans for their future.

Two Deadly Sins: Sloth and Gossip

The other danger of putting young widows on the church rolls is that they are more likely to waste their time: "Besides that, they learn to be idlers, going about from house to house, and not only idlers, but also gossips and busybodies, saying what they should not" (1 Tim. 5:13; cf. 5:6). These women sound like quite the social butterflies. Since the church was paying their rent, they were free to flit here and there, making an endless round of visits to all their friends. This may even mean they were going from church to church, since the first Christians usually met in house churches. In any case, "going about from house to house" stands "in direct contradiction to the good works of the real widows, whose activities are primarily centered in their own homes."[13]

Here the Bible warns against the sin that people often fall into when they have nothing better to do: laziness, or what the Bible calls "idleness." It is also known as "sloth," which is one of the traditional "Seven Deadly Sins." Idleness is the unwillingness to make much of an effort, like a three-toed sloth hanging upside-down all day from a tree, fast asleep. It is an easy habit to fall into when someone else is paying all your bills, which is why Paul did not want Timothy to put young widows on the dole. Human beings were created to work: "Six days you shall labor, and do all your work" (Ex. 20:9). This does not mean that every Christian has to work at a paying job, but every Christian must work. People who depend on one form of public assistance or another need to find something productive

13. Gordon D. Fee, *1 and 2 Timothy, Titus*, New International Biblical Commentary (Peabody, MA: Hendrickson, 1988), 122.

to do with their time, either at home or in the community. If nothing else, there is always plenty of volunteer work to do at the church.

Idleness usually leads to other sins—in this case, gossip. The women Paul was warning Timothy about were not only idlers, "but also gossips and busybodies, saying what they should not" (1 Tim. 5:13). The church in Thessalonica must have faced a similar problem, since Paul had heard that some of them were idle too: they were not "busy at work," he said, "but busybodies" (2 Thess. 3:11). In Ephesus, as such women made their way from house to house they heard all kinds of interesting news, not all of which should have been repeated. But they repeated it anyway.

What were these young widows saying? Some of them may have been spreading false theology, which was a major problem in Ephesus (cf. 2 Tim. 3:6). Others may have been trying to help people who were in trouble, only they did not know how to keep a confidence. Still others may have been spreading malicious rumors. Gossip in all its varieties is a common problem in the church, perhaps especially among Christian women. Through the wonders of the telephone, the internet, and other forms of communication technology, one can be a busybody from the privacy of one's own home, or even one's automobile. All it takes is fingers to type on the keyboard or a chin to prop the cell-phone on one's shoulder. It is good for Christians to stay in close touch with one another, of course, but not just to have something juicy to talk about. Instead, intimate conversations should be directed toward encouraging the weak, helping the needy, saving lost souls, and setting an agenda for prayer. Christian friendships should be spiritual as well as social.

Many people tend to overlook idleness and gossip, but these are serious sins. Consider how destructive they are. Idleness destroys one's property: "How long will you lie there, O sluggard? When will you arise from your sleep? A little sleep, a little slumber, a little folding of the hands to rest, and poverty will come upon you like a robber, and want like an armed man" (Prov. 6:9–11). Idleness also destroys the soul. It simultaneously weakens every other aspect of spiritual life. It is one of the leading contributors to depression. An idle person loses his or her zeal for God, for work, and finally for life itself.

Gossip is equally destructive. It destroys others, especially in their relationships. According to Proverbs, "a whisperer separates close friends" (Prov.

16:28; cf. 17:9). Whispering also fuels the flames of controversy. At some level, gossip has contributed to nearly every conflict and division in the history of the church.

It is because these sins are so destructive that Paul proposes a solution: "So I would have younger widows marry, bear children, manage their households, and give the adversary no occasion for slander" (1 Tim. 5:14; cf. 2:15). The word Paul uses to express his intentions here (*boulomai*) is the same word of authority that he used in 1 Timothy 2:12 and elsewhere. This is not merely Paul's personal advice; it is his apostolic command. That is not to say that each and every single woman must find a husband, which of course is up to the providence of God. However, as a general rule, it is good for young widows to devote themselves to the care of their families, and even to remarry.

What Paul says about remarriage in 1 Timothy 5 is fully consistent with what he says about singleness in 1 Corinthians 7: "I wish that all were as I myself am. But each has his own gift from God, one of one kind and one of another. To the unmarried and the widows I say that it is good for them to remain single as I am. But if they cannot exercise self-control, they should marry. For it is better to marry than to be aflame with passion" (1 Cor. 7:7–9). Notice that widows are specifically mentioned as women who might be better off getting married. The single life is a good life, especially when it is devoted to fruitful Christian service (1 Cor. 7:32–35). Indeed, singleness is Paul's personal preference for those who are so gifted. But there are many good reasons to get married, among them the danger of sexual temptation.

Remarriage is a good solution to the problems Paul was worried about in Ephesus. To begin with, running a household is a terrific remedy for idleness. Once you get married and start having children, you will be so busy you won't have time to be idle, as any mother can testify. You will have enough work of your own to take care of without needing to mind someone else's business!

But what will happen if these instructions are ignored? Rather ominously, the passage ends with Paul wanting to "give the adversary no occasion for slander" (1 Tim. 5:14). The word adversary (*antikeimenō*) may refer to unbelievers. If the young widows of the church do not behave themselves—especially if they fall into sexual sin—the public reputation of the church will be damaged. An even greater adversary, however, is mentioned in the very next verse: "For some have already strayed after Satan" (1 Tim. 5:15).

God's old enemy Satan was lurking in the shadows of the apostolic church. He enticed some young widows to follow him. Possibly this was the result of false teaching, since the false teachers were forbidding people to marry (1 Tim. 4:3). In any case, Satan would like nothing better than to destroy the Christian home.

The reference to Satan is a reminder that mothers at home with their children are engaged in spiritual warfare. Of course their work is difficult, and of course it is filled with temptations and frustrations: this is spiritual warfare! When a Christian mother teaches her child a spiritual lesson, she does so in defiance of Satan. Even daily chores—if they are done in devotion to Christ—are small victories over the devil and his work. The Christian home is never just a home; it is also a military outpost.

Widows Who Are Really in Need

This whole section of 1 Timothy is mainly intended to make sure that widows get the care they need. So after explaining that some widows do not need any help, Paul closes with a reminder that others need to be helped after all: "If any believing woman has relatives who are widows, let her care for them. Let the church not be burdened, so that it may care for those who are really widows" (1 Tim. 5:16).

Scholars have puzzled over why this instruction is given to women only, and not also to men. Bassler surmises that "Christian women of means, perhaps themselves widows, provided material support—food, housing, or clothing—to other widowed women in their congregation."[14] J. N. D. Kelly adds, "The reason why Paul does not impose the same obligation on a Christian man of similar position should be obvious. If such a man were unmarried or a widower, it would be most unsuitable for him to take over responsibility for a group of widows; whereas if he were married, the responsibility in all its practical aspects would naturally devolve upon his wife."[15]

Whether women or men are involved, or both, the important thing is for Christians to provide for their relatives. The family is the first line of defense for the poor. As Calvin put it, "before the Church has to carry the burden,

14. Bassler, *1 Timothy*, 96.
15. Kelly, *Pastoral Epistles*, 121.

let the children do their duty."[16] The early church seems to have understood this principle well, for the chapel of the Villa Albani in Rome contains the following inscription: "To the good Regina her daughter has erected this memorial: to the good Regina her widowed mother, who was a widow for sixty years and never burdened the church after she was the wife of one husband. She lived 80 years, 5 months, and 26 days."[17] The inscription shows how honorable it is for Christians to take care of their own relatives.

The second line of defense for the poor is the church. One of the advantages of belonging to the church of Jesus Christ is always having family to provide for one's needs. Since the finances of the church are limited, it is necessary for Christians to care for their own poor. Then the church will have enough money to assist the truly destitute.

One place where widows really were in need was the city of Kiev in the 1990s after the collapse of communism. As the economy faltered, the streets began to fill with beggars. Poor women approached strangers and cried loudly for a few kopecks to buy bread. What happened to the widows of the church? One evangelical congregation took care of its widows by hosting "Babushka Banquets" at which they served rich feasts of beef, mashed potatoes, vegetables, fruit salad, and bread. That is what the church did in Kiev. But what is being done for the elderly in your own church, especially for the widows? Do you know who they are? Do you know where they live? Do you know what they need? Such questions are important to answer, because looking after widows is of the very essence of true Christianity.

16. Calvin, *Second Epistle of Paul*, 251.

17. Marvin R. Vincent, *Word Studies in the New Testament*, 2d ed., 4 vols. (1888; repr. Peabody, MA: Hendrickson, n.d.), 4:265–66.

16

What Sheep Owe Their Shepherds

1 Timothy 5:17–25

Let the elders who rule well be considered worthy of double honor, especially those who labor in preaching and teaching. For the Scripture says, "You shall not muzzle an ox when it treads out the grain," and, "The laborer deserves his wages." (1 Tim. 5:17–18)

Paul's first letter to Timothy is sometimes treated as a manual of church government. It is much more than that, of course, but some parts of it do sound like something out of a book of church order. This is especially true of chapter 5, which closes with a set of instructions about elders. Since the Greek word for elder is *presbyteros*, this section might be called "practical Presbyterianism," whether one happens to be a Presbyterian or not.

The instructions seem to fall into three categories: remuneration, or how ministers should be paid (1 Tim. 5:17–18); accusation, or how ministers should be disciplined (1 Tim. 5:19–20); and ordination, or how men should be called to the ministry in the first place (1 Tim. 5:22–25). Church government may not seem like a very exciting topic, but consider what happens when these instructions are ignored. If ministers are not adequately paid, then they are distracted by worldly cares and may be tempted to become discontent. If they are falsely accused, then their teaching will be dismissed. If they are not disciplined, then the whole church will fall into disrepute, especially if these men never should have been allowed to become ministers in the first place. In short, if a church fails to practice biblical "Presbyterianism," its ministry is bound to fail.

The Remuneration of Ministers

The apostle introduces this important section of teaching by explaining what sheep owe their shepherds: "Let the elders who rule well be considered worthy of double honor, especially those who labor in preaching and teaching" (1 Tim. 5:17). The "elders" mentioned here are the same men as the "overseers" described in chapter 3. This is certain because when Paul said farewell to these men at Miletus, he used the terms "elder" (or "presbyter"), "overseer" (or "bishop"), and "shepherd" (or "pastor") interchangeably (Acts 20:17, 28; cf. Titus 1:5, 7).

What Paul says to Timothy gives some clues about what these men actually do: they "rule," or as the New International Version has it, "direct the affairs of the church" (1 Tim. 5:17; cf. 1 Tim. 3:4, 12). In other words, these spiritual leaders manage God's household. This means that they teach biblical doctrine, pray for the work of the gospel, and chart a vision for the church's future. They also warn wayward sinners and welcome them back home when they repent.

To one degree or another, all the elders do all these things. But here a distinction seems to be made between two kinds of elders, what Presbyterians usually call "teaching elders" (often referred to as "pastors") and "ruling elders" (or simply "the elders"). Some elders labor as preachers. In the contemporary church they are usually full-time members of the church staff. Since they do the bulk of the public teaching, they are identified as *teaching* elders. The difficulty of their work is suggested by the word "labor," which is a term for strenuous effort. Ruling elders are "able to teach" (see 1 Tim. 3:2), of course, but that is not their primary vocation. Most of them have full-time jobs outside the church, yet one important part of their life's work is to rule or to govern the spiritual affairs of God's household.

This is what elders do. The main point here is what some of them deserve, namely, "double honor." The biblical word for honor (*timē*) was often used to refer to a stipend or an allowance. This meaning is indicated in the English word "honorarium," which is a gift given to a minister for teaching on a special occasion, such as a wedding, a funeral, or a Bible conference. The word "honor" is also used this way earlier in the chapter, when Paul tells Timothy to "honor widows who are truly widows" (1 Tim. 5:3). The kind of "honor" he has in mind is financial support.

What, then, is *double* honor? Some scholars think this has to do with compensation. Teaching elders should be paid twice as much as ruling elders, or perhaps twice as much as the widows. After all, given their qualifications (1 Tim. 3:4), most of them have families to support. However, it seems unlikely that "double honor" refers only to a church's salary scale. There is another kind of honor that may explain what Paul has in mind, for "honor" can also mean "respect." Since the office of teaching elder is sacred, ministers who do their jobs well are worthy of commensurate respect. They deserve honor as well as an honorarium; thus they are "worthy of double honor" (1 Tim. 5:17).

Respect for pastoral ministry can come in many different forms. It starts with how members of the church speak to and about their pastor. The command to honor explains why a minister is sometimes called "Reverend." Honor also includes receiving his counsel and even his correction, insofar as it is in keeping with God's will: "Obey your leaders and submit to them, for they are keeping watch over your souls, as those who will have to give an account. Let them do this with joy and not with groaning, for that would be of no advantage to you" (Heb. 13:17). Another form of respect is to encourage a pastor. Few things are more helpful to a minister of the gospel than specific words of encouragement for his ministry. Honor can also take a tangible form. A thoughtful, generous gift can be another way to show respect for a minister. I will never forget the friend who sent me to a Phillies game with my son, or the couple who gave us a membership at the local swim club one hot summer.

This does not mean that ministers should go around expecting to be treated like kings. Paul has already warned them not to be greedy. In fact, a man who loves money is ineligible to become a teaching elder at all (1 Tim. 3:3). But it is not the church's responsibility to teach their minister to be content by giving him the gift of poverty!

Christianity Today once told the story of Pastor Steve from Montana.[1] With a wife and three children, Pastor Steve tried to make ends meet somewhere below the poverty line. For a while his family managed to scrape by, but eventually the debts began to accumulate. At a certain point Pastor Steve decided to spend a week of vacation taking a class at seminary. The whole family was to drive to Colorado for the week. But just before they were supposed to leave, the transmission on their car went out and they received a surprise medical bill. The summer night before he planned to leave, Pastor Steve sat with his wife out on the deck of the house they were renting and wept. There would be no trip. That week, the family vacationed in the basement of a relative's home several hours away.

Eventually Pastor Steve went to the church board to ask for a raise. The board grudgingly agreed to a small raise, but it was not large enough to meet the family's monthly expenses. The board thus recommended that Steve apply for assistance from Montana Power to help pay his utility bills. They also told him that if he needed more money he ought to become a chaplain with the National Guard. "It's only one weekend a month," they explained. The irony of it all was that the income of the church was exceeding expenses, and there was money in the bank to spare. Not surprisingly, Pastor Steve almost left the ministry. He considered moving to a city and looking for a job that would pay enough to settle his debts. He was a good man. He was not looking to lead an extravagant life. He even was willing to endure hardship in the ministry. But his own church led him into temptation by failing to meet his daily needs.

When a church refuses to pay its minister a decent wage, it is in disobedience to the will of God: "For the Scripture says, 'You shall not muzzle an ox when it treads out the grain,' and, 'The laborer deserves his wages'" (1 Tim. 5:18; cf. 2 Tim. 2:6). Both of these examples come from down on the farm. The first is a direct quotation from Deuteronomy 25:4. (This verse must have impressed the apostle Paul, because he quotes it in a similar context in 1 Cor. 9:9.) When a beast of burden is helping with the harvest, he is entitled to a nibble of grain every now and then. He deserves a share of the proceeds. Besides, he will work longer and harder if he gets something to eat. What is fair for livestock is only fair for clergy. They, too, should be given enough to live.

1. "Why Pastor Steve Loves His Job," *Christianity Today* (May 7, 1997), 12–19.

The second quotation may come from Jesus himself. When Jesus sent his disciples out two-by-two, he told them not to take any money with them. Instead, he told them to stay wherever people would give them a room, because "the laborer deserves his wages" (Luke 10:7; cf. Matt. 10:10; 1 Cor. 9:10). Ministers of the gospel are like farmhands: they deserve room and board in exchange for hard labor.

Sheep have always owed their shepherds a decent wage. The Levites of the Old Testament were supported so they could devote themselves to God's Word. King Hezekiah "commanded the people who lived in Jerusalem to give the portion due to the priests and the Levites, that they might give themselves to the Law of the Lord. As soon as the command was spread abroad, the people of Israel gave in abundance the firstfruits of grain, wine, oil, honey, and of all the produce of the field. And they brought in abundantly the tithe of everything" (2 Chron. 31:4–5). Churches do not need to pay their ministers in oil and honey, necessarily, but the principle is still valid. Every minister should have his basic needs adequately met. Otherwise, he may become distracted from his true calling.

To that end, the trustees of the church should ask their pastor if his needs are being met. A good rule of thumb to follow is that a minister should receive roughly the average wage of the people in his congregation. If the church is poor, then the minister should not expect to become wealthy. But he should receive a decent, living wage. Paul himself was a notable exception to this rule. On occasion, he provided for his own needs by working as a tentmaker (Acts 18:3). The apostle knew he was a special case, however, so he always insisted on the right of a teaching elder to receive a reward for his labor: "The Lord commanded that those who proclaim the gospel should get their living by the gospel" (1 Cor. 9:14; cf. Gal. 6:6).

The Accusation of Elders

The elders who deserve double honor are the ones who do their work well (cf. 1 Tim. 3:4), which suggests that others do not do so well. And in point of fact, delinquent elders were a problem in Ephesus. Although Timothy must deal with them, he must not "admit a charge against an elder except on the evidence of two or three witnesses" (1 Tim. 5:19).

These instructions explain how to handle a grievance against an elder. It almost sounds as if elders get special treatment, yet the Bible always insists it takes at least two witnesses to convict someone. It is like the old saying: "If a brother comes to see you, he has a problem; if two brothers come to see you, *you* have a problem." The Bible is clear on this point: "A single witness shall not suffice against a person for any crime or for any wrong in connection with any offense that he has committed. Only on the evidence of two witnesses or of three witnesses shall a charge be established" (Deut. 19:15; cf. 2 Cor. 13:1). Jesus applied the same rule to everyone in the church, not just to elders (Matt. 18:16).

What is unique for elders is that they may not even be accused of a sin unless there are multiple witnesses. Two or three witnesses are required, not for a conviction, but before an accusation can be entertained at all. The wisdom of this command is self-evident, especially in these scandalous times. In recent decades American politics has been dominated by scandal, often of the "he-said, she-said" variety. In many cases it proves impossible to know the truth, yet the accusations themselves generate no end of gossip. The same thing can happen in the church. A church member stirs up trouble by slandering one of the elders, either publicly or privately. Even if the charge ultimately proves to be unfounded, the man's reputation will be tarnished. This is why every elder should be presumed innocent until he gets a fair hearing. As John Stott wisely observes, "Adherence to this biblical principle would have silenced many a malicious talebearer and saved many pastors from unjust criticism and unnecessary suffering."[2]

One reason to be especially cautious about attacks against the elders of the church is that Satan is out to destroy their ministry. According to Calvin,

> none are more exposed to slanders and insults than godly teachers. This comes not only from the difficulty of their duties, which are so great that sometimes they sink under them, or stagger and halt or take a false step, so that wicked men find many occasions of finding fault with them; but added to that, even when they do all their duties correctly and commit not even the smallest error, they never avoid a thousand criticisms. It is indeed a trick of Satan to estrange men from their ministers so as gradually to bring their teaching into contempt.

2. John Stott, *Guard the Truth: The Message of 1 Timothy and Titus* (Downers Grove, IL: InterVarsity, 1996), 138.

> In this way not only is wrong done to innocent people whose reputation is undeservedly injured, but the authority of God's holy teaching is diminished.[3]

This does not mean that teaching and ruling elders are above the law. Quite the opposite, for the fact that they receive special protection from slander makes their sins all the more reprehensible: "As for those who persist in sin, rebuke them in the presence of all, so that the rest may stand in fear" (1 Tim. 5:20). If the charge against a repeat offender can be proven, his sin should be brought out into the open, as for example Paul brought Peter's hypocrisy to the attention of the church in Antioch (see Gal. 2:11–14). However, public rebuke ought to be a last resort. First an elder should be reproved privately, especially if the sin itself is a private one. But if an elder refuses to repent of a notorious sin, he should be treated the way Paul treated Hymenaeus and Alexander, who were "handed over to Satan that they may learn not to blaspheme" (1 Tim. 1:20).

In these undisciplined times, many churches have allowed discipline to fall into disuse. Christian leaders too rarely have the courage to correct sinners. Sometimes there is some kind of cover-up. Even scoundrels never get punished, so people think they can get away with sin. But according to Chrysostom, such failure to discipline is harmful to all concerned: "For as it is wrong to condemn hastily and rashly, so not to punish manifest offenses is to open the way to others, and embolden them to offend.... For it is a much greater scandal, that the offense should be known, and not the punishment. For as when sinners go unpunished, many commit crimes; so when they are punished, many are made better."[4] Christians must care enough to confront.

When a scandalous minister is rebuked in front of the entire congregation, then "the rest"—meaning the rest of the elders—will be warned not to sin. No doubt the rest of the church will take the hint as well. Literally, they will "stand in fear," fearing not only the consequences of sin, but also God himself, who is so perfectly holy that he ought to be feared by every sinner. One is reminded of the punishment for idolaters in the Old Testament, which

3. John Calvin, *The Second Epistle of Paul the Apostle to the Corinthians and the Epistles to Timothy, Titus and Philemon*, trans. T. A. Smail, Calvin's Commentaries (Edinburgh: Oliver & Boyd, 1964), 263.

4. John Chrysostom, "Homilies on the Epistles of St. Paul the Apostle to Timothy, Titus, and Philemon," trans. and ed. Philip Schaff, *Nicene and Post-Nicene Fathers*, First Series, 14 vols. (Peabody, MA: Hendrickson, 1994), 13:461.

was intended to have the same effect: "And all Israel shall hear and fear and never again do any such wickedness as this" (Deut. 13:11).

Timothy may have been a little afraid himself when he read the apostle's instructions. The reason Paul wrote to him in the first place was to tell him to "charge certain persons not to teach any different doctrine" (1 Tim. 1:3). This put him in an awkward position:

> Given the situation that existed in Ephesus, it is easy to imagine that tempers would have run high. A purge mentality may have set in among those who had resisted the false teachers, leading them to make every effort to root out any elders even remotely associated with the opposition. Then again, pockets of adherents to the false teaching may have brought false accusations against the faithful leaders. In any case, while discipline of the leadership was not to be avoided, it was to be executed carefully and fairly.[5]

It might have been tempting for Timothy to lock himself in his study and hope that his problems would simply disappear. But problems in the church never go away all by themselves, so the apostle gives him a solemn warning: "In the presence of God and of Christ Jesus and of the elect angels I charge you to keep these rules without prejudging, doing nothing from partiality" (1 Tim. 5:21). When it comes to church discipline, Timothy must be even-handed. He must handle each case without prejudice, being careful not to entertain an unfair accusation, even if he thinks it might be true. On the other hand, he must not sweep things under the pews just because the man accused is a fellow elder. Ministers may not play favorites. An accusation against an elder must be judged solely on the merits of the case.

Anyone who has ever been involved in a dispute in the church knows how difficult it is to avoid choosing sides. It was the same in Calvin's day, for the great Reformer confessed: "There is nothing harder than to pronounce judgment with complete impartiality, so as to avoid showing undue favor, or giving rise to suspicions, or being influenced by unfavorable reports, or being excessively strict and in every case to consider nothing but the matter in hand."[6] To help ministers remain impartial, the Bible gives a

5. Philip H. Towner, *1–2 Timothy and Titus*, IVP New Testament Commentary Series (Downers Grove, IL: InterVarsity, 1994), 125–26.

6. Calvin, *Second Epistle of Paul*, 264.

reminder that every act of church discipline is carried out "in the presence of God and of Christ Jesus and of the elect angels" (1 Tim. 5:21).

Here Paul takes Timothy to the throne of God, where the Father and the Son judge the whole world according to the strictest standards of justice. With them are the angels God chose to remain unfallen by his sovereign grace. These divine messengers are mentioned as a reminder that one day there will be a judgment to end all judgments. Jesus said, "When the Son of Man comes in his glory, and all the angels with him, then he will sit on his glorious throne" (Matt. 25:31; cf. Rev. 14:10). This final judgment will be completely impartial, "for there is no injustice with the Lord our God, or partiality or taking bribes" (2 Chron. 19:7). Nor does God show any favoritism (see Rom. 2:11); he is absolutely fair. At the final judgment, therefore, he will give each person exactly what he or she deserves. Those who trust in Jesus Christ will be welcomed into the presence of God, while those who refuse to repent of their sins will be banished from his sight forever.

If God will render perfect justice at the end of history, then justice should be done in the present. Whenever a judgment is called for, the church ought to give the judgment God himself would give, without partiality or favoritism. One day even the ministers who render judgment must appear before the throne of Christ to account for their actions.

The Ordination of Elders

One suspects that the turmoil at the church in Ephesus was stressful, because Paul tells Timothy: "No longer drink only water, but use a little wine for the sake of your stomach and your frequent ailments" (1 Tim. 5:23). It is not entirely clear why Timothy's drinking habits are mentioned. Perhaps he was in danger of becoming too ascetic in his Christianity. He must keep himself pure, of course, but not through self-denial. More likely, pastoral ministry was giving Timothy a bad case of indigestion, and he needed to take some wine for medicinal purposes. Timothy must look after his health. Ambrose of Milan put it like this: "We must drink then not for the sake of pleasure, but because of infirmity, and therefore sparingly as a remedy, not in excess as a gratification."[7]

7. Ambrose, Letter LXIII.27, trans. H. de Romestin, ed. Philip Schaff and Henry Wace, *Nicene and Post-Nicene Fathers*, Second Series, 14 vols. (1896; repr. Peabody, MA: Hendrickson, 1994), 10:460.

As always, the Bible is careful about the use of alcohol. Of course Christians are allowed to drink wine (yes, wine!). As we have seen, like everything else in creation, it is to be "received with thanksgiving," provided that it is "made holy by the word of God and prayer" (1 Tim. 4:4). In fact, the only people who forbid the use of wine are false teachers (cf. 1 Tim. 4:3). However, believers who are tempted to flaunt their Christian liberties should notice Paul's exact words: "a little wine." Moderation is called for. Christians are not commanded to be teetotalers, but they are not allowed to become drunkards, either. This fits in with Paul's earlier injunction that elders must not be drunkards (1 Tim. 3:3).

So much for what Paul tells Timothy about libations. What is more important is what he says about ordinations: "Do not be hasty in the laying on of hands, nor take part in the sins of others; keep yourself pure" (1 Tim. 5:22). The "laying on of hands" is sometimes thought to refer to a special ceremony for welcoming a sinner back to church. In his ecclesiastical history, written early in the fourth century, Eusebius refers to "an old-established custom" of receiving penitents back into fellowship by "prayer combined with the laying on of hands."[8] On this interpretation, the verse would mean something like this: "After passing sentence on the guilty, don't be hasty in revoking it and readmitting the sinners to communion."[9] The practice Eusebius describes came later, however. In the New Testament, the "laying on of hands" usually refers to ordination, as it does throughout the Pastoral Epistles (1 Tim. 4:14; 2 Tim. 1:6). The Holy Spirit committed men to pastoral or evangelistic ministry through the laying on of hands.

Ordination is not something to be taken lightly. If a church is not careful about who gets ordained, it is liable to have a mess on its hands, which is exactly what Timothy had in Ephesus. Sadly, the church is well known for such scandals. A businessman once described his career for me. He worked for IBM . . . until IBM eliminated his division. Then he worked for Exxon . . . until Exxon got rid of his section. And so forth, until finally he was out of a job altogether. I said, "That's the way the business world

8. Eusebius, *The History of the Church from Christ to Constantine*, 7.2, trans. and ed. G. A. Williamson (New York: Penguin, 1965), 288.

9. J. N. D. Kelly, *The Pastoral Epistles: Timothy I and II, Titus*, Harper's New Testament Commentaries (San Francisco: Harper and Row, 1960), 128.

operates these days, isn't it?" He said to me, "I guess that's not a problem in your line of work, although you do have your scandals."

Alas, we do have our scandals. In one case, the minister of a historic church in a major city was removed from his pulpit for committing adultery. A few years later his successor was removed from the same pulpit for the same offense! Anyone who has suffered through such a disaster knows the wisdom of Paul's counsel to Timothy. One of the best ways to avoid ecclesiastical scandal is to be careful whom you ordain in the first place.

Caution about ordination is one of the strengths of many African-American churches, where traditionally it is not uncommon for a black church to wait until a man is forty years old before ordaining him. Many other evangelical churches are willing to ordain men before they turn forty, but they should always be careful. The procedures for ordaining teaching elders in the Presbyterian Church in America offer one good example to follow. First a man becomes a member of his local church. When his elders can testify to "his Christian character and promise of usefulness in the ministry," he "submits himself to the care and guidance of the Presbytery in his course of study and of practical training to prepare himself for this office."[10]

Next the man is licensed to preach the gospel. Before being licensed he will be examined in his Christian experience, his sense of call to the ministry, his practical knowledge of the English Bible, his understanding of biblical doctrine, and his ability to preach. During this time he must complete a one-year internship in pastoral ministry. Normally he will also earn a master of divinity degree at a Bible-teaching seminary. The man will not be ordained until finally he is called to pastor a particular church. At this time he will be examined in his family relationships and in his knowledge of Greek and Hebrew, the sacraments, church history, and church government. Needless to say, all of these requirements help to prevent hasty ordinations!

The requirements for ruling elders are much less strenuous, but they are just as important to follow. A ruling elder must first be nominated by a member of the congregation. Then he is examined as to his life and doctrine. Once the elders have approved him as a candidate for elder, he is presented back to the congregation for election.

10. *The Book of Church Order of the Presbyterian Church in America*, 5th ed. (Atlanta: Committee for Christian Education and Publications, 1997), 18–1, 2.

Ordination to the office of elder is a solemn occasion, not only for the man who is ordained, but also for those who ordain him. Paul tells Timothy to keep himself pure and not to "take part in the sins of others." This may simply mean that he needs to be careful not to fall into scandalous sin himself. It also seems to suggest, however, that Timothy bears spiritual responsibility for the men he ordains. If his elders fall into scandalous sin, it will be a reflection on his ministry. He will be implicated in their scandal. The best way for him to keep his hands clean, therefore, is to refuse to lay them on men who are not qualified to become elders.

One good reason to proceed to ordination with caution is that a person's suitability for ministry is not always immediately obvious: "The sins of some men are conspicuous, going before them to judgment, but the sins of others appear later. So also good works are conspicuous, and even those that are not cannot remain hidden" (1 Tim. 5:24–25).

These verses describe four kinds of people. Some people are such blatant sinners that they can be ruled out for leadership from the outset. Timothy will be able to spot them right away. Their reputation will precede them. They are running headlong to judgment. In fact, they already have one foot in hell, where they will surely go, unless they turn away from their sins and come to Christ in faith and repentance.

Other sins are much less conspicuous, especially in the church, where one typically finds the most sophisticated sinners of all. Some sins take a while to surface. But eventually—when the peace of the church is disturbed or when there is trouble in a family—the sin will come to light. Such sins trail behind like the brown stain a slug leaves on the garden path. Therefore, the church should take its time to discern whether a man is really qualified to be an elder. In fact, the more pushy someone becomes about leading a ministry, the more reason there is to be cautious.

This principle can be applied positively as well as negatively: "So also good works are conspicuous" (1 Tim. 5:25). True godliness shines like the sun. Thus there are some candidates who obviously belong in the ministry. They not only have strong gifts; they also have servants' hearts. Not every good deed is equally obvious, of course, but "even those that are not cannot remain hidden" (1 Tim. 5:25). Good deeds done in secret are still known unto God. To apply this to ordination, some men who do not have obvious gifts for pastoral ministry will eventually realize their potential. So Paul wants

Timothy to give them a second chance to make a first impression. He should not rule out a man who may later develop into a good minister. This applies not just to ministers, of course, but to the quiet work of every humble Christian servant.

To summarize, there are four kinds of people in the visible church. Jerome described them as follows: "Certain persons sin so deliberately and flagrantly that you no sooner see them than you know them at once to be sinners. But the defects of others are so cunningly concealed that we only learn them from subsequent information. Similarly the good deeds of some people are public property, while those of others we come to know only through long intimacy with them."[11]

The obvious practical question is this: What kind of person are you? What will people find out about you in days to come? Will your sins catch up with you? Or will people discover that you are much godlier than they ever expected?

Some sinners will not be found out until the day of judgment. But they will be found out in the end, be sure of that. In the pure light of God's justice all of their sins will be revealed, and they will perish with them. Happily, many good deeds will also be brought to light on that day. In this life some worthy Christian men and women seem completely overlooked. Yet they have received the grace that is to be found only in Jesus Christ. In the strength of that grace, they quietly perform many beautiful acts of self-sacrifice. One day all their good works will be revealed, to the praise of God's glory.

There is a wonderful example of this in *The Great Divorce* by C. S. Lewis. In the story a man travels to the outskirts of heaven, where he sees a most magnificent woman. All around her are dancing lights, with Spirits scattering flowers, and boys and girls singing beautiful songs. The visitor imagines her to be some famous person from earth:

> "Is it? . . . is it?" I whispered to my guide.
>
> "Not at all," said he. "It's someone ye'll never have heard of. Her name on earth was Sarah Smith and she lived at Golders Green."
>
> "She seems to be . . . well, a person of particular importance."

11. Jerome, Letter LIV.8, trans. W. H. Fremantle, ed. Philip Schaff and Henry Wace, *Nicene and Post-Nicene Fathers*, Second Series, 14 vols. (1896; repr. Peabody, MA: Hendrickson, 1994), 6:105.

> "Aye. She is one of the great ones. Ye have heard that fame in this country and fame on Earth are two quite different things."[12]

Many things will look very different in the light of eternity. By the power of God's grace, we are called to perform the kind of good deeds that cannot be hidden forever, especially if we are shepherds who serve Christ's sheep.

12. C. S. Lewis, *The Great Divorce* (New York: Macmillan, 1946), 107.

17

Yes, Master!

1 Timothy 6:1–2

Let all who are under a yoke as slaves regard their own masters as worthy of all honor, so that the name of God and the teaching may not be reviled. (1 Tim. 6:1)

The Puritan Cotton Mather once set out to provide biblical support for the American slave trade. He began by collecting biblical passages which he believed supported the practice of slaveholding. Then he went on to write a set of "Rules for the Society of Negroes." Among other things, Mather argued that slaves who disobeyed their masters were to be beaten and barred from the church.[1]

There are a number of lessons to be learned from Mather's example. The first is that the church of Jesus Christ bears part of the guilt for the sins of slavery in human history. In the words of Henry Highland Garnet, while slavery "stretched its dark wings of death over the land, the Church stood silently by—the priests prophesied falsely, and the people loved to have it

1. See Martin Luther King Jr., *Where Do We Go from Here: Chaos or Community?* (Boston: Beacon, 1967), 73.

so."[2] For at least until the end of the nineteenth century, the institution of slavery was widely accepted by Christians in Europe and America.

In his book *The Problem of Slavery in Western Culture*, David Brion Davis documents "The Failure of Christianization."[3] Slavery held such a pervasive influence that when John Newton gave his life to Christ, he did not immediately resign as the captain of a slave ship. Instead, he ran a tighter ship and even celebrated communion on the main deck while African slaves groaned in their chains below.[4] It was only later that Newton repented for buying and selling human beings. Perhaps Newton can be excused because he was a new convert. But others had no excuse because they were among the greatest teachers of the church. Jonathan Edwards owned a slave, although he was critical of the African trade. So did George Whitefield, who opposed cruelty to slaves, but considered slavery itself to be lawful. In fact, in order to help maintain his Orphan House, Whitefield acquired a plantation and purchased some seventy-five slaves. James Henley Thornwell, the great southern Presbyterian theologian, concluded that "the Scriptures not only fail to condemn slavery, they as distinctly sanction it as any other social condition of man."[5]

Christians cannot blame the rest of the world for the sins of slavery, but must bear part of its shame. For many years I took comfort in the fact that my Dutch ancestors were not slaveholders. In fact, when they settled on the Iowa plains, they committed themselves to the cause of emancipation. Yet I have since discovered that the first slaves ever to set foot on American shores were transported by a Dutch ship in 1620. Worse still, they were brought here by the Puritans, on whom we depend for so much sound theology.[6] Would that it were not so! But it is so. The church of Jesus Christ bears part of the guilt for the sins of slavery in human history. That guilt cannot be ignored; it can only be confessed and forgiven on the basis of the blood Jesus Christ shed on the cross.

2. Henry Highland Garnet, "An Address to the Slaves of the United States of America," in Henry Louis Gates Jr., and Nellie Y. McKay, eds., *The Norton Anthology of African American Literature* (New York: Norton, 1997), 280–85 (p. 281).

3. David Brion Davis, *The Problem of Slavery in Western Culture* (Ithaca, NY: Cornell University Press, 1966), 197ff.

4. Ibid., 388.

5. James Henley Thornwell, *The Collected Writings of James Henley Thornwell*, ed. John B. Adger and John L. Girardeau, 4 vols. (Richmond: Presbyterian Committee of Publication, 1871–81), 4:386.

6. Robert L. Dabney, *A Defence of Virginia* (1867; repr. Harrisonburg, VA: Sprinkle, 1991), 27.

What Paul Really Said about Slavery

The other thing to be learned from Cotton Mather is how important it is to get the Bible straight. In part, the views of Mather and other Reformed theologians on slavery were based on a misunderstanding of the Mosaic law and how it applies (or doesn't apply) to believers today. These men rightly observed that the Old Testament permits certain forms of slavery. What they failed to fully appreciate were the discontinuities between the Old and New Testaments and the differences between the way slavery was practiced in the ancient world and the way it was practiced in their own times. However, their defense of slavery was also based on the New Testament teaching that slaves should be obedient to their masters, which shows why it is so necessary to know how to interpret the Bible properly. These men were trying to be faithful to Scripture. In many cases they personally opposed the worst abuses of slavery and worked to ensure that slaves received the gospel. Yet partly as a result of their exegetical errors, countless human beings made in the image of God continued to endure untold misery and suffering.

What does the New Testament really teach about slavery? It is sometimes thought that the apostle Paul, especially, was soft on the slave trade. For example, he once met a fugitive slave named Onesimus and led him to Christ. Then he sent him back to his master Philemon with a letter in which he never once told Philemon to give Onesimus his freedom. Then there are all the passages in Paul's letters that tell slaves to behave themselves: "Slaves, obey in everything those who are your earthly masters," and so forth (Col. 3:22; cf. Eph. 6:5–8; 1 Tim. 6:1–2; Titus 2:9–10).

If Paul was soft on slavery, then it becomes rather difficult to defend the New Testament. We know that slavery denied the dignity of the human person and brought great suffering into the world, so why doesn't the Bible denounce it?

Usually, scholars say something like this: The Roman Empire was not ready for the abolition of slavery. There were millions of slaves in those days, possibly comprising as much as one third of the world population.[7] If slavery had been abolished all at once, the entire empire would have come

7. Thomas C. Oden, *First and Second Timothy and Titus*, Interpretation (Louisville: John Knox, 1989), 107.

crashing to the ground. Any attempt at a slave revolt would have turned into a bloodbath, and Christians would have been unable to evangelize the world. As Guthrie cautiously concludes, "The time was unpropitious for overturning this deeply rooted system."[8]

Instead of trying to abolish slavery, the argument goes, the New Testament sets forth principles for its gradual elimination. Paul writes, for example, "There is neither Jew nor Greek, there is neither slave nor free, there is neither male nor female, for you are all one in Christ Jesus" (Gal. 3:28). What the apostle was trying to do was to "undermine the very essence of slavery by preaching the love of Christ to all."[9] Eventually, once the principles of biblical Christianity started to have an influence on world culture, people would figure out that slavery was contrary to the will of God. Paul did not have to tell Philemon to free Onesimus; he would be able to figure it out on his own by reading between the lines of the New Testament.

These arguments may have a good deal of merit. Christianity eventually did become the single greatest force in history for the eradication of slavery. Sadly, there are still too many places in the world today where people traffic in slaves. However, wherever Christianity has come to dominate a culture, the institution of slavery has been legally eliminated. Indeed, "the more fully Christianity is realized in any society, the more thoroughly will slavery be destroyed."[10]

What is often overlooked, however, is that the New Testament does take a strong stand against slavery. To begin with, in contrast to what it says about other social relationships, the Bible never teaches that slavery is part of the created order—an omission that shows it is not part of God's permanent will for humanity.[11] More importantly, Paul himself has already condemned the buying and selling of human beings at the beginning of his first letter to Timothy: "The law is not laid down for the just but for the lawless and disobedient, for the ungodly and sinners, for the unholy and profane, for those who strike their fathers and mothers, for murderers, the sexually immoral,

8. Donald Guthrie, *The Pastoral Epistles*, Tyndale New Testament Commentaries (Downers Grove, IL: InterVarsity, 1957), 109.

9. Oden, *First and Second Timothy*, 108.

10. William M. Ramsay, *Historical Commentary on the Pastoral Epistles*, ed. Mark Wilson (Grand Rapids: Kregel, 1996), 87.

11. George Knight, *The Pastoral Epistles*, New International Greek Testament Commentary (Grand Rapids: Eerdmans, 1992), 242.

men who practice homosexuality, *enslavers*, liars, perjurers, and whatever else is contrary to sound doctrine, in accordance with the glorious gospel of the blessed God" (1 Tim. 1:9–11, emphasis added).

Paul mentions the slave trade almost in passing, but his condemnation could hardly be stronger: anyone who traffics in slaves is "lawless" and "disobedient." Here it is important to note that the Mosaic law condemned man-stealing as a capital crime. The Old Testament permitted some forms of slavery, including the capture (as opposed to killing) of foreign slaves in a holy war and voluntary servitude for Israelites who needed to pay off their debts (but only for up to six years, after which they were set free). However, the Mosaic law also regulated slavery to prevent abuse, and kidnapping slaves was punishable by death (see Ex. 21:16; Deut. 24:7); so was negligent homicide (see Deut. 22:8). This means that the whole Western institution of slavery—which began with the capture of African slaves and included the death passage to the Americas—directly violated the law of God.

The unlawfulness of the slave trade was recognized by many Christians, including Reformed theologians like Richard Baxter, who called slave traders the "common enemies of mankind" and said that anyone who bought slaves (except for the purpose of freeing them) committed a "heinous sin."[12] This was Paul's view as well. Slave trading is "lawless," the apostle said, and anyone who participates in it is an "ungodly sinner"; he is "unholy and profane." Furthermore, he is unsound in his doctrine. Thus a man who buys or sells human beings stands opposed to the gospel itself. He is condemned by God's law and subject to God's judgment.

The subject of slavery comes up again in chapter 6. Slaveholders have often twisted these verses to their own advantage, but Paul has not changed his mind and decided that slave-trading is permissible after all. In fact, he is not speaking to slaveholders at all; he is speaking to slaves themselves. The Bible is always bound to be misinterpreted when people start listening to what God is saying to someone else instead of what he is saying to them. These instructions are not for masters, but for "all who are under a yoke as slaves" (1 Tim. 6:1). Without approving of slavery in all its forms, Paul gives pastoral counsel to people who are enslaved.

12. Richard Baxter, *A Christian Directory*, quoted in Davis, *Slavery*, 338.

It helps to understand what slavery was like in the Roman world, for it was different in many respects from the institution that later developed in Europe and America. In the ancient world slavery generally was not based on the color of someone's skin, except for slaves captured in ethnic warfare. This is in contrast with the inherently racist premises of slavery in the West, which denied the full dignity of people of color as human beings made in the image of God. Also, in the ancient world many people were enslaved because of economic necessity. In some cases slavery was voluntary; people sold themselves as slaves in order to clear their debts, or in order to learn a trade. There were other differences as well. Because slaves were members of a household, most of them had a fair degree of security, with opportunities for advancement. They enjoyed "a good deal of freedom and social mobility. Many earned a living or worked in partnership with their owners. Some actually held positions of authority within businesses or administrative posts in lower levels of government."[13] They worked in highly skilled occupations such as education or medicine. There were even slaves who owned their own slaves![14] Most important of all, slavery was not necessarily permanent, because there were a variety of ways for slaves to win or to buy their freedom.

When Your Boss Is a Pagan

Slavery was still slavery, of course. It meant that one human being belonged to another human being as a living possession. Slaves did not have the free rights of citizens and many were vulnerable to abuse, including physical and sexual abuse. The phrase "under the yoke" describes their situation well. Some slaves were indeed treated like livestock; their owners considered them little more than cattle.[15]

13. Philip H. Towner, *1–2 Timothy and Titus*, IVP New Testament Commentary Series (Downers Grove, IL: InterVarsity, 1994), 131.

14. Wayne E. Meeks, *The First Urban Christians: The Social World of the Apostle Paul* (New Haven, CT: Yale University Press, 1983), 20.

15. For more information about slavery in the New Testament world, see J. M. G. Barclay, "Paul, Philemon and the Dilemma of Christian Slave Ownership," *New Testament Studies* 37 (1991): 161–86; S. Scott Bartchy, *First Century Slavery in 1 Corinthians 7:21*, Society of Biblical Literature Dissertation Series 11 (Missoula, MT: Scholars Press, 1973); James S. Jeffers, *The Greco-Roman World of the New Testament Era: Exploring the Background of Early Christianity* (Downers Grove, IL: InterVarsity, 1999), 220–36.

Even though slavery has been largely abolished in the West, what the Bible says to slaves is still relevant today. To begin with, the term Paul used for "slave" (*doulos*) can also be translated "servant" or "bondservant," and thus it covers a wide range of work situations. Just as the relationship between master and slave was the primary economic relationship in the ancient world, so the relationship between boss and employee is the primary economic relationship in the world today, and we should apply the biblical teaching accordingly.

Furthermore, it may fairly be said that many modern workers are "under the yoke," as Paul called it (1 Tim. 6:1), because their work is deeply dehumanizing. Some jobs are boring; they involve the same routine day after day after day. Other workers are at the mercy of their executives, or their stockholders, who treat them as little more than slaves. One company buys another and then the whole organization is reorganized. As a result, people get right-sized right out of a job, like so many cattle being led to market. Still other jobs are stressful. They demand such long hours or so many days on the road that it becomes difficult to live a balanced life or nurture strong family relationships. Many modern workers have to slave away at their jobs.

Therefore, what Paul says to slaves applies generally to nearly everyone who holds down a job: "Let all who are under a yoke as slaves regard their own masters as worthy of all honor, so that the name of God and the teaching may not be reviled" (1 Tim. 6:1). The way to apply this verse today, very simply, is that every boss deserves a full-day's work from every Christian employee.

Paul has used the word "honor" (*timē*) several times already. It defines the kind of recognition that Christians ought to show to godly widows (1 Tim. 5:3), or the kind of respect they should give to good ministers (1 Tim. 5:17). Masters deserve the same kind of treatment, even if they are not Christians, which is what Paul mainly seems to have in mind.

When it comes to honoring one's boss, the Bible does not grant any exceptions for bad work situations. The apostle Peter was even more direct: "Servants, be subject to your masters with all respect, not only to the good and gentle but also to the unjust" (1 Peter 2:18). If God gave these commands to slaves, they apply all the more to free men and women in the marketplace. Respect is something every Christian worker owes to every boss, even in the very worst working environments.

The word "regard" is important: slaves are to "*regard* their own masters as worthy of all honor" (1 Tim. 6:1). This clearly allows for the possibility that someone's master may not actually be worthy of respect. He may be incompetent. He may be immoral. He may be unreasonable or overbearing. Nevertheless, he must be *regarded as* worthy of respect. This is because God has placed him in his position of authority. To show honor to one's earthly master is to show honor to one's heavenly Father. Furthermore, the Bible tells Christians to show "all" honor. It does not say that workers need to show respect only when their bosses are in the office. It does not give employees the right to gossip about management as long as they are in the break room when they do it. It does not even allow Christians to complain about their jobs when they go back home. No, the Bible says that workers and servants should "regard their own masters as worthy of all honor."

Work before a Watching World

Showing full respect is necessary to the missionary purpose of the church. Paul gives two reasons why Christians need to respect their masters—"so that the name of God and the teaching may not be reviled" (1 Tim. 6:1)—and both reasons have to do with God's saving purpose for the world. If Christians are poor workers, then God and his gospel will be brought into disrepute.

God cares about his reputation. He is concerned about what outsiders think of Christianity. This concern shows up again and again in 1 Timothy. In chapter 2 Christians are instructed to "lead a peaceful and quiet life, godly and dignified in every way" (1 Tim. 2:2), with the hope that all men will "be saved and come to the knowledge of the truth" (1 Tim. 2:4). In chapter 3 it is stated that church elders "must be well thought of by outsiders" (1 Tim. 3:7). In chapter 5 Christians are told to provide for their widows "so that they may be without reproach" (1 Tim. 5:7), where reproach may refer to an accusation from outside the church. In short, God wants his people to be careful how they are coming across. He wants them to have the respect and admiration of their neighbors, including their coworkers. Thus the way that a Christian behaves on the job is a major part of his or her testimony.

This was an important issue for slaves in the early church, because the Romans typically started to get suspicious whenever their slaves decided to worship some new god. According to Cicero, they commonly believed that slaves who dabbled in foreign religions would turn against their masters and overthrow the social order.[16] If Christian slaves showed disrespect to their masters, then all of the Romans' worst suspicions about Christianity would be confirmed, bringing dishonor to both the name and the gospel of God. The famous archaeologist William Ramsay described the situation like this: "It would bring discredit on the church and cause ill-feeling against the church in the society of the Roman Empire if Christian slaves were found to be discontented or disobedient. The slave must cheerfully sacrifice his freedom, reconcile himself to his lot, and do the work that is ordered. The Name and the Teaching will thus be saved from discredit and vilification."[17]

Two things are at stake every time a believer punches the time clock. The first is "the name of God," which stands for God's character—his holiness, love, justice, and all the rest of his divine attributes. Since God's people bear God's name, the way they work is a reflection on God himself. Paul's reference to the name of God here echoes a quotation from the prophet Isaiah: " 'And now what do I have here?' declares the Lord. . . . 'All day long my name is constantly blasphemed' " (Isa. 52:5 NIV). God's name was under attack because the sins of his people were an embarrassment to him. The nations saw what was happening in Israel, and God was being slandered as a result.

The same thing is likely to happen whenever Christians do a lousy job. Anyone who calls himself a Christian represents Christ to the world. So every time a Christian makes a delivery, turns in a project, hands in an expense account, makes a decision at a board meeting, pushes to get a sale, closes a deal, takes care of a patient, mops the floor, grades an exam, or decides it is time to leave work and go home, he or she is making some kind of statement about who Jesus is. A Christian who gives anything less than the very best effort puts Jesus Christ in a bad light.

One man who took the responsibility to stand up for God's name on the job was Joseph, the son of Jacob. Joseph was a slave in the house of Potiphar, a captain of the Egyptian guard. He was such a good worker that he became indispensable to his master. So Potiphar "left all that he had in Joseph's charge, and because of him he had no concern about anything but the food he ate" (Gen. 39:6). Eventually Potiphar's wife began to lust after Joseph and tried to entice him into a sexual relationship. But even though "she spoke to

16. Cicero, *Laws*, 2.7.19–27.
17. Ramsay, *Historical Commentary*, 88.

Joseph day after day, he would not listen to her, to lie beside her or to be with her" (Gen. 39:10). The reason that Joseph refused to sin with Potiphar's wife was that he was God's servant, first of all: "Behold, because of me my master has no concern about anything in the house, and he has put everything that he has in my charge. He is not greater in this house than I am, nor has he kept back anything from me except yourself, because you are his wife. How then can I do this great wickedness and sin against God?" (Gen. 39:8–9). Joseph understood that the way he handled himself on the job was a reflection on the name and character of almighty God.

The other thing that is at stake every time a Christian shows up for work is the gospel of Jesus Christ. Slaves need to respect their masters "so that the teaching may not be reviled" (1 Tim. 6:1). By "the teaching" Paul meant the basic content of the Christian faith. The teaching is that God sent his Son Jesus Christ to save sinners by dying on the cross. Everyone who accepts this teaching receives eternal life. But whether people will accept it or not partly depends on the way Christians handle themselves on the job. So every Christian who works in a non-Christian environment is a missionary. Paul said something similar when he wrote to Titus: "Slaves are to be submissive to their own masters in everything; they are to be well-pleasing, not argumentative, not pilfering, but showing all good faith, so that in everything they may adorn the doctrine of God our Savior" (Titus 2:9–10).

A wonderful example of how to "adorn the doctrine of God our Savior" is the little slave girl who served in Naaman's household. Naaman was a valiant general, the commander of the Syrian army. He had great wealth and many possessions, but he also had leprosy, and this was his torment (2 Kings 5:1). One of Naaman's servants was a young Jewish girl who had been captured during the wars and carried back to Syria as a slave. The little girl had heard about her master's disease. One day as she went about her duties she sighed, "Would that my lord were with the prophet who is in Samaria! He would cure him of his leprosy" (2 Kings 5:3). Eventually her words got back to Naaman and he went off to Samaria to find a cure. Not only did God's prophet Elisha give him a cure, but he also led him to faith in the living God.

This all came about because the little slave girl was an on-the-job evangelist. She wasn't pushy. She didn't leave tracts on her master's pillow. She didn't go around pointing out people's sins. Instead, in the most natural way, as she cleaned up the breakfast dishes or did her daily chores, she gave a testimony of God's saving power. God used her testimony to bring her master to saving faith.

In the same way, every believer is called to be a witness on the job, and not a closet Christian. Be sure that your employer and your fellow-employees know that you are a Christian, so that your work will be evaluated in the context of your faith. When you are offered a promotion, consider the implications it will have for your family and ministry in the church. When you talk about your weekend, mention what happened at church the day before. When people are talking about some current issue around the water cooler, give an answer from the biblical point of view. When you are on a business trip with your coworkers, take advantage of the opportunity to get to know them on a personal basis.

A Christian who is committed to reaching the workplace for Jesus Christ will find plenty of natural situations in which to speak about supernatural things. Your coworkers may not be very interested in your Christianity. On occasion, they may even ridicule your faith. But when the day of trouble comes, to whom will they go for counsel? When they are confronted with death, to whom will they go for comfort? And when the Holy Spirit awakens them to their spiritual need, to whom will they go for the words of life? They will turn to the man or woman who has loved them with the love of Christ from the very first day they walked into the office. Then you will be able to share the good news about Jesus Christ, so that they can know his love, too.

When Your Boss Is a Believer

What if your boss is a Christian already? What do you do when you walk through the company parking lot and discover—to your amazement—that he has a fish symbol on the back of his car, too? How is the work relationship different when both the manager and the employee are servants of the Lord Jesus Christ?

This problem was particularly acute in the early church. Some of the first Christians were slaves, so masters and slaves worshiped side by side. In the church, slaves had absolute equality before God (cf. Gal. 3:28), but in society as a whole they were considered inferior. What did this mean for their work? No doubt some slaves wanted to take advantage of their new-found Christianity. "For freedom Christ has set us free!" they said (cf. Gal. 5:1). "Because our masters are our brothers," they reasoned, "they can no longer be our masters, and we can no longer be their slaves." Therefore, they concluded that the coming of Christianity meant the end of their captivity.

The fact is, however, that the New Testament never tells slaves to throw off their own yokes. They can pray to God for deliverance, of course. They can also purchase their freedom through legal means, as Paul encourages them to do (1 Cor. 7:21: "But if you can gain your freedom, avail yourself of the opportunity"). But the New Testament does not tell slaves to escape from their bondage. In this respect, slavery is like any other kind of suffering. God does not tell his people to avoid suffering at all costs. Instead, he gives us the grace to endure it for the sake of Jesus Christ. And when it comes to the sufferings of slavery, the Bible says, "Those who have believing masters must not be disrespectful on the ground that they are brothers; rather they must serve all the better since those who benefit by their good service are believers and beloved" (1 Tim. 6:2).

Apparently, some slaves were starting to be disrespectful to their masters. They thought they could take advantage of them because they were brothers in Christ. People often treat their own family members worse than they treat guests. "It's only my brother," they say. "He'll get over it." Sometimes Christians face the same temptation in their work relationships with other believers—their brothers and sisters in Christ. Some Christian workers take advantage of Christian bosses. They assume they are entitled to special favors because they are brothers and sisters in Christ. They know their boss will be more forgiving (after all, he is a Christian!) so they take liberties they would never dream of taking in a secular workplace. If they did try to take them, in fact, they would soon find themselves looking for another job.

Anyone who has worked in a church, or in a Christian school, or in some other ministry knows how unpleasant it can be to work in a Christian organization. Everyone has high expectations for how everyone else will behave. But eventually someone does something that does not quite measure up to Christian standards, and then everyone else gets very offended. "I can't believe he did that! And here I thought the whole time that he was a Christian!" At the same time that some people take advantage of their coworkers because they are Christians, others forget that the Christians they work with are human beings, and therefore sinners. As a result of all this, the work environment in some Christian businesses is as toxic as anything in the secular marketplace.

Christian organizations ought to be the very best places to work, and they can be, provided the workers behave like Christians. The distinguishing mark of Christian fellowship is love. Therefore, Christians in the marketplace should treat one another with deep affection. They must serve their brothers and sisters "all the better since those who benefit by their good service are believers and beloved" (1 Tim. 6:2). The word "service" (*douleuetōsan*) is used in an unusual way in this verse. It usually describes a donation given by some wealthy benefactor. Therefore, some scholars conclude that "service" is something slaves receive from their masters. Paul's point is just the opposite, however. In the economy of God everything is reversed. Through humble service, Christian slaves even become the generous benefactors of their Christian masters.

The reason these slaves are so generous is that their masters are so dear to them. The word "beloved" (*agapētoi*) is the same word Paul used when he told Philemon to welcome Onesimus "no longer as a slave but more than a slave, as a beloved brother—especially to me, but how much more to you, both in the flesh and in the Lord" (Philem. 16). Masters should remember the love they have for their servants because they belong to Christ. In the same way, Christian bosses ought to have real affection for the believers who work for them.

Master and Slave

What the Bible says about working for God in the marketplace is not easy teaching. A Christian in a difficult work situation may find some of these biblical principles very hard to put into practice. Who ever wants to be a slave?

Yet there are two compelling reasons to work in a way that pleases God. The first is that God is your Master. This is a lesson Paul taught the Ephesians in an earlier letter: "Slaves, obey your earthly masters with fear and trembling, with a sincere heart, as you would Christ, not by the way of eye-service, as people-pleasers, but as servants of Christ, doing the will of God from the heart, rendering service with a good will as to the Lord and not to man, knowing that whatever good anyone does, this he will receive back from the Lord, whether he is a slave or free" (Eph. 6:5–8; cf. Col. 3:22–25). If a slave belongs to Christ, then Christ is his ultimate Master. To serve an earthly master is actually one way to serve God himself. To put it in contemporary English, every Christian is on God's payroll.

Not only is God your Master, but he has also become your servant, even your slave. The Bible says that God the Son "made himself nothing, taking the form of a servant" (Phil. 2:7). The word for "servant" in Philippians 2:7 is the same word used for "slave" in 1 Timothy 6:1 (*doulos*). The Son of God became a slave when he became a man. He became *our* slave. He obeyed the law of God perfectly in our place. He suffered the penalty we deserved. He paid for our sins when he died on the cross. While it is one thing to obey a master, it is another thing to obey a master who is so generous that he has willingly served as your slave. Since Jesus Christ has already done more for us than we will ever do for him, we should at least do all that we can for him, and we should do this at work as much as anywhere else.

18

The Christian Attitude toward Money

1 Timothy 6:3–10

Now there is great gain in godliness with contentment. . . . But those who desire to be rich fall into temptation, into a snare, into many senseless and harmful desires that plunge people into ruin and destruction. For the love of money is a root of all kinds of evils. (1 Tim. 6:6, 9–10)

There was land for sale, and Vasili Andreevich wanted to buy it. In fact, he wanted to arrive early enough to buy the property before it went up for auction. So he loaded up his sledge and foolishly ventured out into the darkness of a long Russian winter's night. The wind was harsh, the snow was heavy, and eventually Andreevich lost his way. When his sledge got stuck in a snowdrift, Vasili had to spend the night trying to survive a raging blizzard: "He did not wish to sleep. He lay and thought: thought ever of the one thing that constituted the sole aim, meaning, pleasure, and pride of his life—of how much money he had made and might still make, of how much other people he knew had made and possessed, and of how those others had made and were making it, and how he, like them, might still make much more."[1] But Vasili's grandiose plans came to nothing. In the morning, when the villagers dug his sledge out of the snow, they found the man frozen stiff.

The story of Vasili Andreevich, which was told by Leo Tolstoy, shows how "those who desire to be rich fall into temptation, into a snare, into many senseless and harmful desires that plunge people into ruin and destruction" (1 Tim. 6:9; cf. Luke 12:13–21).

When Theology Becomes Pathology

There were false teachers in the church at Ephesus who were in danger of meeting the same unhappy end, and for the same reason: they were in love with money. Before mentioning their greed, however, the apostle Paul reminds Pastor Timothy of their basic theological error: "If anyone teaches a different doctrine and does not agree with the sound words of our Lord Jesus Christ and the teaching that accords with godliness" (1 Tim. 6:3; cf. 1:3). This is the basic problem with every form of bad theology, or, as Paul terms it, "different doctrine." In one way or another, such heterodoxy does not adhere to what the Bible teaches about the person and work of Jesus Christ.

What the Bible teaches about Jesus Christ is "sound." This medical term is used throughout the Pastoral Epistles (cf. 1 Tim. 1:10; 2 Tim. 1:13; Titus 1:9; 2:1; etc.) to mean "healthy" or "wholesome." Solid biblical teaching—especially "the sound words of our Lord Jesus Christ"—produces spiritual well-being. This phrase may refer to the apostolic teaching *about* Jesus, or it may refer to Jesus' own words as recorded in the Gospels. It may even refer to both, since, as John Stott reminds us, "Paul regarded his own words as the words of Christ" (cf. Luke 10:16; 2 Cor. 13:3).[2] In any case, "the sound words of our Lord Jesus Christ" comprise the Christian gospel. This gospel teaches that Jesus is the one and only Son of God, man as well as God, who was conceived by the Holy Spirit in the womb of the virgin Mary, who suffered and died on the cross of Calvary, who was buried in a tomb, and who was raised again from the dead to give eternal

1. Leo Tolstoy, "Master and Man," in Darryl Tippens, Stephen Weathers, and Jack Welch, eds., *Shadow and Light: Literature and the Life of Faith* (Abilene, TX: ACU Press, 1997), 132–73 (pp. 158–59).

2. John Stott, *Guard the Truth: The Message of 1 Timothy and Titus* (Downers Grove, IL: InterVarsity, 1996), 147.

life to everyone who believes in him. This is the sound instruction of our Lord Jesus Christ; anything else is unsound. Indeed, the only word for it is heresy.

The difference between true religion and false religion always comes down to Jesus Christ—who he is and what he has done. The reason that Reformation Christians oppose the teaching of the Muslims, the Mormons, the Jehovah's Witnesses, and others, is not that those religions are immoral. No, we oppose them because they are unsound in their teaching about Jesus Christ. The first question to ask of any cult or any religion is, "What does it teach about Jesus Christ?" The same question should be asked of every man, woman, or child: "What do you think of Jesus Christ?" Most cults—Mormons and Jehovah's Witnesses would be good examples—are wrong about the *person* of Jesus Christ. They deny his deity, and thus reduce him to the status of a mere human being. What other world religions deny, primarily, is the *work* of Jesus Christ. They do not accept his sacrifice for sin or his bodily resurrection. But true religion demands a true understanding of Jesus Christ, both in his person and in his work. This understanding comes only through the Scriptures of the Old and New Testaments. This, and this alone, is "the teaching that accords with godliness" (1 Tim. 6:3; cf. Titus 1:1).

Paul reminded Timothy of his own role as a godly teacher at the end of verse 2: "Teach and urge these things." This is a good, short summary of the work of a gospel minister. First and foremost, a pastor is a teacher. He expounds the Word of God, which is the only remedy for false doctrine. He teaches "these things" (orthodoxy), not "different doctrine" (heterodoxy). But the minister's work does not end with teaching. To "urge" is "to appeal to those who are also being taught to apply the teaching to their lives."[3] Therefore, a good preacher exhorts as well as explains. As Charles Spurgeon used to say, "Where the application begins, there the sermon begins."[4]

What a minister teaches and applies in his preaching is mainly Jesus Christ, who is the beginning and the end of all sound theology. Martin Luther said:

> I have found and noted in all histories of the whole Christian Church that all those who have maintained the central doctrine of Jesus Christ in its integrity

3. George Knight, *The Pastoral Epistles*, New International Greek Testament Commentary (Grand Rapids: Eerdmans, 1992), 248.

4. John A. Broadus, *On the Preparation and Delivery of Sermons*, 4th ed., ed. Vernon L. Stanfield (San Francisco: Harper & Row, 1979), 165.

> have remained safe and sound in the true Christian faith. Although they erred and sinned in other respects, yet they were finally saved. For if anyone stands firm and right on this point, that Jesus Christ is true God and true man, all the other articles of the Christian faith will fall in place for him and firmly sustain him.[5]

Sadly, the same could not be said of the false teachers in Ephesus. Because they did not maintain "the central doctrine of Jesus Christ," they did not remain "safe and sound in the true Christian faith." This is why Paul condemned them so harshly, saying that anyone who teaches false theology "is puffed up with conceit and understands nothing" (1 Tim. 6:4; cf. 3:6). He thinks he knows everything, yet in fact he knows nothing at all, and thus he is as ignorant as he is arrogant. C. K. Barrett calls the man "a pompous ignoramus."[6]

The result of his theological error was (and always is) trouble in the church. Do not blame orthodox Christians when there is controversy. It is the unsound theologian who "has an unhealthy craving for controversy and for quarrels about words, which produce envy, dissension, slander, evil suspicions, and constant friction among people who are depraved in mind and deprived of the truth" (1 Tim. 6:4–5; cf. 1:4). The word "unhealthy" shows the difference between orthodoxy and heresy. Orthodoxy is healthy; it consists of "sound words." But heterodoxy will make the church sick. Its champions are jealous, resentful, abusive, irritable, and depraved. In other words, they are everything that qualified elders are not (see 1 Tim. 3:1–7). John Stott thus calls their contentious spirit "positively pathological."[7]

There is a certain kind of churchman who enjoys a good fight. He (I say "he" because this mentality seems especially prevalent among men) is argumentative. He majors on minors. The more speculative the doctrine, the more tenaciously he debates for it. He not only splits hairs, but he tries to do so with a chainsaw. In the end he robs himself of the truth. This means that part of being a good theologian is knowing when *not* to fight. Consider these wise words from the great Scottish preacher Alexander Whyte, which

5. Martin Luther, in James Atkinson, *Martin Luther: Prophet to the Church Catholic* (Grand Rapids: Eerdmans, 1983), 184.

6. C. K. Barrett, *The Pastoral Epistles* (Oxford: Clarendon, 1963), 83.

7. Stott, *Guard the Truth*, 147.

a friend once shared with me: "Eschew controversy, my brethren, as you would eschew the entrance to hell itself! Let them have it their own way. Let them talk, let them write, let them correct you, let them traduce you. Let them judge and condemn you, let them slay you. Rather let the truth of God itself suffer than that love suffer. You have not enough of the Divine nature in you to be a controversialist."

In It for the Money

Unfortunately, there were plenty of controversialists in Timothy's church. The last thing Paul says about them explains how they got that way—it had to do with their profit motive. The bottom line for them was, well, "the bottom line." They thought that "godliness is a means of gain" (1 Tim. 6:5; cf. Titus 1:11), meaning financial gain. In other words, they were in the ministry for the money.

How were these false teachers turning a profit? Remember that religion was big business in Ephesus, the home of the goddess Diana. So the false teachers may have tried to market Christianity. Perhaps they went on the religious lecture circuit, or received compensation for their services in some other way. In those days many popular teachers charged their disciples a small fee. More likely, these hucksters were teaching an early version of the health-and-wealth gospel. They were not interested in religion for its own sake. Instead, they taught that good morals were the pathway to financial security. But in one way or another, they were guilty of the sin of avarice, which is "extreme greed for money or gain" (*Oxford English Dictionary*).

Greed has always been a great danger for the church. This was true in the Middle Ages, when the sale of indulgences made salvation something that only money could buy, but it is equally true today. The bookstores and mail-order catalogues are full of religious merchandise. The Christian television programs spend a great deal of time appealing for money, or telling you how to make more money. "Name it and claim it!" they say. "All you need to do is ask . . . and send us a small donation."

The world can hardly be blamed if it concludes that Christianity is mainly about money. The scandals of the church almost always involve what used to be called "filthy lucre." Consider the secretary who embezzled hundreds of thousands of dollars from denominational funds, or the minister who used church money to buy a mansion for his mistress. It always has something to do with money.

This is why Paul himself was so careful in his use of money. He refused to sell out the gospel, to "peddle the word of God for profit," as he once put it (2 Cor. 2:17 NIV). The apostle understood that the Holy Spirit's work does not require money. Of all the resources the church needs to do its work, money is by far the least important. Tertullian once put it like this: "Nothing that is God's is obtainable by money." A church (or an individual, for that matter) that becomes preoccupied with money is on the pathway to theological error.

Content with Christ

Godliness is not the means to financial gain; godliness *is* the gain. Here the Bible turns a surprising phrase: although godliness is not a means of gain, "there is great gain in godliness with contentment" (1 Tim. 6:6). By "godliness" is meant the knowledge of Jesus Christ in the mind and the heart that is worked out through the Christian life (cf. 1 Tim. 3:16). Such godliness is not a means to something else more valuable; it is supremely valuable all by itself.

Godliness is not merely gain, it is *great* gain! It is, said Calvin, "itself a sufficiently great gain to us, because through it we become not only heirs of the world but are enabled to enjoy Christ and all His riches."[8] The great gain of knowing Christ is not only for this life, but it is also for the life to come, as Paul has already explained (1 Tim. 4:8; cf. 6:19). Faith in Jesus Christ is the ultimate investment because it yields eternal life.

Godliness is great gain, provided that we learn how to be content with our present circumstances. The Revised English Version emphasizes the need for contentment: "[People] think religion should yield dividends; and of course religion does yield high dividends, but only to those who are content with what they have." The word "contentment" (*autarkeia*) was often used in Greek philosophy to describe a man who had all his

8. John Calvin, *The Second Epistle of Paul the Apostle to the Corinthians and the Epistles to Timothy, Titus and Philemon*, trans. T. A. Smail, Calvin's Commentaries (Edinburgh: Oliver & Boyd, 1964), 274.

resources within himself. He did not need to depend on anyone or anything else. He was completely self-sufficient. When Paul talks about contentment, however, he means something slightly different. The Puritan Jeremiah Burroughs described contentment as "a work of the Spirit indoors."[9] He wrote, "I find a sufficiency of satisfaction in my own heart, through the grace of Christ that is in me."[10] The person who has what Burroughs called *The Rare Jewel of Christian Contentment* has all his or her resources in God.

A Christian is not self-sufficient, but Christ-sufficient.[11] Anyone who has Jesus Christ has everything he or she needs. The trouble is that we are not always content. Some of our discontent comes from the natural frustration of living in a fallen world; we are waiting for Jesus to make everything new. But a good deal of our discontent also comes from not being satisfied with Jesus himself. We want something more or something else.

Our discontent begins in childhood, as indicated by this "introduction to property law from a toddler's perspective":

> If I like it, it's mine.
> If I can take it away from you, it's mine.
> If I had it a while ago, it's mine.
> If I say it is mine, it's mine.
> If it looks like mine, it's mine.
> If I say I saw it first, it's mine.
> If you're having fun with it, it's mine.
> If you lay down your toy, it's mine.
> If it is broken, it's yours.[12]

This may sound childish, but some people remain childish all their lives, never learning the secret of being content. I once heard Charles Swindoll quote a little poem he had received from a teenager:

9. Jeremiah Burroughs, *The Rare Jewel of Christian Contentment* (London, 1648; repr. Edinburgh: Banner of Truth, 1964), 20.

10. Ibid., 19.

11. Gordon D. Fee, *1 and 2 Timothy, Titus*, New International Biblical Commentary (Peabody, MA: Hendrickson, 1988), 143.

12. From the Joke Distribution Network.

It was Spring, but it was Summer I wanted:
The warm days and the great outdoors.

It was Summer, but it was Fall I wanted:
The colorful leaves and the cool, dry air.

It was Fall, but it was Winter I wanted:
The beautiful snow and the joy of the holiday season.

It was Winter, but it was Spring I wanted:
The warmth and the blossoming of nature.

I was a child, and it was adulthood I wanted:
The freedom and the respect.

I was 20, but it was 30 I wanted:
To be mature and sophisticated.

I was middle-aged, but it was 20 I wanted:
The youth and the free spirit.

I was retired, but it was middle-aged I wanted:
The presence of mind without limitations.

My life was over,
and I never got what I wanted.

Discontent is life's burglar. It robs every other experience of its God-given joy. Someone who is discontent is always operating at a loss.

You Can't Take It with You

The only way to make great gains is through "godliness with contentment" (1 Tim. 6:6). There are three reasons for this, and the first is that "you can't take it with you." Here is the apostle Paul's version of that famous expression: "For we brought nothing into the world, and we cannot take anything out of the world" (1 Tim. 6:7).

These are the two undeniable, unchangeable truths about human possessions: nothing in, nothing out. Every person who has ever lived enters and exits the world the same way. All belongings must be checked at graveside. This was true of our first parents. Adam and Eve came into the world with nothing, and they left the world with nothing. "For you are dust," God said to Adam, "and to dust you shall return" (Gen. 3:19). Ashes to ashes, dust to dust.

The same was true of Job, the wealthiest man in the ancient world. Job had fabulous possessions, riches beyond compare, but they were all taken away. In rapid succession the man lost his oxen, his donkeys, his sheep, his camels, his servants, his children . . . everything. When it happened, Job "fell on the ground and worshiped. And he said, 'Naked I came from my mother's womb, and naked shall I return' " (Job 1:20–21). In this respect, Job was no different from anyone else. Every human being dies penniless. It is like the old story about the millionaire. When he died, everyone wanted to know what was in his will. So they whispered to the minister, "How much did he leave behind?" "Everything!" the minister said. "He had to leave it all behind!"

The Monday morning philosopher who wrote Ecclesiastes observed the same phenomenon: "As he came from his mother's womb he shall go again, naked as he came, and shall take nothing for his toil that he may carry away in his hand" (Eccl. 5:15). Every mortal will return to the dust. Even the great Pharaohs of Egypt, who were buried with all their riches and had their bodies carefully embalmed, couldn't take it with them. The psalmist said it like this: "Be not afraid when a man becomes rich, when the glory of his house increases. For when he dies he will carry nothing away; his glory will not go down after him" (Ps. 49:16–17).

Enough Already!

The second reason to be content with what you have is that what you have is enough (probably more than enough). If you come into the world with nothing, and leave with nothing, then what do you need in the meantime? Not much: "But if we have food and clothing, with these we will be content" (1 Tim. 6:8).

It may seem surprising that the Bible fails to mention shelter along with food and clothing. Yet the word for clothing (*skepasma*) means "covering," and thus also refers to shelter. Jesus said much the same thing: "Do not be anxious about your life, what you will eat or what you will drink, nor about your body, what you will put on" (Matt. 6:25). The reason Jesus said not to worry is that the same God who feeds the birds and clothes the lilies provides food and shelter for all his children. If this seems overly austere, it may be because we live in such an affluent society, in which "what some people mistake for the high cost of living is really the cost of high living."[13]

Every Christian ought to be content with the basic necessities of life. The *Westminster Shorter Catechism* puts it well when it speaks of "a competent portion of the good things of this life."[14] We do not need luxuries, only necessities. "For," as John Stott advises, "possessions are only the traveling luggage of time; they are not the stuff of eternity. It would be sensible therefore to travel light."[15] If God provides more than we need, there is nothing wrong with that. In fact, there are instructions for the rich near the end of this chapter (see 1 Tim. 6:17–19). But the Bible calls Christians to be content with a simple lifestyle, even to be downwardly mobile. Clement of Alexandria said that "those who are in earnest about salvation must settle this beforehand in their mind: all we possess is given to us for the sake of self-sufficiency, and one may attain that with only a few things. . . . God has given to us, I know well, the liberty of using things—but only so far as necessary; and he has determined that our use of them should be shared."[16] One good set of guidelines for sharing comes from the Evangelical Commitment to Simple Lifestyle produced by the Lausanne Committee for World Evangelization in 1980:

> We resolve to renounce waste and oppose extravagance in personal living, clothing and housing, travel and church buildings. We also accept the distinction between necessities and luxuries, creative hobbies and empty status symbols, modesty and vanity, occasional celebrations and normal routine, and between the service of God and slavery to fashion. Where to draw the line requires conscientious thought and decision by us, together with members of our family.

13. Doug Larson, *Leadership* (Fall, 1997), 75.

14. *The Shorter Catechism*, in *The Westminster Standards* (Norcross, GA: Great Commission Publications, 1991), A. 104.

15. Stott, *Guard the Truth*, 150.

16. Clement of Alexandria, "True Wealth," condensed from *The Tutor* and reprinted in *Re:generation Quarterly* 4.4 (1998): 14.

But the best document I have ever read on contentment is still the statement my mother-in-law posted over her kitchen sink: "Contentment is knowing that if I am not satisfied with what I have, I will not be satisfied with what I want, either." Discontent always wants something more or something else. It always thinks about what it lacks. But even when you get what you think you want—a new home, a better job, another outfit, more toys, whatever—you soon find that you are discontent all over again. This is because, like a noxious weed, discontent is rooted in the heart. Discontent comes from what a man is, not from what he doesn't have.

This also explains why contentment is completely unrelated to how many possessions a person has. In fact, often the more possessions a person has, the more empty life becomes. The German philosopher Arthur Schopenhauer observed that "Gold is like sea water—the more one drinks of it, the thirstier one becomes."[17] For once Schopenhauer was right, and Herbert Schlossberg explains why: "All true needs—such as food, drink, and companionship—are satiable. Illegitimate wants—pride, envy, greed—are insatiable. By their nature they cannot be satisfied . . . enough is never enough."[18] The Bible describes the insatiably addictive power of money like this: "He who loves money will not be satisfied with money, nor he who loves wealth with his income" (Eccl. 5:10).

The London preacher Dick Lucas tells the story of a man he met who went to a church in the most prosperous county in England. Among other things, the minister told him that if he trusted in Jesus, God would give him a Jaguar automobile. The trouble was, the man already owned a Jaguar. So he went to the church just down the road, walked up to the minister and said, "I went to such-and-such a church and they told me that God wants me to have a Jaguar. But you see, I already have a Jaguar, and my life is still empty and meaningless. Doesn't Christianity have anything more to offer me than another automobile?"

Christianity does have more to offer. What it offers is Jesus Christ, the true treasure of the soul. What the human heart really craves is not gold, but God. Anyone who comes to God through Jesus Christ finds meaning,

17. Arthur Schopenhauer, quoted in Stott, *Guard the Truth*, 152.

18. Herbert Schlossberg, *Idols for Destruction*, quoted by J. Robert Vannoy in "The Seven Deadly Sins: Greed," as published in a newsletter from Biblical Theological Seminary (Fall, 1997), 5.

purpose, joy, and even satisfaction with life. It is like the wonderful line by Charles Wesley in his hymn "Jesus, Lover of My Soul," which goes: "Thou, O Christ, art all I want; more than all in thee I find."

One man who discovered that Jesus Christ was all he really needed was the apostle Paul. And Paul was more than willing to share his secret: "I know how to be brought low, and I know how to abound. In any and every circumstance, I have learned the secret of facing plenty and hunger, abundance and need. I can do all things through him who strengthens me" (Phil. 4:12–13). The secret of contentment is to be satisfied with Jesus Christ.

Think of it this way: Contentment is the best furniture for your home. If you add contentment to your living room, you have all the furnishings you need. Contentment is the best fashion accessory. Wrap contentment around your collar, and voilà, you have reached the height of true fashion. Or add "contentment" as a line item in your portfolio; then you have the ultimate financial security. The more content you are in Christ, the more you discover that godliness with contentment is great gain.

The Root of All Evil

The last reason to be content with what God has given you is that discontent leads to disaster. Apparently, people who want to get rich have never read to the end of Paul's letter to Timothy, where it says, "But those who desire to be rich fall into temptation, into a snare, into many senseless and harmful desires that plunge people into ruin and destruction. For the love of money is a root of all kinds of evils. It is through this craving that some have wandered away from the faith and pierced themselves with many pangs" (1 Tim. 6:9–10).

One thing leads to another. First, there is the desire to get rich, which seems harmless enough. Then there is some temptation to get rich by immoral means. But that is actually a snare of the devil which leads to more and more evil desires. Eventually the greedy man plunges into ruin and destruction. And "plunge" is just the word for it. He is drowning, submerged in the sea of his own avarice. Soon he will surely come to "ruin," meaning moral failure in the present life, and "destruction," meaning spiritual death in the life to come (cf. Mark 8:36).

It is not people who *are* rich who fall into this trap, notice, but people who want to be richer than they already are. What the Bible condemns is people who live for money, "who have fixed their desires on material wealth and made it their overriding motive."[19] Nor is money the root of all evil. This may be the most frequently misquoted verse in the Bible. "Money is the root of all evil," people say, when actually it is the *love* of money that causes the trouble. Money itself is morally neutral. It can be used for many good and noble purposes. Greed is not rooted in money, therefore, but in the fallen nature of the human heart. John Stott wisely observes that this passage is "not for poverty against wealth, but for contentment against covetousness."[20]

Notice as well that money is not the root of *all* evil, which is the way this verse appears in the King James Version: "Money is the root of all evil" (1 Tim. 6:10). Literally, the verse reads, "money is the root of all evils." However, this statement is proverbial, and thus it is not intended to be understood as an absolute rule, universally applicable to all situations. Strictly speaking, there are many evils in the world that do not come from greed. Some come from the lust for power, or the desire for sex, or the longing for fame. If anything, *pride* is the root of all evil—the desire to unseat God and climb onto his throne. But greed remains one radical source of evil; it is the kind of sin that leads to many other sins. The English Standard Version and New International Version capture the sense of the verse well, even if they are somewhat interpretive: "the love of money is *a* root of *all kinds* of evil" (1 Tim. 6:10). Clement of Alexandria said, "Wealth, when not properly governed, is a stronghold of evil."[21] "Take away therefore the love of money," Chrysostom argued, "and you put an end to war, to battle, to enmity, to strife and contention."[22]

Almost wistfully, Paul remembers what happened to some of the money-lovers he knew. They wandered from the Christian faith, of course. They gave up faith in Christ as the "central desire and love of their life."[23] They

19. J. N. D. Kelly, *The Pastoral Epistles: Timothy I and II, Titus*, Harper's New Testament Commentaries (San Francisco: Harper and Row, 1960), 137.

20. Stott, *Guard the Truth*, 154.

21. Clement of Alexandria, "True Wealth," 14.

22. John Chrysostom, "Homilies on the Epistles of St. Paul the Apostle to Timothy, Titus, and Philemon," trans. and ed. Philip Schaff, *Nicene and Post-Nicene Fathers*, First Series, 14 vols. (Peabody, MA: Hendrickson, 1994), 13:469.

23. Knight, *Pastoral Epistles*, 258.

had to, because the love of God and the love of money are incompatible. "No one can serve two masters," Jesus said. "You cannot serve God and money" (Matt. 6:24). Either you love God and use money, or you love money and use God to get it.

Paul often witnessed this dilemma in the early church, maybe even in Ephesus. He had heard the story of Ananias and Sapphira, who exaggerated how much they were putting in the offering plate, and as a result were struck down dead at the doors of the church (Acts 5:1–10). Later, he would lament the loss of Demas, who deserted him because he was "in love with this present world" (2 Tim. 4:10), and warn that in the terrible times of the last days, people will be "lovers of money" (2 Tim. 3:2).

Nor is it hard to come up with examples from the Old Testament. There was Achan, of course, who stole a beautiful robe because it had a designer label from Babylon. He and his family were stoned and buried under a pile of rocks (Josh. 7:1–26). There was King Solomon, who did not even set out to be wealthy, yet the love of money caught up with him in the end. Another man who was royally greedy was King Ahab, who pouted when Naboth refused to sell his vineyard (1 Kings 21:1–22). Ahab wanted the property so badly that he lost his appetite. Eventually, he killed Naboth to get the vineyard, but even before he tasted his first grape, God pronounced disaster on his household. Or consider Gehazi (2 Kings 5:20–27), who was unhappy that Elisha was giving God's grace away for free. By the time he was finished, Gehazi had told every lie in the book in order to "get something" from Naaman the Syrian. But God witnessed his theft, and Gehazi was punished with leprosy as a result.

The wounds caused by greed are self-inflicted. In his sermon on this text, Chrysostom said, "Desires are thorns, and as when one touches thorns, he gores his hand, and gets him wounds, so he that falls into these lusts will be wounded by them, and pierce his soul with griefs."[24] Is there a sadder example of this truth than Judas Iscariot? He was a follower of Jesus Christ. He had the gifts of an apostle. Yet he sold the Lord of glory for thirty pieces of silver. In the end, pierced with bitter grief, Judas took his own life (Matt. 27:3–5). The Bible means what it says: the love of money leads to no end of evil, and ultimately to eternal death.

24. Chrysostom, "Homilies," 469.

The frightening thing, of course, is that so many of us have money-loving hearts. Our greed must be rooted out. Acquisitiveness must be replaced with godliness. The only thing to do is to repent for every covetous desire and ask God to fill us with love for Christ, which is what Vasili Andreevich did. As Vasili struggled vainly to keep himself warm during the last night of his life, he had what can only be described as a conversion experience. He heard the call of God, responded in faith and repented of his greed. This is the way Tolstoy described his dying moments:

> And he remembered his money, his shop, his house, the buying and selling . . . and it was hard for him to understand why that man, called Vasili . . . had troubled himself with all those things with which he had been troubled.
>
> "Well, it was because he did not know what the real thing was," he thought, concerning that Vasili. . . . "He did not know, but now I know and know for sure. Now I know!" And again he heard the voice of one who had called him before. "I'm coming! Coming!" he responded gladly, and his whole being was filled with joyful emotion. He felt himself free and that nothing could hold him back any longer.
>
> After that Vasili Andreevich neither saw, heard, nor felt anything more in this world.[25]

What Vasili Andreevich heard was the voice of God, calling him home. What he repented of was his greedy, money-loving heart. And what he discovered in the life beyond this world is the truth of what Paul said to Timothy: "There is great gain in godliness with contentment" (1 Tim. 6:6).

25. Tolstoy, "Master and Man," 171.

19

Rules of Engagement

1 Timothy 6:11–16

But as for you, O man of God, flee these things. Pursue righteousness, godliness, faith, love, steadfastness, gentleness. Fight the good fight of the faith. Take hold of the eternal life to which you were called and about which you made the good confession in the presence of many witnesses. (1 Tim. 6:11–12)

The United States military engagement in Somalia—commonly known as Black Hawk Down—is a well-known military debacle.[1] In the armed conflict following the downing of two American Blackhawk helicopters in the streets of Mogadishu, the city became a scene of unimaginable confusion. Somali women and children were gunned down with automatic weapons. American soldiers were captured and dragged through the streets. It was not always clear who was fighting whom. Eventually, military discipline broke down, and it was every unit for itself. When the fighting was over, members of the United States Army walked around the Somali soccer stadium in a daze, trying to figure out what had happened.

1. For a full account, see Mark Bowden, *Black Hawk Down: A Story of Modern War* (New York: Atlantic Monthly Press, 1999).

There are many military lessons to be learned from the street-fight in Mogadishu. One of the most obvious is that soldiers need to know their rules of engagement—the guidelines that tell them what they can and cannot do in a particular conflict. Once discipline and communication broke down in Somalia, the American soldiers essentially had to make up their own rules as they went along.

There are times when similar confusion reigns in the church. Christians lose track of what they are fighting for and whom they are fighting against. Sometimes they even fire at random. The sad result is that many Christians are wounded by "friendly fire." Fortunately, God has given his church rules of engagement, some of which are listed at the close of Paul's first letter to Timothy. These rules not only have personal application to Timothy as a minister, but they also help every Christian know how to "fight the good fight of the faith" (1 Tim. 6:12).

Know When to Run

The first thing a soldier needs to know is what dangers to avoid. Good soldiers do not knowingly and carelessly walk into minefields. So Timothy's first rule of engagement is an order to make a tactical withdrawal: "But as for you, O man of God, flee these things" (1 Tim. 6:11). Each word in this phrase is significant. Dick Lucas, who formerly preached at St. Helen's Bishopsgate in the financial district of London, liked to point out that the words "but you" are a standard refrain in the Pastoral Epistles. Each time they appear, they follow a description of the kind of pastorate that Paul hoped that Timothy would avoid, and thus they are used to show the absolute contrast between the true and the false ministry of the gospel. In 2 Timothy 3, for example, Paul warned Timothy that "evil people and impostors will go on from bad to worse, deceiving and being deceived. *But as for you*, continue in what you have learned and have firmly believed" (2 Tim. 3:13–14a; cf. v. 5; 4:16). Or again, "The time is coming when people will not endure sound teaching. . . . *As for you*, always be sober-minded, endure suffering, do the work of an evangelist, fulfill your ministry" (2 Tim. 4:3, 5).

There are many false teachers in the world. There always have been, and there always will be. But a minister like Timothy must have nothing to do with them. When others are false, he must remain true. When others take ministry as a professional career, he must receive it as a sacred calling. When others teach the wisdom of the world, he must teach the wisdom of God revealed in Holy Scripture. When others preach themselves, he will preach Christ crucified and risen from the dead.

What makes Timothy different is that he is a "man of God" (1 Tim. 6:11; cf. 2 Tim. 3:17). This may be the highest commendation that Paul ever gave young Timothy. The title "man of God" is used but rarely in the Old Testament, where it is reserved almost exclusively for great heroes of the faith—men like Moses (Deut. 33:1), Samuel (1 Sam. 9:6), David (Neh. 12:24), Elijah (1 Kings 17:18), and Elisha (2 Kings 4:7). Like those great men before him, Timothy had been given a message from God. Like them, he must remain true to God in the face of danger. If he remains faithful at his post, then he, too, will be called a "man of God."

What the man of God is told to do is to "flee these things." By "these things," Paul clearly means the things he has just been warning about in verses 3 through 10. Timothy is to run away from the love of money and its bitter fruits: discontent, foolish desire, dissension, and false doctrine. Ministers must not be greedy (cf. 1 Tim. 3:3). When it comes to money they should follow the example of the apostle Paul, who knew when to run. Paul recognized, of course, that ministers need their daily bread. He even defended their right to draw a salary (1 Tim. 5:17–18). But he himself was not in the ministry for the money. Thus, when he said farewell to the elders from Timothy's church, he was able to state that he had "coveted no one's silver or gold or apparel" (Acts 20:33; cf. 1 Thess. 2:5).

The command to "flee these things" reminds me of an incident that took place on the campus of Wheaton College in the 1980s. A popular prank in those days was (and probably still is) to use surgical tubing to launch water balloons at students going in and out of the freshman dorm. One night, as unsuspecting freshmen were being bombarded from long-distance, two cars suddenly drove up and the pranksters were surrounded by public safety officers. One of the officers smirked at the unexpected success of their sting operation. "What do you guys think you're doing?" he said.

"Running!" answered one of the students, and before public safety could do anything about it, he ran into the bushes and disappeared. The point is that you have to know when to run. When it comes to the love of money and its associated dangers, it is not enough to walk away. The only thing to do is run for dear life. In order to stay away from the dangers of greed, the man of God must take "constant evasive action."[2]

IN HOT PURSUIT

There is more to avoiding sin, however, than simply beating a hasty retreat. If all we do is run away from one sin, we will run right into the arms of another. The human heart is like a popular ride at the amusement park: sins are lined up at the entrance, waiting for a chance to get on and enjoy the ride. Satan is happy for a sin to get off the ride every now and then, provided another sin can climb on board. So a man finally masters sexual temptation, but then he becomes a glutton instead. Or a woman learns to control her tongue, but she still harbors proud and jealous thoughts. Real growth in godliness means more than just trading in one sin for another. It means replacing the don'ts with the dos. It means getting rid of vices and replacing them with virtues. And it means developing the complete character that enables a Christian to serve God well in the world.

This is why Paul tells Timothy to do more than retreat. He also gives him a rule for pursuit: "Pursue righteousness, godliness, faith, love, steadfastness, gentleness" (1 Tim. 6:11). In a similar vein, Paul will later tell him to "flee youthful passions and pursue righteousness, faith, love, and peace" (2 Tim. 2:22). The Christian needs to know what to run after as well as when to run. Here the Bible gives the man of God six things to pursue. These are not the only things to pursue, of course, but they are all essential character traits of the Christian life.

Righteousness has to do with conduct before other human beings. It means to be upright, to handle one's responsibilities at home, at work, at church, and everywhere else with complete integrity. *Godliness*, which has to do with piety before God, has turned out to be virtually Paul's favorite word (*eusebeian*) in this epistle. In one form or another, it appears eight times, more than anywhere else in the Bible. It is in 1 Timothy that we are told to "lead a peaceful and quiet life, *godly* and dignified in every way" (1 Tim. 2:2), that "great indeed is the mystery of *godliness*" (1 Tim. 3:16),

2. Ronald A. Ward, *Commentary on 1 and 2 Timothy and Titus* (Waco, TX: Word, 1974), 103.

that "*godliness* is of value in every way" (1 Tim. 4:8), and that "there is great gain in *godliness* with contentment" (1 Tim. 6:6). One of the main messages of the entire letter is "train yourself for *godliness*" (1 Tim. 4:7).

Faith and *love* are included whenever Paul lists the cardinal virtues of the Christian life. *Endurance* is the ability to persevere in difficult times—to "persist," as Timothy was told at the end of chapter 4. It is the staying power that is necessary for the kind of military campaign in which Timothy is engaged. At the same time, the young minister must be *gentle*. Gentleness is not usually considered a desirable quality in a soldier. The poster at the army recruiting office does not say, "We're looking for a few gentle men." But gentleness has great value in the church, and never more so than when dealing with doctrinal error. In his subsequent letter, Paul would advise Timothy in "correcting his opponents with gentleness" (2 Tim. 2:25). Even though Timothy must stand up to the false teachers, he must not be harsh. As Jonathan Edwards once wrote,

> It is the duty of God's people to be steadfast and vigorous in their opposition to the designs and ways of such as are endeavoring to overthrow the kingdom of Christ and the interest of religion. . . . If therefore we see any of the followers of Christ, in the midst of the most violent, unreasonable and wicked opposition of God's and his own enemies, maintaining, under all this temptation, the humility and quietness and gentleness of a lamb, and the harmlessness and love and sweetness of a dove, we may well judge that here is a good soldier of Jesus Christ.[3]

When it comes to gentleness, as well as righteousness, godliness, faith, love, and endurance, the man of God is in hot pursuit. These attributes are doubly necessary for a minister of the gospel. "Entering for the ministry," we read in the diary of Kenneth MacRae, "means something more than merely preaching the gospel; it means also the consecration of the whole life to the service of God; it means a holiness of walk and conversation far exceeding that expected of a Christian in a less responsible sphere."[4]

3. Jonathan Edwards, quoted in *Banner of Truth* 416 (May 1998): 27.

4. Kenneth MacRae, "Thoughts on Preaching from 'The Diary of Kenneth MacRae,'" *Banner of Truth* 415 (April 1998): 26–32 (27).

The Good Fight of the Faith

So far Paul has given Timothy two rules of engagement: one for flight and one for pursuit. Next, he gives him one for actual combat: "Fight the good fight of the faith" (1 Tim. 6:11). This command has to do with doctrine. What the Christian fights for is "the faith," meaning orthodox Christianity, which Paul has previously described as "the sound words of our Lord Jesus Christ" (1 Tim. 6:3). The faith is the body of doctrine about salvation in Christ that was taught by the apostles and is recorded in the pages of the New Testament.

Here the Bible brings together two things that never can be separated. Verse 12 is about Christian doctrine, whereas the previous verse was about the Christian life (cf. 1 Tim. 4:16: "Keep a close watch on yourself and on the teaching"). Life and doctrine—they are like bread and butter, or cookies and milk. You cannot have one without the other. Doctrine without life is dead orthodoxy; life without doctrine is reckless faith. But put life together with doctrine—add the ethical to the theological—and you get the light and the heat of authentic Christianity.

Sound doctrine does not preserve itself, however. It must be defended. The word Paul uses for fighting is the Greek word for struggle (*agōnizō*). It sometimes refers to an athletic competition such as a boxing match or a wrestling tournament.[5] Here it may also be taken in a military sense, especially since it echoes a similar command from the beginning of the letter (1 Tim. 1:18; cf. 2 Tim. 4:7). What this rule means, rather obviously, is that there are times when Christians—especially Christian ministers—will have to fight for it. Not that they are belligerent, of course. Paul has just told Timothy to "pursue gentleness" (1 Tim. 6:11). But there is a fight to be fought, and every loyal soldier in Christ's army must fight it. As Calvin said, "Christ calls all His servants to warfare."[6]

In the novel *Excalibur*, Bernard Cornwell writes that "a man should love peace, but, if he cannot fight with all his heart, then he will not have peace."[7]

5. Gordon D. Fee, *1 and 2 Timothy, Titus*, New International Biblical Commentary (Peabody, MA: Hendrickson, 1988), 149–50.

6. John Calvin, *The Second Epistle of Paul the Apostle to the Corinthians and the Epistles to Timothy, Titus and Philemon*, trans. T. A. Smail, Calvin's Commentaries (Edinburgh: Oliver & Boyd, 1964), 276.

7. Bernard Cornwell, *Excalibur: A Novel of Arthur* (New York: St. Martin's, 1999), 192.

An army which lacks the courage to fight must either surrender or be defeated. Sadly, there were men in Ephesus who lacked the courage to fight for the truth. Instead of defending the faith, they simply wandered away from it (1 Tim. 6:10, 21).

It is never pleasant to fight, of course, but there are some things worth fighting for. What makes a fight good is a good cause, and the Christian has the best of all causes: the honor and glory of God displayed in the truth of Jesus Christ. "Choose your battles," people often say, and there are times when this is good advice. However, it is not the counsel Paul gives to Timothy. For the minister of the gospel, the lines have already been drawn. The battle has already been joined.

A gospel minister must defend the faith. He must fight for the infallibility, inerrancy, and sufficiency of Holy Scripture, maintaining that the Bible is the Word of God, written. He must fight for the deity of Jesus Christ, maintaining that Jesus is fully God as well as fully human. He must fight for the depravity of humanity, maintaining that all mankind are born in sin and misery. He must fight for the holiness of God, maintaining that God will judge the world in righteousness. He must fight for the efficacy of the substitutionary atonement, maintaining that Christ died on the cross in the place of sinners. He must fight for the bodily resurrection, maintaining that Jesus Christ is the risen Lord. From beginning to end, he must fight for the sovereignty of God's grace, maintaining that salvation is the choice and the gift of God, to the praise of his glory. The fight for such truths is the good fight of the faith.

Reach for Victory

No sooner has Paul drawn the battle lines, than he looks forward to the end of the war entirely: "Take hold of the eternal life to which you were called" (1 Tim. 6:12). This provides a fourth rule of engagement: reach for the victory, here described as eternal life.

Timothy received eternal life when he first came to Jesus Christ in faith. Every Christian does. Eternal life is God's free gift to everyone who comes to him trusting Jesus Christ and asking for forgiveness of sins. As Paul mentioned at the beginning of this letter, those who believe on Jesus Christ "receive eternal life" (1 Tim. 1:16). But Timothy still needed to "take hold of the eternal life" (1 Tim. 6:12). That is, he needed to appropriate it, to grasp it and hang on to it for all he was worth. The apostle Paul tried to do the same thing himself. "Not that I have already obtained all this," he wrote to the Philippians, "or have already been made perfect, but I press on to take hold of that for which Christ Jesus took hold of me" (Phil. 3:12 NIV). What these verses teach is that eternal life is for now as well as later. Christians not only get "a piece of the pie, by-and-by," but they also get a slice of it right now. Eternal life is "both a present possession and a future hope."[8]

Timothy had the hope of eternal life because he was called to receive it by God's own Spirit. This is known as the doctrine of "effectual calling," which simply means that God's call is effective. God's call is like a military summons: it has an irresistible, saving influence on God's chosen people. The Puritans defined effectual calling as "the work of God's Spirit, whereby, convincing us of our sin and misery, enlightening our minds in the knowledge of Christ, and renewing our wills, he doth persuade and enable us to embrace Jesus Christ, freely offered to us in the gospel."[9]

Timothy answered God's call when he made his "good confession in the presence of many witnesses" (1 Tim. 6:12). There has been a good deal of scholarly discussion about exactly when this took place. What event did Paul have in mind? One strong possibility is Timothy's ordination, which is mentioned more than once in these letters (e.g. 1 Tim. 4:14; 2 Tim. 1:6). Timothy undoubtedly confessed his faith in Jesus Christ at his ordination. This practice continues to the present day. In many African American churches, for example, ministers give a detailed public testimony of their saving faith in Christ.

It is more likely, however, that Timothy made his good confession at his baptism. Ordination is a call to the ministry of the gospel. But what is mentioned here is the call to eternal life itself, a call that comes with baptism for the remission of sins. Like his ordination, Timothy's baptism would have taken place in the presence of many witnesses, for Christian baptism has always been part of the public worship of the church (cf. Rom. 10:9–10). By mentioning his confession in this way, Paul was appealing to Timothy's sense

8. John Stott, *Guard the Truth: The Message of 1 Timothy and Titus* (Downers Grove, IL: InterVarsity, 1996), 157.

9. *The Shorter Catechism*, in *The Westminster Standards* (Norcross, GA: Great Commission Publications, 1991), A. 31.

of honor. He had made a public confession of his faith in Jesus Christ and had vowed to follow him to the death. Not only that, but he had made his vow in the presence of the church. As Timothy looked back on that momentous occasion and remembered the faces of the beloved friends who had witnessed his baptism (or ordination), he would be inspired to obey his orders until the glorious end.

Timothy's vow would be reason enough to keep on fighting, but Paul gives him an even more solemn charge: "I charge you in the presence of God, who gives life to all things, and of Christ Jesus, who in his testimony before Pontius Pilate made the good confession, to keep the commandment unstained and free from reproach" (1 Tim. 6:13–14). Paul may be Timothy's commanding officer, but ultimately his orders come from his Commander-in-Chief, who is the creator and sustainer of all life.

What did Paul mean by "the commandment"? He may have been referring to the rules of engagement given in verses 11 and 12, or to the vows Timothy made at his baptism (or his ordination). J. N. D. Kelly thinks the language in these verses may even come from an early baptismal liturgy. The commandment, then, is "the whole law of Christ, the rule of faith and life enjoined by the gospel, to which Timothy has pledged himself at his baptism."[10]

In case he needs any further encouragement, Paul reminds Timothy that his Commander-in-Chief made good on his own confession. Jesus Christ made his confession before Pontius Pilate, the Roman governor of Judea who ordered his execution. As it says in the Apostles' Creed, "he suffered under Pontius Pilate." Pilate himself does not have any particular theological significance, but he does have historical significance. He is included in the Apostles' Creed in order to fix the work of Jesus Christ to a specific time and place in human history. For many years skeptical Bible scholars denied the existence of Pontius Pilate because he was not mentioned in any historical documents outside the Bible. But then in the 1960s archaeologists made a discovery that confirmed the biblical history. In the steps of the theater in Caesarea they found the following Latin inscription: "Pontius Pilate, Prefect of Judea, has dedicated to the people of Caesarea a temple in honor of Tiberius."[11]

10. J. N. D. Kelly, *The Pastoral Epistles: Timothy I and II, Titus*, Harper's New Testament Commentaries (San Francisco: Harper and Row, 1960), 144.

11. John McRay, *Archaeology and the New Testament* (Grand Rapids: Baker, 1991), 145.

This is the same Pontius Pilate before whom Jesus of Nazareth was tried and condemned. Jesus appeared before him to testify that he was the Messiah. Pilate asked him a simple question: "Are you the King of the Jews?" (John 18:33). Jesus answered by saying, "You say that I am a king. For this purpose I was born and for this purpose I have come into the world—to bear witness to the truth" (John 18:37; cf. Matt. 27:11; Luke 22:70). This was Jesus' good confession. He was confessing himself as Lord. At every Christian baptism the same confession is made: Jesus is Lord.

The phrase "before Pontius Pilate" can also mean "in the days of Pontius Pilate." It is possible, therefore, that this verse refers to something more than what Jesus said at his trial. His good confession was made in deed as well as word. It included his work on the cross, the way he "suffered under Pontius Pilate." Thus Calvin explains that "Christ made his *confession before Pilate* not in many words but in reality, that is by His voluntary submission to death. . . . For He ratified [his testimony] with His own blood and with the sacrifice of His death better than with any words." Whether this is the best interpretation of 1 Timothy 6:13 or not, it is certainly true that even on the cross Jesus bravely maintained his bold confession. And as Calvin goes on to say, this gives courage to Timothy and every other soldier of the cross: "Thus whenever our hearts waver, let us remember immediately to look to the death of Christ for strength. What cowardice it would be to desert such a leader who goes before us to show us the way."[12]

Help Is on the Way

The fifth and final rule of engagement encompasses all the others: keep fighting until the end. Reinforcements are coming; help is on the way. So although Timothy must follow his rules of engagement, he will not have to follow them forever. They will remain in force only "until the appearing of our Lord Jesus Christ, which he will display at the proper time" (1 Tim. 6:14–15; cf. 2 Tim. 4:1, 8).

This short, simple sentence summarizes virtually everything anyone needs to know about the second coming of Jesus Christ. First, the return of Jesus Christ is definite: God *will* display the "appearing," or epiphany (*epiphaneia*),

12. Calvin, *Second Epistle of Paul*, 278.

of our Lord Jesus Christ. The personal, visible, triumphant return of Jesus Christ has been a certainty since the day he left this earth and ascended to his Father in heaven. After Jesus departed, while the apostles stood gazing confusedly into the heavens, angels appeared and said, "Men of Galilee, why do you stand looking into heaven? This Jesus, who was taken up from you into heaven, will come in the same way as you saw him go into heaven" (Acts 1:11). God has guaranteed the return of Jesus Christ.

Second, the time of his coming is known only to God. God will bring it about "at the proper time" (1 Tim. 6:15). Paul is as uncertain about the time as he is certain about the event itself. Only God knows when Christ will return, and that is his business. The Bible repeatedly warns Christians not to speculate about when Jesus will come again. This was the plain teaching of Jesus himself. "But concerning that day and hour no one knows," Jesus said, "not even the angels of heaven, nor the Son, but the Father only" (Matt. 24:36). "Well," some have said, "maybe you can't know the day or the hour, but you can know the month, or the year!" Nonsense. When Jesus said "day" and "hour," he was not speaking literally, but figuratively, and his point was that we cannot know the time of his return at all. As he went on to say, "the Son of Man is coming at an hour you do not expect" (Matt. 24:44). God will bring about the glorious appearing of our Lord Jesus Christ in his own good time.

God always has perfect timing, and when it comes to the glorious return of Jesus Christ, he is holding strictly to his own timetable. His return will bring total triumph for the people of God. We are not on a suicide mission, doomed to destruction. On the contrary, our King has promised to come again before the last battle, when he will come with heavy reinforcements to sweep our enemy from the field. In the meantime, every soldier in God's army must keep fighting, blamelessly, the good fight of the faith: "For if earthly soldiers do not hesitate to fight when the outcome is uncertain and they are in danger of death, how much more bravely ought we to fight under the guidance and banner of Christ, where we can be certain beforehand of victory, more especially since a reward awaits us, far beyond the rewards usually given by commanders to their men, a glorious immortality and heavenly blessedness."[13]

13. Ibid., 276.

A Victory Song

Certain of this victory, Paul ends his letter with a short victory song: "He who is the blessed and only Sovereign, the King of kings and Lord of lords, who alone has immortality, who dwells in unapproachable light, whom no one has ever seen or can see. To him be honor and eternal dominion. Amen" (1 Tim. 6:15–16). These words may come from a baptismal liturgy, an early Christian hymn, or even a hymn from the synagogue. They also echo the doxology Paul sang back in the first chapter: "To the King of ages, immortal, invisible, the only God, be honor and glory forever and ever. Amen" (1 Tim. 1:17).

Whatever its origins, Paul's concluding doxology emphasizes God's transcendence. God is far, far above and beyond everyone and everything else. He is invincible, the "blessed and only Sovereign, the King of kings and Lord of lords" (1 Tim. 6:15; cf. Deut. 10:17; Rev. 17:14). God is the absolute potentate over all that is, all that was, and all that will be. He is the only sovereign being inside or outside the entire universe. All powers and dominions are subject to him. He is King of kings, ruling over all the kings of the earth, including both the emperors of Rome and the superpowers of modern times. And he is Lord of lords, ruling over all the deities of world religion, including Diana of the Ephesians and all the gods of this age. God is to be praised for the invincibility of his power.

God is also immortal. The Roman emperors claimed to be immortal, but God "alone has immortality" (1 Tim. 6:16). This does not mean, of course, that nothing else will last forever. The new heavens and the new earth will stand forever. So will the blessed angels, as well as the bodies and souls of human beings, which are destined to heaven or to hell for all eternity. But only God "has life in himself" (John 5:26). He alone is immortal of his very nature. Every other creature depends upon God for its existence. Even those that have immortal souls are living on borrowed time, for "in him we live and move and have our being" (Acts 17:28). Therefore, God is to be praised for the immortality of his existence.

Finally, God is invisible. He "dwells in unapproachable light, whom no one has ever seen or can see" (1 Tim. 6:16). Here the Bible speaks of the blinding, luminescent radiance that streams from the glory of God. Yet God himself remains invisible. As he said to Moses, "You cannot see my face, for man shall not see me and live" (Ex. 33:20). God is to be praised for the invisibility of his essence.

Invincible, immortal, invisible, altogether inaccessible—this is the great Commander we serve. What else can we do but trust, serve, and worship him? If invincibility, immortality, and invisibility belong to him, then all praise and worship belong to him as well: "To him be honor and eternal dominion. Amen" (1 Tim. 6:16).

20

The Ultimate Investment

1 Timothy 6:17–21

As for the rich in this present age, charge them not to be haughty, nor to set their hopes on the uncertainty of riches, but on God, who richly provides us with everything to enjoy. They are to do good, to be rich in good works, to be generous and ready to share, thus storing up treasure for themselves as a good foundation for the future, so that they may take hold of that which is truly life.
(1 Tim. 6:17–19)

In the year 1923, nine of the world's wealthiest men held a meeting at the Edgewater Beach Hotel in Chicago. In attendance were the presidents of the world's largest steel, gas, and utility companies, the world's greatest wheat speculator, the president of the New York Stock Exchange, a member of the presidential cabinet, a Wall Street tycoon, the head of the world's largest monopoly, and the president of the Bank of International Settlements.

The men who met at the Edgewater that day knew all the secrets of generating and manipulating capital. They could own anything and everything that money could buy. There was one more thing they held in common, which is that within the next decade they all lost everything they had:

> The president of the largest independent steel company, Charles Schwab, lived on borrowed money for the last five years of his life and died bankrupt. The president of the largest gas company, Howard Hopson, went insane. The president of the largest utility, Samuel Insull, died in a foreign land, penniless and a fugitive from justice. The greatest wheat speculator, Arthur Cotton, also died abroad and insolvent. The president of the New York Stock Exchange, Richard Whitney, was sent to the infamous Sing Sing penitentiary. The member of the presidential cabinet, Albert Fall, was pardoned from prison so he could go home to die. The Wall Street tycoon, Jesse Livermore, committed suicide. The head of the world's largest monopoly, Ivan Krueger, committed suicide. The president of the Bank of International Settlements, Leon Fraser, committed suicide.[1]

Although it is sad, and shocking, the story of these nine men should not be surprising, for the Bible warns the rich not "to set their hopes on the uncertainty of riches, but on God" (1 Tim. 6:17).

A P.S. for the Wealthy

This word for the wealthy comes in the postscript Paul added to his first letter to Timothy. The main body of the epistle ended with the doxology of verse 16: "To him be honor and eternal dominion. Amen" (1 Tim. 6:16). But then, it seems, the apostle went back and reread his letter, and by the time he was finished, he realized something was missing.

Near the close of his letter, the apostle had warned that "those who desire to be rich" are headed for destruction (1 Tim. 6:9). That warning was not just for the poor; it was for anyone who wanted more money. Left by itself, however, it might give the impression that it is wrong for Christians to be rich. This would have been the wrong impression, for there is nothing wrong with money, in and of itself. The gospel is for the haves as well as the have-nots. The kingdom of heaven belongs to all the poor in spirit (Matt. 5:3), whether they are economically impoverished or not.

1. Patrick Morley, *The Seven Seasons of a Man's Life* (Grand Rapids: Zondervan, 1997), 84–85.

The Ephesians needed to hear this. Although there were many poor Christians in Ephesus, including a number of slaves (see 1 Tim. 6:1–2), Paul also knew committed Christians there who happened to be rich. It was with them in mind that he told Timothy: "As for the rich in this present age, charge them not to be haughty, nor to set their hopes on the uncertainty of riches, but on God, who richly provides us with everything to enjoy" (1 Tim. 6:17). This word to the wealthy obviously assumes that some Christians will be rich already in this life. As if to emphasize how very wealthy they are, the Greek vocabulary for rich (*plousios*) is used four different ways in this verse—as an adjective, a noun, an adverb, and a verb.

In the providence of God, some Christians live in comfortable circumstances. They own their own homes. They wear nice clothes. They have more than enough food to eat. And Christians who are blessed with such material prosperity do not need to feel guilty about it; nor do they need to divest themselves of their wealth. They are even allowed to enjoy themselves. For everything we own comes from God himself, "who richly provides us with everything to enjoy" (1 Tim. 6:17). God is no miser. He provides for the rich and the poor alike, and whatever he provides is for our enjoyment. Paul first introduced this principle back in chapter 4, when he criticized the false teachers for their asceticism. There he said that God created good food and married sexuality "to be received with thanksgiving by those who believe and know the truth. For everything created by God is good, and nothing is to be rejected if it is received with thanksgiving" (1 Tim. 4:3–4). The Bible celebrates the good things of life.

This does not mean that we should live for luxury. Paul has already warned against that kind of attitude: the widow "who is self-indulgent," he said, "is dead even while she lives" (1 Tim. 5:6). Earthly pleasures can give no lasting joy. The only real and lasting joy is God himself, but anyone who finds joy in the Giver will also enjoy his gifts. "Enjoyment," writes Gordon Fee, "does not mean self-indulgent living. The reason everything may be enjoyed lies in the recognition that everything, including one's wealth, is a *gift*, the expression of God's gracious generosity."[2]

2. Gordon D. Fee, *1 and 2 Timothy, Titus*, New International Biblical Commentary (Peabody, MA: Hendrickson, 1988), 157.

Paul's postscript to Timothy must come as a great relief to Christians in the West. Compared to the rest of the modern world, not to mention the ancient Ephesians, we are very rich. We need not feel guilty about this, but grateful for what God has provided for our enjoyment.

In God We Trust

Yet the Bible has more to say about our prosperity than simply to say that we should enjoy it. Although there is nothing wrong with our money in and of itself, the Scripture hastens to say that it is not to be trusted: "As for the rich in this present age, charge them not to be haughty, nor to set their hopes on the uncertainty of riches" (1 Tim. 6:17). This verse mentions two sinful attitudes that are common among the rich—a false sense of importance and a false sense of security.

First, wealthy people often have a false sense of importance. Some rich people are proud of what they can accumulate, and this makes them rather arrogant. They boast about their latest acquisitions. They feel so important that they expect to be treated with a degree of deference. In the church, they think they are entitled to influence simply because they are wealthy. These attitudes are all too common in the business world. My own adopted city of Philadelphia is home to the Wharton School of Business, one of the last bastions of capitalism. Christian students at Wharton often find it difficult to know how to live for Christ in corporate America. One student reported to me what a classmate said when they started to talk about business ethics: "Well, I'm going to Wall Street, and we live by a different set of standards." Since this kind of arrogance is a common sin among the wealthy, Paul charged young pastor Timothy to tell the rich people in his congregation not to think too highly of themselves. He must remind them that the only reason they are prosperous is that God has made them prosper.

Another common attitude among the wealthy is a false sense of security. Instead of relying on God, they depend on their financial instincts and trust in their own resources. Since the United States is a wealthy nation, these are common American attitudes. If the economy is good, the mood in the country is good, and the politicians will stay in office. If the economy is bad, the mood in the country is bad, and the politicians will have to go. This is a sure sign that our culture bases its ultimate sense of security on money.

This false sense of security even pervades the church. Kenneth Kantzer, who formerly served as the editor of *Christianity Today*, was once asked what he considered the greatest problem facing the contemporary church. "It is not what you might expect me to say," he answered. "It is not liberalism or neo-orthodoxy or wrong views of revelation or inspiration or other controversial points in theology. . . . The most serious problem facing today's church is materialism—materialism not as a philosophical theory, but as a way of life."[3] The "American way of life" it is usually called.

The reality is that money is a shaky foundation. It is *so* uncertain, as the Scripture says. Consider the three Japanese businessmen, each of them on the verge of bankruptcy, who met at the hotel for one last round of drinks, and then went into their separate rooms and hanged themselves. They had misplaced their confidence, building their lives on the sandy bottom of worldly wealth (see Luke 6:48–49).

Or consider the American economy at the turn of the millennium. The 1990s were a decade of economic strength, the longest peace-time expansion in Western history. Investors were holding on to the stock market for the ride of their lives. Yet there were continual reminders of the instability of wealth: a trillion dollar budget deficit for the federal government; wide-scale layoffs caused by corporate mergers; trouble in the Asian markets; fears of global computer crashes; predictions about when Social Security would run out of money. Almost all of these worries are still with us, for when it comes to the economy, there are no guarantees. The writer of the Proverbs put it well: "Cast but a glance at riches, and they are gone, for they will surely sprout wings and fly off to the sky like an eagle" (Prov. 23:5 NIV). Riches are here today, gone tomorrow. They cannot be trusted.

The only safe place to put our trust is in God himself. All prosperity comes from him. Daily bread comes from him, not from one's paycheck. Tuition payments come from him, not from a scholarship fund. Security for old age comes from him, not from a retirement account. Thus the only place to put all true confidence is in God, in whom we have everything we need. Those who do trust in him are able to say, "Lord, you have blessed me with more

3. Kenneth Kantzer, as quoted by J. Robert Vannoy in a newsletter published by Biblical Theological Seminary, Hatfield, PA.

than I could ever deserve. But you could take it all away tomorrow and I would still be full of joy, for I have everything I need in Jesus Christ."

You cannot trust both God and money (see Matt. 6:24)—it is either one or the other. So which will it be? The best answer to that question can be found in a pocket full of change. Every quarter, dime, nickel, or penny stamped by the United States Mint bears the motto "In God We Trust." The motto is sound theology, and there is no better place for it than on American currency. In God we trust, not money.

The Generous Lifestyle

One of the best ways to learn how to trust God rather than money is to give our money away, which is what Paul wants Timothy to tell the wealthy people in his congregation to do: "They are to do good, to be rich in good works, to be generous and ready to share" (1 Tim. 6:18). In other words, rich Christians are to be good and generous.

There are several surprises in this verse. One surprise comes from the way Paul plays with his words. He actually commands the rich to *be* rich . . . in good deeds. This splendid phrase completely reverses the values of this world. Everyone wants to be rich, but are you rich in good deeds? The trouble is that when it comes to doing good deeds, most Christians are lower middle class: we have never learned that the way to be truly wealthy is to give our lives away for Jesus Christ. True riches "are found in the giving, not in the having."[4]

Another surprise is that God does not come begging for money. The first two things the Bible mentions do not require any cash. Someone can "do good" and "be rich in good deeds" without spending a cent. The first thing God wants from the rich is not their money. What he values most of all is a servant's heart. He wants us to be "rich toward God," as Jesus put it when he explained the parable of the rich fool (Luke 12:21). This means that it is not enough for the wealthy to give money to charity, although of course there is a place for that. What God demands first is active service. It is one thing to pay for someone else to feed the hungry or care for the sick; it is another thing to feed the hungry yourself, or to dress a sick man's wounds. Rich

4. Fee, *1 and 2 Timothy*, 158.

Christians are called to do *both*, and not just to try to solve everything—including God's demand for mercy—by spending more money. There are no idle rich in the kingdom of God. Every Christian is called to active, personal involvement in deeds of mercy.

Some deeds of mercy also require money. Thus another way that wealthy Christians can glorify God is through the wise use of their money. God calls all his children "to be generous and ready to share" (1 Tim. 6:18), to embrace a lifestyle of giving. Instead of considering godliness as a means to gain (see 1 Tim. 6:5), he wants them to use their gain as a means of godliness. The stewardship of personal wealth is an important aspect of a rich Christian's calling.

In the days of the early church it was generosity, more than anything else, that showed the difference between Christianity and paganism. The pagans did not care for the poor because the poor could give them nothing in return. What made Christians different is that they *did* care for the poor: "There was not a needy person among them" (Acts 4:34). Not only did Christians care for their own poor, but they also cared for the pagan poor. The followers of Christ were the ones who fed the hungry, cared for lepers, and rescued children who had been left to die. By the second century, Tertullian was able to boast that Christians spent more on the poor in the street than the pagans spent at the temple. The result was the rapid, worldwide expansion of the gospel.

Generous Christians could have the same worldwide impact today. More capital is being generated now than at any other time in human history, yet the disparity between the rich and the poor has never been greater. At the same time, many valuable Christian ministries are hindered by lack of funds. The problem is not that there are not enough Christians, but that most Christians are not Christ-like enough in their giving. We scarcely realize what the church could accomplish in the world if we gave our money away for Jesus with the same liberality that Jesus gave his life for us.

One way for us to become more like Christ in our giving is to train ourselves to be generous in the little sacrifices of daily life. Take the small piece of cake. Let someone else have the parking space. Leave hot water in the tank for the next shower. Do someone else's chores. Share your power tools with your neighbor. Look to pass the basketball before you shoot. Put a little extra in the offering plate. For the Christian, generosity ought to be a way of life.

The reason we are able to be so generous is that we serve a generous God. God is richer than the richest man who ever lived. He not only owns the cattle on a thousand hills (Ps. 50:10), he also owns the hills! Yet God does not hoard his treasure. As Paul playfully puts it, he "*richly* provides us with everything to enjoy" (1 Tim. 6:17). It is impossible to think of God's rich giving without thinking of his most lavish gift of all: "For you know the grace of our Lord Jesus Christ, that though he was rich, yet for your sake he became poor, so that you by his poverty might become rich" (2 Cor. 8:9).

This is the basic law of the divine economy: the rich became poor so that the poor might become rich. Those who have become rich by the grace of God must therefore be willing to enrich others. "In the end," said Clement of Alexandria, "it is not the one who keeps, but the one who gives away, who is rich; and it is giving away, not possession, which renders a man happy."[5]

Saving Up for Eternity

The command to be generous and willing to share is hard for some wealthy people to follow. After all, if a rich man gives his riches away, he won't be rich anymore. Remember that this was why the rich young man refused to follow Jesus. Jesus told him, "If you would be perfect, go, sell what you possess and give to the poor, and you will have treasure in heaven; and come, follow me" (Matt. 19:21). Unfortunately, the man was not ready to be so generous: "When the young man heard this he went away sorrowful, for he had great possessions" (Matt. 19:22). As Jesus watched the rich young man slowly walk away, he said to his disciples, "Truly, I say to you, only with difficulty will a rich person enter the kingdom of heaven" (Matt. 19:23).

The apostle Paul understood how hard it is for the rich to be godly too. So in order to encourage them to be generous, he appealed to their business instincts. People who are generous and willing to share are "thus storing up treasure for themselves as a good foundation for the future, so that they may take hold of that which is truly life" (1 Tim. 6:19). This verse introduces another curiosity of the divine economy. Storing up earthly treasure actually turns out to be a bad investment! The goal of any investor is to gain long-

5. Clement of Alexandria, "True Wealth," condensed from *The Tutor* and reprinted in *Re:generation Quarterly* 4.4 (1998): 14.

term financial security. But even if a man spends his whole life trying to build up a fortune, he will lose all his assets at death. As the apostle has already said, "we brought nothing into the world, and we cannot take anything out of the world" (1 Tim. 6:7).

One man who discovered this to his dismay was Jay Gould, the nineteenth-century financial genius. The man was worth one hundred million dollars, but he died in utter despair. His dying words were, "I'm the most miserable devil in the world."[6] Although Gould had made plenty of long-term investments, none of them was long-term enough. It was not until he lay on his death bed that he realized how foolish he had been for failing to invest in any eternal securities.

According to the Bible there are really two kinds of wealth. Paul hinted at this when he referred to "the rich in this present age" (1 Tim. 6:17). This phrase suggests that there is also a coming age, and that being rich then and being rich now are two entirely different matters. Where earthly treasure is concerned, the old saying is true: "you can't take it with you." When it comes to spiritual capital, however, you *can* send it on ahead! This explains why the Bible often describes the blessings of heaven as treasures. This was the teaching of Jesus Christ, who said, "Do not lay up for yourselves treasures on earth, where moth and rust destroy and where thieves break in and steal, but lay up for yourselves treasures in heaven, where neither moth nor rust destroys and where thieves do not break in and steal. For where your treasure is, there your heart will be also" (Matt. 6:19–21; cf. Luke 12:33).

When Paul talks about the kind of treasure that will make a solid foundation for the age to come, what he has in mind is the treasure of eternal life. One thing money cannot buy is life itself. Earthly riches have no life-giving power. But a man who gives his possessions away for the sake of Jesus Christ has begun to "take hold of that which is truly life" (1 Tim. 6:19). This is the same kind of life that was mentioned back in verse 12—eternal life, which is life indeed.

The Bible thus encourages us to amass a fortune in heavenly treasure, and thereby to take hold of eternal life. This is not salvation by works. The passage does not teach, as some have thought, that wealth is "a means to secure

6. John Stott, *Guard the Truth: The Message of 1 Timothy and Titus* (Downers Grove, IL: InterVarsity, 1996), 153.

one's salvation."[7] There is no way to buy one's way into heaven. God cannot be bribed. Eternal life is his free gift. But anyone who is good and generous out of gratitude to God for salvation in Jesus Christ has already begun to enter the joy of eternal life.

This prospect is bound to appeal to anyone who has good business sense. A smart investor is happy to part with substantial assets, provided that he will get something better in return. The Bible promises that when earthly treasure is given away in the name of Jesus Christ, it is exchanged for heavenly treasure. A "good foundation for the future" is the ultimate investment. Unlike earthly treasure, heavenly treasure cannot be lost. It is a lucrative investment because it secures the infinite riches of heaven. It is a long-term investment because it will last for all eternity. It is a stable investment because it is backed by the full faith and credit of almighty God. As Chrysostom wisely said, in heaven "nothing is uncertain, for the foundation being firm, there is no instability, all is firm, fixed, immovable, fast, and enduring."[8]

A P.P.S. for Timothy

One more thing. At the very end of his epistle Paul repeats his main message: "O Timothy, guard the deposit entrusted to you" (1 Tim. 6:20). This post-postscript is intensely personal. Although Paul sometimes dictated his correspondence to a secretary (e.g. 1 Cor. 16:21), in this instance he has taken the pen into his own hand. "O Timothy," he says, making a personal and heartfelt appeal, "guard the deposit."

Here the apostle is using the language of commerce. There were no safe-deposit boxes in the ancient world. When a man went on a long journey, he left his most valued possessions with someone he could trust. Once the valuables were deposited, it was up to the agent to keep them safe. So what had Paul entrusted to Timothy? He may have been referring to the young man's personal faith, or to his ministry in the church. But Timothy had received something even more valuable: the apostolic doctrines of the Christian faith.

7. Jouette M. Bassler, *1 Timothy, 2 Timothy, Titus* (Nashville: Abingdon, 1996), 120.

8. John Chrysostom, "Homilies on the Epistles of St. Paul the Apostle to Timothy, Titus, and Philemon," trans. and ed. Philip Schaff, *Nicene and Post-Nicene Fathers*, First Series, 14 vols. (Peabody, MA: Hendrickson, 1994), 13:472.

This must be what Paul means because back at the beginning of the letter he mentioned that he himself had been "entrusted" with the gospel (1 Tim. 1:11). The same idea comes up again in his next letter, in which he again tells Timothy to "guard the good deposit entrusted to you" (2 Tim. 1:14). Timothy, in turn, is to entrust the same saving truths "to faithful men who will be able to teach others also" (2 Tim. 2:2).

To say this in another way, Timothy was a trustee of the gospel. Like every gospel minister, he had received the message of salvation in Jesus Christ as a sacred trust. According to ancient legal doctrine, a trustee was obligated to preserve a deposit "unharmed and unchanged."[9] Therefore, a minister is not free to make up his theology as he goes along. On the contrary, he must proclaim that very same message that he himself has received. His task is not to innovate, but to preserve. Orthodox Christianity is not to be reinvented, re-envisioned, or reinterpreted; it is to be cherished, guarded, and defended. The suggestion here "is that the Christian message is not something which the church's minister works out for himself or is entitled to add to; it is a divine revelation which has been committed to his care, and which it is his bounden duty to pass on unimpaired to others."[10] The world seeks some new doctrinal idea or some new spiritual experience, but the church offers the same old gospel. In his sermon on this text, Leo the Great asked, "What is meant by *the deposit*?" This was the answer that Leo gave: "That which is committed to thee, not that which is invented by thee; that which thou hast received, not that which thou hast devised; a thing not of wit, but of learning; not of private assumption, but of public tradition; a thing brought to thee, not brought forth of thee; wherein thou must not be an author, but a keeper; not a leader but a follower. Keep the deposit."[11]

Part of that sacred trust is deposited in this very letter. Paul has reminded Timothy of the most basic truths of the gospel. He has stated "that Christ Jesus came into the world to save sinners" (1 Tim. 1:15). He has claimed that "there is one God, and there is one mediator between God and men, the man Christ Jesus, who gave himself as a ransom for all" (1 Tim. 2:5–6). He

9. Bassler, *1 Timothy*, 121.

10. J. N. D. Kelly, *The Pastoral Epistles: Timothy I and II, Titus*, Harper's New Testament Commentaries (San Francisco: Harper and Row, 1960), 150.

11. Leo the Great, quoted in Thomas C. Oden, *First and Second Timothy and Titus*, Interpretation (Louisville: John Knox, 1989), 127.

has revealed the great mystery of godliness, that God "was manifested in the flesh, vindicated by the Spirit, seen by angels, proclaimed among the nations, believed on in the world, taken up in glory" (1 Tim. 3:16). Paul was banking on Timothy to guard these precious doctrines of the incarnation, the atonement, the redemption, the resurrection, the proclamation, and the glorification of Jesus Christ.

What made this task so urgent was that there were so many false teachers to oppose Timothy. Paul had frequently reminded him of the danger of "vain discussion" (1 Tim. 1:6) or "irreverent, silly myths" (1 Tim. 4:7). Now he reminds him, yet again, to "avoid the irreverent babble and contradictions of what is falsely called knowledge" (1 Tim. 6:20; cf. 2 Tim. 2:16). Calvin described the kind of discourse Paul was warning about as "the high-sounding talk and the bombastic verbosity of those who are not content with the simplicity of the Gospel but turn it into profane philosophy."[12] What this means is that the church of Jesus Christ is no place for the traditions of men, the jargon of academic theology, or the speculations of cult leaders.

The result of such teaching can only be a denial of the Christian faith. Apparently, this was already starting to happen in Ephesus, for by professing this so-called knowledge, "some have swerved from the faith" (1 Tim. 6:21; cf. 1:19b–20; 4:1; 5:15; 6:10). These men were to be avoided. In what appears to have been an early form of Gnosticism, they had laid claim to special knowledge. But the doctrines they professed—literally, their counter-affirmations—were antithetical to the gospel. These men did not set out to abandon the faith, of course. Few people ever do. They simply drifted away.

Timothy had vowed that he himself would never wander from the sound doctrines of orthodox Christianity. He would guard what the apostle had entrusted to his care. But in order to defend the faith, he needed God's grace, which is what God promised to give him. The letter thus ends the way it began. The first thing Paul extended to Timothy was "grace, mercy, and peace from God the Father and Christ Jesus our Lord" (1 Tim. 1:2). Similarly, his closing benediction is "grace be with you" (1 Tim. 6:21).

There is something familiar about this blessing, but there is something strange about it, too. The letter was addressed to Timothy. But the word

12. John Calvin, *The Second Epistle of Paul the Apostle to the Corinthians and the Epistles to Timothy, Titus and Philemon*, trans. T. A. Smail, Calvin's Commentaries (Edinburgh: Oliver & Boyd, 1964), 284.

"you" in the farewell is expressed in the plural rather than the singular. A more accurate way to translate the phrase is "Grace be with you all." This is a reminder that 1 Timothy was not simply a private letter for Timothy, but a public letter for the whole family of believers in Ephesus. It is also for the Christian church throughout the ages. As we defend the faith in our own times, the God of Paul and Timothy gives us the promise of his blessing: "Grace be with you."

Index of Scripture

Index of Subjects and Names

Available in the Reformed Expository Commentary Series

New Testament

The Incarnation in the Gospels, by Daniel M. Doriani, Philip Graham Ryken, and Richard D. Phillips
Matthew, by Daniel M. Doriani
Luke, by Philip Graham Ryken
John, by Richard D. Phillips
Romans, by Daniel M. Doriani
Galatians, by Philip Graham Ryken
Ephesians, by Bryan Chapell
Philippians, by Dennis E. Johnson
1 & 2 Thessalonians, by Richard D. Phillips
1 Timothy, by Philip Graham Ryken
2 Timothy & Titus, by Daniel M. Doriani and Richard D. Phillips
Hebrews, by Richard D. Phillips
James, by Daniel M. Doriani
1 Peter, by Daniel M. Doriani
1–3 John, by Douglas Sean O'Donnell
Revelation, by Richard D. Phillips

Forthcoming

Mark, by Douglas Sean O'Donnell
2 Corinthians, by Trent Casto